Opioids 360

Opioids 360

A Multidisciplinary Examination of an American Tragedy

Edited by
Sarah A. See
Eric S. See

ROWMAN & LITTLEFIELD
Lanham • Boulder • New York • London

Published by Rowman & Littlefield
An imprint of The Rowman & Littlefield Publishing Group, Inc.
4501 Forbes Boulevard, Suite 200, Lanham, Maryland 20706
www.rowman.com

86-90 Paul Street, London EC2A 4NE

British Library Cataloguing in Publication Information available

Library of Congress Cataloging-in-Publication Data available

ISBN 978-1-5381-9256-6 (cloth)
ISBN 978-1-5381-9257-3 (paper)
ISBN 978-1-5381-9258-0 (electronic)

♾™ The paper used in this publication meets the minimum requirements of American National Standard for Information Sciences—Permanence of Paper for Printed Library Materials, ANSI/NISO Z39.48-1992.

Contents

Acknowledgments

This book is dedicated to our children, Cameron, Lauren, and Stephanie, as well as our extended families and friends who have supported us on these long and difficult projects.

Additionally, *Opioids 360* is dedicated to all of those who have suffered from opioid use, misuse, and abuse. Those who have died or suffered from these medications, or from being denied medications, need to be remembered and championed as we continue to work in this field and develop policy. The faces, names, families, and stories behind the gruesome statistics must never be forgotten.

Finally, we want to thank Rebecca King and the Methodist University Writing Center for their assistance with this book. Your hard work and dedication have made this a much better volume.

Sarah A. See and Eric S. See

Foreword

In an American era where the opioid crisis has moved beyond the boundaries of individual experience to transform into a national emergency, *Opioids 360* serves as an essential tapestry of insights, analyses, and reflections on a multidimensional issue that continues to reshape societal norms and public health policies. The book's chapters are written by authors who address issues, often complex in nature, surrounding opioid addiction, exploring narratives that have often been oversimplified or misconstrued by government officials and pharmaceutical companies. From changing the script on prevailing stigmas to examining the elaborate maze of international connections and domestic policies, the authors offer a well-rounded exploration of the forces at play in this ongoing crisis. By weaving together perspectives from criminal justice, psychology, economics, ethics, and medical practice, *Opioids 360* not only contributes to the academic discourse but also elicits a broader understanding of a topic that affects millions worldwide.

The book's comprehensive approach allows readers to grasp the underlying mechanisms that have fueled the opioid epidemic, including the role of government regulation, the role of pharmaceutical companies, and the influence of the news media in shaping public perceptions. An examination of state and federal responses, particularly through litigation against pharmaceutical companies, sheds light on the proactive measures underway at various levels to address the crisis. Furthermore, the inclusion of a dedicated chapter centered on opioid use on college campuses provides a fresh, relatable perspective, as undergraduates offer their perspectives on this serious problem on many college campuses.

Ultimately, this book advocates for commonsense reforms, framed in critical thinking, that balance the serious need for public safety with the rights of patients requiring access to necessary medications. The book serves as a valuable resource for criminal justice practitioners and any organization impacted by the current opioid crisis. It stimulates thinking by offering practical advice on navigating the complexities of opioid use and addiction. By expanding the knowledge base on the opioid crisis and promoting interdisciplinary collaboration, the editors, See and See created a book that not only informs but should inspire criminal justice practitioners, government leaders, and citizens to take action to prevent opioid abuse in America. Action that cannot be delayed.

Darl Champion
Faculty Emeritus, Justice Studies,
Methodist University
Instructor, Law Enforcement Executive
Program, North Carolina State University
Adjunct Graduate Faculty, Master's in
Criminal Justice Program, Guilford College

Introduction

Eric S. See and Sarah A. See

Almost 1,000,000 people have died from opioid overdoses in the United States since 1999. While the numbers of deaths from prescription opioids such as OxyContin and Roxycontin are down significantly, deaths from synthetic opioids such as fentanyl continue to rise. Opioids in the form of prescription medications, heroin, and synthetic fentanyl have created a crisis of epic proportions destroying individuals and families across the country. The epidemic has impacted all levels of government, as well as our systems of health care and criminal justice.

This book takes a full 360 macro-to-micro approach to understanding the problems presented by opioids. The macro approach examines the international role played by other nations in the production of foreign-made fentanyl currently flooding the streets of the United States. This approach continues when looking at the responses of various state and local governments but takes a micro approach when looking at the effects on individuals such as athletes, students, and patients in pain. This full spectrum approach allows the reader to gain an understanding of the opioid epidemic in a way that has never been presented in other sources.

Opioids 360 addresses and explains critical issues. It carries on the tradition of *Guns 360*, by having experts from various fields come together to focus their attention and knowledge on a specific problem affecting our nation. The chapters in *Opioids 360* were written by experts in the fields of criminology, medicine, economics, psychology, sociology, communication, religion, and ethics. In addition, a critical and innovative feature from *Guns 360* has been replicated in *Opioids 360*, and that is students talking to students. In chapter 13, five Methodist University undergraduate students talk directly to students across the country about medication issues involving posttraumatic stress disorder (PTSD), anxiety, depression, attention-deficit/hyperactivity disorder (ADHD), and drug-seeking behavior. This chapter is instrumental in helping students in your classroom connect to complex and challenging topics.

Opioids are not taken in isolation or in a vacuum. This macro-to-micro approach involving experts in the field, as well as undergraduate students, presents the complex issues surrounding opioids in a comprehensive yet accessible manner. This approach and the information it brings is long overdue and is designed to educate, inform, and ultimately improve and save lives.

1

Flipping the Script on Narratives About Opioid Addiction

J. Scott Lewis

The use of potentially habit-forming drugs such as nicotine, caffeine, alcohol, and psychoactive drugs is a ubiquitous feature of human cultures (Croq, 2007). Drug use encompasses a variety of social functions, including ceremonial religious functions, medicine, and even as commodities for common consumption. Opium is one of the earliest documented drugs, being mentioned at least as far back as the Homeric hymns of the ninth century BCE. This highly addictive and often deadly substance goes beyond merely medicinal, religious, or recreational use. The drug and the way that we think about it are bound up in the fabric of social myth and narrative. This chapter explores the history of the narrative of opioid addiction and how that narrative construction influences public understanding of opioid addiction. Specifically, the modern social narrative about opioid addiction contributes to social stigmas that not only create barriers to effective treatment of opioid abuse but also obscure broader questions about persistent social problems.

Opioid addiction is not just a matter of science or medicine, but it is a product of an evolved social narrative that has deep roots in values forged in the Enlightenment, and that remain with us today. To put it more esoterically, the modern concept of addiction is the product of a specific historical and cultural trajectory rather than an inevitable unfolding of psychological or medical knowledge. Modern understanding of opioid addiction places addicts in one of two specific but related positions in the social hierarchy. Although each position carries with it its own assumptions and narrative constructions, they often converge in the same place. In both cases, the person grappling with addiction finds themselves on the bottom rung of a complex social hierarchy that includes elements of racial and gender bias. This placement has implications for the treatment of opioid addiction because it inevitably locates addiction in "otherness." Narratives about opioid addiction also supply a convenient scapegoat for many of society's most pressing problems, diverting attention from the actual causes of the problems. In fact, rather than a cause of social ills, opioid addiction is a consequence of social dislocation rooted in failed Enlightenment promises.

EARLY USES OF OPIUM

Opium and its many derivatives come from the opium poppy, a plant likely indigenous to Mesopotamia and Asia Minor, including India and Persia (Hamarneh, 1972). In these cultures, opium has traditionally been used medicinally as a pain reliever and to induce sleep. Opium was imported to other areas of the world through established trade routes. Interestingly, although it seems that while opioids were widely used, there is little mention in the existing literature or histories of these cultures of anything resembling addiction. Hamarneh (1972) notes that "it seems safe to state that there was no spread of drug abuse or addiction in Islamic lands of either poppy or hemp plants during the nineteenth century" (p. 228). Yet, at the same time, opium addiction appeared to be rising in the Occident. But what is addiction, and in what ways is our modern understanding of addiction a social construct?

THE ORIGINS OF ADDICTION

In the history of non-Western cultures, the concept of addiction is virtually nonexistent. Drug use was primarily medicinal or ritualistic. Ritualistic use included imbibing the mind-altering substance as a means of reaching another realm of existence or understanding, or as a means of communicating with gods, spirits, or ancestors. Although dependence or addiction in the clinical sense probably did exist, it was likely exceedingly rare and not understood in those cultures because the term is absent from the cultural lexicon. The term "addiction" and its modern meanings are constructions of Occidental culture.

The meaning of the term addiction has changed significantly over time. Today, the term is most often used pejoratively, especially in the broad, nonspecialized social narrative. While the clinical definition of addiction is defined as a chronic, relapsing disorder characterized by compulsion for the drug or behavior, and its continued use despite negative consequences (US Department of Health and Human Services, n.d.), the pejorative usage often describes a person who is somehow less than complete or less than whole. The term has become weaponized in two specific ways. First, the term is used as a social scapegoat, something often blamed for social problems with deeper and more complex causes. Relatedly, the term addiction has become weaponized against specific types or groups of people in a narrative that places them rigidly at the bottom of the social hierarchy.

Thus, addiction is a culture-bound phenomenon, influenced by social factors (Weinberg, 2011). For most of history, the narrative of drug use has been socially positive or neutral. Only in recent history has the idea of drug use taken on a negative connotation and used as a means of social control. The pejorative narrative of drug use has its roots in the Enlightenment, which ushered in a new way of thinking about human society and the individuals that comprise it. These new ways of thinking emphasized a change in values that made drug use socially problematic (Hickman, 2007).

The term addiction derives from the Latin root *dicere*, meaning to speak or dictate. Attaching the preposition *ad* is translated into "to address" or "to judge." So *addicere* was to speak judgment. In Roman society, the term found common usage in two primary areas of social life—a legal usage and a religious usage. Both usages of the term addiction remain in altered but intact form in the modern world. The legal usage concerned civil law, encapsulating the powers of a judge. *Do, doci, addico* translates to "I give, I say, I adjudge" (Black et al., 1990, p. 37). The *addictus*—the individual upon whom the adjudication was pronounced, was often before the court for indebtedness and ended up chained and imprisoned or sold into slavery. According to White (2004), the popular usage of the time signified surrender to one's superior.

The second usage of the term in early Roman society refers to the communication of the gods as augurs. Positive responses to inquiries about conditions to do battle—*addixerunt*—were judgments by the gods (Rosenthal & Faris, 2019). Significantly, in both cases, the word is rooted in institutions of power: the power of the legal system and power of the gods and institutional religion. In both cases, there is an implication that the individual—*the addictus*—lacks efficacy. Rosenthal and Faris (2019) conspicuously note that the two institutions in which early understanding of addiction are intimately connected. The religious practice of divination was strongly associated with gambling—a significant cause of indebtedness.

In the Middle Ages, the term addiction was placed in a mostly religious context (Rosenthal & Faris, 2019). The term was used to encourage behaviors the Church considered socially desirable while discouraging choices that current dogma considered sinful. For example, being addicted to physical pleasures such as alcohol or gluttony was strongly discouraged, though not necessarily sinful (Lemon, 2018). This idea of addiction extended as well to gaming, tobacco, music, dancing, and other things that were perceived to weaken devotion to God. By contrast, devoting all your time and thought to religious activities was also seen as a form of addiction—albeit a positive one. How addiction was perceived and judged was dependent on the object of devotion, either positive or negative.

In the 17th century, addiction was seen mostly as a positive attribute (Alexander & Schweighofer, 1988; Rosenthal & Faris, 2019) and was used to refer to someone who was a strong adherent to a particular cause. A religious document from 1670 describes addicts devoting most of their day to study, devotion, and other spiritual activities. Other writings from the period describe addicts to God and even addicts to art and poetry. The meaning of the term referred to devotees and how addiction was understood was primarily focused not on the person, but rather on the object of devotion.

By the 19th century, the focus of the term addiction shifts closer to contemporary understanding. Driven by the simultaneous emergence of alcoholism as an increasingly recognized social problem, cultural historians such as Hickman (2007) locate this change in what some have termed the crisis of modernity brought on by the Enlightenment. The Enlightenment was a social, political, and philosophical movement that fundamentally shifted the direction of society. Key value changes included, but were not limited to, an emphasis on individuality and self-efficacy; the rise of science; the emergence of global capitalism; the weakening of religious institutions; and the belief in the perfectibility of society and the power of social institutions to effect positive social change. Each of these values had the latent consequence of changing the social narrative of opioid addiction.

Many names were offered to describe these new addictions, rooted in the increasing social complexity of modern life. While the term "alcoholism" was straightforward and easily outcompeted rival terminology, the situation was more complicated with regard to drugs. While alcohol is a singular category, there are many categories of drugs. Even within the category of opioids, there are many distinct types. Not surprisingly, many terms emerged to describe the emerging concept of addiction. Many of these terms were drug-specific, such as morphism and opiumism. Another highly specific term that shows a clear connection with the parallel development of addiction narratives by combining narcotic use with the effects of alcohol is the term "opium drunkenness" (White, 2004).

The term opium drunkenness is of special note since it shows not only how narratives of opium dependence are intertwined with narratives of alcohol dependence but also how addiction was constructed as volitional. Drunkenness is most often not something that is forced upon a person. Rather, it is something that an individual takes on, something that they do to themselves. This strongly reflected the values of the time.

An emphasis on individualism appeared primarily through the writing of English and Scottish philosophers advocating for natural rights and the efficacy of each person to decide the trajectory of their own life. The emergence of capitalism expanded the horizon of the individual through trade and exploration. Quality of life also improved under capitalism and the subsequent popularization of science and discovery. The rise of science paralleled this newfound individualistic freedom to experiment, ultimately driving the Industrial Revolution. A rapid expansion of wealth accompanied these trends. At the same time, many social problems such as inequality, crime, and poverty became concentrated in cities and thus became more visible to an increasingly urbanized population. Science—including the new sciences of psychology and sociology—promised to solve many of society's most pressing social problems.

These new values brought many benefits to Europeans emerging out of the Middle Ages. However, the emergence of modernity brought new challenges and concerns. Among them was an increase in anomie. The term, popularized by French sociologist Emile Durkheim, refers to a sense of normlessness, or a disconnect from the integrating forces of society for the identity of the individual. This usually accompanies significant social change. The crisis of modernity, as Hickman (2007) calls it, is a crisis of identity. Changing cultural values emphasizing a powerful sense of self-reliance and a decline of religious institutional control threatened traditional ways of life that had prevailed for hundreds of years.

Opioid use in Europe and America was already relatively common as a medicine. Opium in its variety of forms was commonplace among physicians in the middle of the 19th century (Jones, 2020). In its various forms, it was used to treat conditions as varied as chronic pain, headaches, persistent cough, menstrual cramps, vertigo, and insomnia. Laudanum, a mixture of opium and alcohol, was often used to quiet babies who cried too much, and as an anti-anxiety medication. This usage of the drug can be seen in Mary Shelley's novel *Frankenstein*. Victor Frankenstein, a medical student, doses himself with laudanum after the monster he created kills his best friend.

Opioid abuse, though known about, was not a problem that was widely discussed. It was stereotypically seen as a problem of Asian culture, something from a different place and a different time and among a different group of people. The stereotype, exemplified by descriptive accounts that painted Chinese opium users as unindustrious and completely at the mercy of the drug, created an image that juxtaposed Oriental and Occidental culture and served to "otherize" non-Western peoples and confirm the superiority of European civilization. This mythology began to deteriorate, however, with the publication of Thomas De Quincey's *Confessions of an English Opium Eater* in 1821. This serialized publication detailed the author's struggles with opium dependency. Although De Quincey (1852) contributes to the Asiatic stereotype about opioid use, he makes the startling point that opioid addiction is not merely a problem of Asiatic cultures. Rather, the problem is more ubiquitous, affecting white Europeans as well.

De Quincey is careful to balance his assessment of opium. On one hand, he describes the effects of opium as something to increase the imagination and expand creativity. On the other hand, he details in striking fashion the pains of opium addiction, including nightmares and the inability to maintain a sense of reason and efficacy.

At the time, De Quincey's essay was read in a mostly positive light, influencing opium usage by others. Asiatic indulgence, expanded consciousness, and enhanced creativity trumped Enlightenment values of reason and self-determination. Many people—Europeans and Americans alike—were turning to opium as a means of escaping the demands of an increasingly rational world. Critics of De Quincey's essay were quick to point out that opium threatens human faculties. If the Enlightenment promise is to be realized, individuals need to be in complete control of their physical and mental faculties. Opium threatened not just the individual, but also the very fabric of the Enlightenment promises of Utopia. This reveals the challenge of understanding addiction. While nonwhite populations were already living contradictorily in a society that promised freedom but exploited them, the newly emergent cultural values of modernity and capitalism began to isolate members of the dominant society as well. Always being in command of one's faculties is demanding work, straining the identity of the individual and the social institutions that support them. The forces of modernity that created the demand and desire for opium were the same forces that discouraged its usage, thus creating a contradiction that exacerbated anomie and social dislocation among the white population.

There is a parallel between the early antidrug movement and the temperance movement (in reality a series of movements). One of the major effects of alcohol is disinhibition. Alcohol was blamed for domestic violence, crime, indebtedness, and other social ills (Nathan et al., 2016). Alcohol corrupted the values of independence and virtue that were central values of the Enlightenment. The passion of liquor overwhelmed the senses and led to the degradation of the individual. The root of the temperance movement was a refrain against a loss of reason and personal efficacy.

The narrative of the temperance movement came in two fundamental parts. First was the narrative of alcohol and its effects, as noted above. The second, and more important for the current analysis, is the narrative of the person who used alcohol. What kind of a person would allow himself to give in to intoxication at the expense of industry and reason? Although complex and nuanced, the general portrait of the chronic alcoholic was a male who lacked willpower. A lack of self-respect and an unwillingness to work were also common in the narrative. Thus, alcoholism became a narrative about the person rather than about the specific drug of choice. The stereotype strongly reflects a willful dissent from the Enlightenment values that shaped the modern world. In most cases, alcoholism was seen as something that the person chose to do, rather than something that happened to them. Addiction was a sign and symbol of personal weakness.

So powerful was the temperance movement in America that for a while it overshadowed the looming problem of opioid use (Hickman, 2007), which in many ways paralleled alcoholism. The temperance movement and the anti-opioid movement both demanded an elevated level of individual self-control and efficacy (Weinberg, 2011), with the drugs seen as antithetical to the full human realization of Enlightenment values. However, while the temperance movement saw alcoholism as a choice, narratives about opioid addiction were more complicated. Hickman (2007) makes a compelling argument that a dual understanding of addiction appeared. In addition to the volitional definition of opioid addiction as a choice (which mirrored closely the temperance movement), there also emerged a juridical understanding of addiction rooted in medical practice. In this narrative addiction was imposed rather than chosen. As doctors prescribed opium for various maladies, many people who would not have otherwise taken the drug became dependent.

Levine (1978) suggests that the modern concept of addiction is rooted in a change in the way in which the medical profession understood the concept of addiction. This change saw addiction as disease-like, placing the condition in a framework familiar to the profession. The framing of addiction as a disease placed the problem of alcohol dependence—and drug dependence more broadly—in the purview of the medical profession, giving control of the problem and the population affected by it to medical professionals.

In many ways opioid addiction reflected Enlightenment values. Advances in medical sciences revealed increasingly more uses for opioids, and doctors were encouraged to prescribe them for a variety of ailments. As more patients were given opioids, they increasingly became dependent upon the drugs. This juridical addiction was rooted in the science of medicine, supported by the Enlightenment promise of a Utopian society free of pain and suffering. Volitional addiction was also connected to the Enlightenment but in a more complex way. The Enlightenment was a European phenomenon, and the values promoted by Enlightenment thinking scaffolded the belief in the superiority of Occidental culture. As noted, Opium was seen as a primarily Asiatic drug, and its effects were described as creating lethargy and an unwillingness to work. As opioid use seeped into Western culture, there were increasing fears that the superiority of Occidental cultures would be threatened. Volitional opium addiction was described in many texts as making the Europeans more like Asians. This was an interpretation of degrading the Enlightenment promise. As one slips into addiction, one slips away from the values of reason and rationality that form the cornerstone of the Enlightenment. Thus, the narrative of addiction became inexorably entangled with narratives of race. Narratives about addiction and race functioned both to position nonwhite racial groups as other—less than human—and disconnected from progressive Occidental Enlightenment values, as well as to locate these others in a subordinate position relative to the dominant social groups. By associating race with drug use and abuse, social control of those groups became legitimated through other means.

The American Civil War accelerated the rise of the medical profession as an important institution in society. More soldiers died from battle wounds and disease than from direct death on the battlefield. Many wounded soldiers lived in constant pain, and morphine supplied the best option for managing chronic pain. Courtwright (1978) notes that "opiate addiction increased markedly in America during the latter half of the nineteenth century. Estimates of the magnitude and duration of that increase vary; it is likely, however, that there were at least 200,000 addicts by 1900" (p. 101). As we have seen, there are many reasons for the increase in opioid addiction. Yet it is clear from historical evidence that the war was a driving force in the increase in opioid addiction in the United States (Courtwright, 1978). With over 10 million morphine pills issued by the Union army alone, nearly three million ounces of other opium products, and with the emergence of the hypodermic needle an uncountable number of morphine injections, opioids were a drug of choice for many medical problems during the war. Morphine dependence was identified during the war.

As a product of modernity, the war certainly contributed to the increase in addicts. The increasing anomie that accompanied the aftermath of the war also contributed to increasing dependency on drugs. Jones (2020) notes that the conditions of addiction that many soldiers found themselves in "violated prevailing ideals of masculinity and morality, undermining veterans' good character and manhood" (p. 186). Jones goes on to say that medical understanding of opioid addiction at the time believed that addiction resulted in insanity, "a diagnosis that often resulted in a literal loss of freedom when addicted veterans were involuntarily committed to mental institutions" (p. 186). Thus, many veterans suffering from addiction were involuntarily committed to mental institutions, thus forfeiting their freedom. Institutions of that time were not recuperative institutions. Rather, they functioned primarily to remove the mentally ill from society. A poorly understood phenomenon, mental illness was seen as enfeebling. In other words, opioid addiction, a condition brought on by the demands of modern society, disconnected veterans from Enlightenment ideals about what it means to be a noble and good person.

MODERN ADDICTION

The emergence of modern opioid addiction during the American Civil War had another important effect. The medical profession became more legitimized, capitalizing on rapid scientific advances that preceded and followed the conflict. The juridical addict was born—an addict who was given drugs under the supervision of the medical profession. Ironically, juridical addiction gave rise to much of the modern control of addiction to the medical profession (Acker, 2004). As addiction became more widespread, it gained increasing attention from the medical community. Doctors made an increasingly vocal case to the government to do something about what was perceived to be a growing crisis unique to the modern world. In America, the scope of government intervention in drug use was seen to be limited by the Constitution. Drugs have been legal and unregulated since the founding of the nation, with many of the Founding Fathers using drugs for various maladies. However, with the emergence of the concept of addiction after the war and the positioning of addicts as socially undesirable and threatening to the American way of life, federal legislation became more likely.

Initially, the federal government had little interest in regulating narcotics. Alcohol dependency was seen as a more widespread problem, and thus more worthy of attention. Additionally, opium and other narcotics were still seen by many as foreign problems that, while seeping into American culture, were characteristics of other cultures and peoples. The federal government did not take the drug problem seriously until 1898, after the United States took control of the Philippine Islands after the Spanish-American War (Drug Enforcement Administration (DEA) The Early Years, n.d.). Calls from the medical profession for the government to legislate power to doctors and pharmacies to control access to opioids eventually led to the passage of the Harrison Narcotics Act in 1914. Due to Constitutional considerations, the legislation lacked any real means of addressing the emerging narcotics problem and was passed mostly as a revenue stream for the government. Because the Harrison Narcotics Act was a revenue bill, enforcement of the legislation was given to the Treasury Department. The relevant aspect of the legislation rests in the broad ability of physicians to prescribe narcotics in the course of their professional practice, so long as that prescription was prescribed in good faith.

Drug use was thus increasingly seen as a legal and medical problem. Both frameworks reflect the dominance of Enlightenment values: the first as a function of new political philosophies and the second as a function of the increasing dominance of science and rationality. Ironically, there is some evidence that narcotic usage was declining prior to the passage of the Harrison Narcotics Act (Courtwright, 2001). The decline was likely the result of the same forces that gave rise to medico-legal dominance in the first place (Campbell, 2007).

At first, the connection between medical control of opioids and legal regulation of the drugs was limited to government sanction of the medical profession. The requirement for a prescription to have opioids was created and enforced by federal statute, but the practice was relegated to physicians and pharmacies (Hickman, 2007). One hope for this regulation was to reinforce the emerging disease model and move toward the destigmatization of individuals suffering from addiction.

Federal regulation and medical control of drugs did little to destigmatize drug use, however. In fact, in some ways, it made the problem worse. Medical diagnoses seek causal clarification and separating addicts into juridical or volitional further placed addicts in subordinate positions. The only difference was which institution gained control over the addict. In the case of the juridical addict, the addict was put at the mercy of the medical profession and their expertise. The volitional addict was more often controlled by the criminal justice system.

After the constitutionality of the Harrison Narcotics Act was affirmed by the Supreme Court, the way was cleared for increased government regulation and control of the drug market. The fledgling Narcotic Division of the Internal Revenue Service, headed by Levi Nutt, included more than 150 narcotic agents (Drug Enforcement Agency, n.d.). Nutt often clashed with physicians because he was opposed to addiction maintenance strategies which were becoming increasingly common among the medical profession at the time. By 1921, Nutt's agents closed 44 narcotics clinics, unquestioningly making worse the problem that he was tasked with solving.

Although not officially declared as a government initiative, a tacit war on drugs had begun. The war was escalated by the government with the creation of the Federal Bureau of Narcotics in 1930. The Federal Bureau of Narcotics merged two small agencies and had substantially more power to shape drug policy than its predecessors. The bureau was headed by Harry Anslinger, a charismatic and morally obsessive character. He was also a racist. Anslinger's obsession with increasing the power and scope of agency was facilitated by a patina of scholarly research. Anslinger's agency publicized studies that supported increased federal control of drugs while suppressing studies that suggested that drugs were not as dangerous as many people suspected. He promoted his own department's claim that drug use was rising and stifled research that concluded the opposite.

Anslinger's tactics renewed the connection between race and drugs and created the connection between drugs and violence. His agency promoted the idea that Mexicans were importing marijuana and that it made them violent and lustful. Specifically, he argued before Congress that marijuana made Mexicans desire white women. He made similar accusations about African Americans about their use of marijuana, cocaine, and opioids. Such claims were, of course, nonsense, but they perfectly illustrate how the narratives of drug use represented a clash between dominant and subordinate cultures. Drugs threatened the dominance of white cultural values. Thus, the idea that addicts were somehow different from everyone else now had the sanction of the federal government.

The war on drugs officially began in 1971 with a declaration by Richard Nixon that aimed at his political enemies. Former White House counsel and assistant to the president for Domestic Affairs John Ehrlichman said in a 1994 interview that:

> We knew we couldn't make it illegal to be either against the war or black, but by getting the public to associate the hippies with marijuana and blacks with heroin, and then criminalizing both heavily, we could disrupt those communities. We could arrest their leaders, raid their homes, break up their meetings, and vilify them night after night on the evening news. Did we know we were lying about the drugs? Of course we did. (Garza, 2016)

As the quote suggests, drug use is seen as antithetical to organized civilization, framed as distinctly antigovernment and anti-utilitarian—something in direct opposition to the Enlightenment values that frame modern conceptions of opioid addiction. The image of drug use is given a racial profile, even though rates of addiction as a percentage of the population are similar across racial lines. More importantly, juridical addiction is absent from this narrative construction. The idea that addicts are victims of the medical profession or other forces outside the control of the addict has been surpassed by the volitional model that suggests that addiction is solely the fault of the drug user. The common picture of an opioid addict is often a poor Black male, even though data show that those new to heroin use in the past decades are 90% white (Mendoza et al., 2019).

In the 1980s President Ronald Reagan expanded the war on drugs with a narrative that Hawdon (2001) describes as a moral panic. A moral panic is defined as a condition in which a group of persons is defined as a threat to dominant social values or interests (Cohen, 1972). Even though evidence suggests that drug use was declining in the 1980s, a politically motivated narrative supplied a convenient scapegoat for a myriad of social problems. Claims that drug use was an epidemic, particularly among youth, equated to a call for action against what was described as a pernicious evil.

This vilification offered politicians a ready-made scapegoat for several social ills. The Reagan administration blamed drugs for many pressing social problems, such as teen pregnancy, rising juvenile and adult crime, poverty, and rising numbers of welfare recipients. Volitional addiction became increasingly entwined with the political and legal system. Juridical addiction became increasingly relegated to the margins of public discourse on addiction.

Succeeding President Reagan, George Bush failed to maintain the moral panic of drug use (Hawdon, 2001). Yet, while his narrative was less forceful than Reagan's, it was certainly more racist. While Reagan's narrative claimed drugs as a pervasive problem that crossed racial, gender, and social class boundaries, the narrative constructed by the Bush administration and the legal reform that flowed from that narrative saw drugs as a problem primarily in poor, Black, inner-city neighborhoods. This is most exemplified in legislation that increased criminal penalties for crack cocaine but not for powdered cocaine. Powdered cocaine was commonly seen as a drug associated with rich white men, with movies and television portraying white CEOs snorting cocaine through rolled-up hundred-dollar bills. Conversely, crack cocaine, which is chemically similar to the powdered form, was associated with hyperviolent and hypersexual Black males residing in areas of concentrated disadvantage. Both parts of this narrative support a strongly volitional model of drug use, but the narrative is divided in the way in which each race tolerated and used the drugs. White drug use was seen as done in a context of fun and success. Black drug use was seen in the context of crime and poverty. Critically, both narratives reflect Enlightenment thinking. While white drug use as an individual choice is rooted in the capitalist ideal—a symbol of decadence—Black drug use is rooted in the poverty of failure within a culture that believes everyone can be successful.

The history of addiction makes it clear that addiction is most often seen as a failing of the individual. Although the medical profession and academia have ostensibly abandoned this position, it remains the dominant social belief about addiction in the broader society (Santoro & Santoro, 2018). The social narrative that addicts are primarily volitional, and that they are responsible for many of our most visible social problems, is still prevalent. However, juridical addiction has also made a resurgence, despite claims by Goldstein (2001) that "medically caused addiction is today truly a rarity, practically a myth" (p. 159), more recent research from Cicero et al. (2014) belies Goldstein's claim. Using self-report data on past drug use, Cicero and colleagues found that 75% of drug users in their sample were introduced to opioids through prescription drugs. Data collected by Han et al. (2015) suggest that nonmedical use of prescription opioids has decreased over time. However, high-risk opioid use has increased. The authors echo earlier research (Jones et al., 2014) that attributes this increase in high-intensity prescription opioid use to an increase in prescribing opioids in the general population. Prescribing more opioids increased not only the propensity for juridical addiction but also the number of opioids in circulation (Centers for Disease Control and Prevention, 2023).

This trend can be seen in media portrayals of opioid use. Netherland and Hansen (2016) conducted a content analysis of popular press articles discussing heroin users. Results showed a clear difference in the way in which opioid use was portrayed across racial lines. Whites were portrayed as juridical users, sympathetic users of prescription painkillers; Black people and Hispanics were portrayed as volitional users, criminalized users of injected heroin.

These trends have caused a shift in academic approaches to opioid addiction but have done little to change the narrative of addiction. Data suggests that to at least some degree juridical addiction drives the current public health crisis of opioid addiction. However, this effect may be overstated. Most people who use drugs, including opioids, do not become addicts. Most drug scares are manufactured crises emerging from racist or classist political narratives (Murakawa, 2011) and have little basis in reality. The narrative about opioid addiction, for example, suggests that once a person begins using opioids, regardless of the source of first use, the results end up the same. The social opprobrium of addiction applies to both juridical and volitional addiction. Volitional addicts should never have chosen to use drugs, while juridical addicts should know enough to stop using them. Opioid addicts are vilified because the social narrative suggests that they can just stop. This narrative is reinforced by government policy and medical practice that advocates methods of treatment that emphasize an abstinence-only model. The American government at every level has refused to support addiction maintenance programs with demonstrated treatment efficacy while financially supporting abstinence-only models with dubious records of success.

It seems likely that opioid use and associated deaths are on the rise (Wood & Elliott, 2019), with the largest increase in deaths occurring among Black opioid users (Haider Warraich, 2022). The influx of fentanyl—a potent synthetic opioid—appears responsible for the increase in deaths overall, while gaps in access to healthcare and disparities in treatment seem to account for the increases in deaths among African Americans.

STIGMA

Regardless of the source of the addiction, the addict is subject to the effects of stigma. The concept of stigma is most often used to refer to a negative label that is applied to a person, which becomes part of the person's identity and disqualifies the person from full social acceptance or full participation in society. Although many people have written about stigma, the most widely cited comes from Goffman (1963). Goffman (1963) names several kinds of stigma: tribal stigma, physical deformations, and deviations in personality. More recently, Falk (2001) named two kinds of stigmas: existential and achieved. Existential stigmas are stigmas that a person is born with, such as a congenital birth defect; or stigmas that are imposed upon the individual. Achieved stigmas are those that a person takes on during their lifetime, such as opioid addiction.

Volitional addiction is situated as an achieved stigma. However, the status of juridical addiction is less clear. Although the origins of juridical addiction are indeed imposed in the sense that the first drug use is sanctioned by the medical profession, continued usage beyond the immediate need for medical care doubtless contains a degree of volition. As Han and colleagues (2015) point out, nonmedical use of prescription opioids is on the rise. Increasing regulation of physicians by the government in the wake of this knowledge has also blurred the line between government approaches to opioid addiction and medical approaches to opioid addiction. Thus, the space between types of stigmas—and the narratives that accompany each—has become increasingly blurred.

The blurring of juridical and volitional addiction becomes clearer when one considers how the government has come to address juridical addiction. After the Harrison Narcotics Act granted power to the medical profession to prescribe opioids, the government has increasingly regulated opioids and other drugs. Government sanctions have increasingly replaced medical expertise. Most recently, in the wake of an uptick in opioid addictions allegedly caused by overprescription of painkillers, the criminal justice system began placing increasingly restrictive rules on medical practitioners and arrested and prosecuted those who were seen to have overstepped the power granted to them by federal fiat. Additionally, the federal government has prohibited addiction maintenance strategies and significantly limited drugs used to treat opioid addiction, such as Suboxone, buprenorphine, and naloxone. Thus, when it comes to opioids and other drugs, even the medical profession is subordinate to the federal government.

The arrest and prosecution of doctors and pharmaceutical companies for their role in the opioid crisis has added to the public narrative of drug addiction by implicating the medical profession and fomenting distrust in modern medicine. The effects of these policies will have a negative impact on the treatment of opioid addiction in three main ways. First, the criminalization of the medical profession erodes trust in the medical profession. Mistrust makes it less likely that individuals addicted to opioids will seek help. Relatedly, doctors may be less willing to offer help, both in the realm of pain management as well as in the prescribing of addiction maintenance medications. Finally, the criminalizing of doctors for prescribing needed medication that leads to addiction further places the addict in the position of "other," stigmatizing them as something to be criminalized and scapegoated rather than as victims to be treated.

Several excellent studies document these concerns. McCracken et al. (2006) note that fear of professional sanction is still a challenge for doctors seeking to help patients with opioid addiction. Patients also expressed concern. Nearly 45% of patients seeking opioids for chronic pain expressed apprehension about addiction. Even more, 75% expressed concern about developing tolerance to the drug, one step in the process of addiction. Patients also expressed apprehension of being questioned about the medication, refilling medication, and experiencing a relationship of mistrust with their physician.

Some of this mistrust appears warranted. Increasing regulation of the medical profession by the government when it comes to prescribing opioids has led to concerns about over-monitoring both the medical profession and the patient. Although tight monitoring is justified by the political elites as necessary to reduce opioid addiction, it is unclear whether it has the desired effect or not. Additionally, strict control may have the latent effect of deterring patients who need pain control from seeking treatment, as well as deterring doctors from prescribing medication that may be needed for normal functioning. Indeed, according to the Centers for Disease Control and Prevention (2023) rates of opioid prescriptions as measured per capita have declined since 2019. Yet, as previously noted, nonmedical opioid use is on the rise.

Research does suggest a shift in physician attitudes toward prescribing opioids to patients who need them. A study by Turk et al. (1994) revealed little moral or legal concern for physicians prescribing opioids. However, just four years later, Gallagher (1998) suggests some apprehension by doctors about prescribing opioids to patients. The first successful conviction of a physician prescribing opioids was for manslaughter occurred in 2016, when patients under the care of

Dr. Hsui-Ying Tseng died from opioid overdoses. Dr. Tseng was sentenced to 30 years to life for her role in facilitating the deaths of three patients she had recklessly prescribed opioids for chronic pain management (Yang & Haffajee, 2016). This conviction drove home the fear of opioid addiction that is manifest in the social narrative. The medical community, once given control of opioids by the government, now found itself in the line of fire in the face of a growing concern over opioid use.

Mistrust between doctors and patients is high (Merrill et al., 2002). Because of the shift in the legal landscape regarding physicians prescribing opioids, doctors report significant fear of being deceived by patients about the degree of medical need for the drugs. Many doctors seem to second-guess themselves when it comes to prescribing opioids, even when the patient and their medical history are known. Overly invasive questioning by physicians may lead to mistrust by the patient who believes that their opioid use may be revealed by the doctor and criminalized.

These concerns are amplified when the patients are Black. Hall et al. (2022) report that mistrust in the medical profession is higher among African American populations seeking treatment for opioid addiction. This is both a cause and consequence of well-documented racial disparities in health access and drug treatment. Given the history of addiction as a foundationally racist narrative connected to violence and a myriad of other social problems, this mistrust is understandable. The volitional model cuts both ways, creating a mindset both in the social world and in the minds of addicts that they are somehow less than whole. The problem of addiction is both a social problem—as exemplified in the juridical model—and an individual problem when seen as volitional.

In either case, the addict is seen as an "other," as something outside of the normal. The stigma attached to the process of "otherization" places the addict at the bottom rung of the social hierarchy. This is made worse by the intersection of race and social class with the label of addict. In other words, while being a member of a historically marginalized group places a person low in the social hierarchy; and being poor places a person low in the social hierarchy; being poor and Black and an addict creates layers of social opprobrium that significantly affects treatment in several ways.

Regardless of whether drug use is seen as volitional or juridical, the social construction of addiction places the addict in a subordinate relationship. In the case of juridical addiction, the addict finds themselves subordinate to a medical profession that may have caused the addiction in the first place. The power granted to the medical profession by the government now looks to solve a problem that it, however inadvertently, created. Juridical addicts are dependent on the medical profession for support, treatment, and follow-up. Volitional addicts are in a subordinate position to the criminal justice profession, which is by nature punitive and rooted in the belief that the addict is the cause of their addiction. In both cases, the addict is relegated to a subordinate place in the hierarchy of treatment. Treatment of opioid addicts is still rooted in Enlightenment thinking, with drug use continually seen as a willing rejection of dominant social values.

CONCLUSION

Social narratives about opioid addiction are rooted in Enlightenment values and are a product of modernity (Alexander, 2008). These narratives are intertwined with narratives about race and otherness and form part of a broader scapegoat mentality. Increasing demands on time; increased pressure of capitalism toward unachievable material wealth; scientism; and the deconstruction of identity have outpaced cultural coping mechanisms. Drugs offer a convenient and ready escape from the pressures of modern life. Drugs are symptoms of modern problems, not the cause of them. If society is genuinely interested in mitigating the problem of drugs in society, and in the treatment of persons who are victims of addiction, we should carefully consider the position that current models of addiction narratives create. Positions of subordination are positions that lack power. As Alexander (2008) has pointed out, people who lack social power and social efficacy are often the ones most likely to turn to drugs as a coping mechanism and are more likely to become addicts. Continuing to put addicts into subordinate positions in their treatment process reinforces the conditions that may have caused them to first use drugs. A better approach might be to construct a new narrative along two fronts.

First, a reevaluation of social expectations and norms is warranted. Opioid use is a conditional response to anomie—a sense of normlessness. The conflict or frustration that is felt when a discrepancy emerges between social expectations and personal beliefs and abilities creates a profound inner tension that must be resolved (Raymond, 1975). When people feel disconnected from institutions and social forces that form the foundations of their society and their social identity, anomie results. Alexander (2008) developed the dislocation theory of addiction, in which globalization and strong individualistic tendencies characteristic of late-stage capitalism create a sense of nonbelonging and psychosocial integration, which fuels drug use as an escape. Alexander is describing anomie. He writes that "people can endure dislocation for a time. However, prolonged dislocation eventually leads to unbearable despair, shame, emotional anguish, boredom, and bewilderment" (Alexander, 2008, p. 59). Alexander suggests that drug use offers a readily available means of coping with anomie. Opioids are particularly common because the effects they have on the body and mind are numbing. Addiction is merely a byproduct of significant drug use. Alexander reminds us that while many people use drugs, most drug users never become addicts. "Only chronically and severely dislocated people are vulnerable to addiction" (Alexander, 2008, p. 63).

Narratives are important for society. They supply convenient unifying stories and myths that help to organize society. They often serve the function of alerting members of society to problems that need to be addressed. However, they often place the blame for social problems on groups who are marginalized or powerless. Such scapegoating distracts from the real cause of the problem. Dominant narratives of opioid addiction are problematic because they make addicts the cause of social problems when in fact the social problems are the ultimate cause of opioid addiction. People turn to drugs to cope with the increasingly isolating effects of modernity.

Opioid addiction is a consequence of the failure of modern Enlightenment values to deliver on its promises. In the absence of adequate social support and mental health care, drugs offer an available and affordable salve for the increasingly commonplace anomie of modernity. People use drugs to cope with the normlessness that results from increasing social demands for individual perfection. Too often, addiction is the result.

Psychiatrist Thomas Szasz (1960, 1974) suggested that mental illnesses are really nothing more than problems of living—an inability to function in an increasingly demanding modernist world. Just as Hickman (2007) located addiction in modernity, so does Szasz. Addiction is a problem of living, of modern life. As Peele (2012) puts it, "at its core, addiction is more than a physical problem; it is a problem with how we live and experience our lives" (p. 24). Reducing stigma around job loss, family dissolution, educational inequity, and other important drivers of anomie are all important aspects of reducing initial drug use. Rather than seeing opioid addiction as something about the person, we should approach addiction as a problem of functioning or living in a world that demands more and more—institutionally through more laws and thus more obedience; more regulation of thought and behavior; and greater expectations for achievement—and individually through the securing of a solid social identity at seemingly younger and younger ages while at the same time encouraging the growth of technologies that make social connectedness more and more of a challenge. Addressing the social problems at the root of anomie or dislocation places less burden on addicts and reduces stigma associated with opioid addiction.

The effectiveness of opioids as a means of physical and mental pain relief makes it an ideal choice for the relief from modern anomie. New narratives of opioid addiction need to be constructed to avoid the historical racism and classism that characterizes current social opprobrium of drug use. New narratives should consider addicts in the most human way possible, victims of societal failings, rather than causes of it. If society is committed to combating opioid addiction, a new narrative that places opioid use as a consequence of a dislocating modernity, rather than as a cause of social problems, is necessary. Such an understanding reinforces the humanness of addicts. Focus should be placed on reducing social dislocation and anomie. Solving the problems of living in an increasingly demanding modern world, rather than blaming and attacking victims of modernity should be prioritized.

REFERENCES

Acker, C. (2004). Portrait of an addicted family: Dynamics of opiate addiction in the early twentieth century. In S. W. Tracy & C. J. Acker (Eds.), *Altering the American consciousness: The history of alcohol and drug use in the United States, 1800–2000* (pp. 164–81). University of Massachusetts Press.

Alexander, B. K. (2008). *The globalization of addiction: A study on poverty of the spirit.* Oxford University Press.

Alexander, B. K., & Schweighofer, A. R. (1988). Defining "addiction." *Canadian Psychology/Psychologie Canadienne, 29*(2), 151–62. https://doi.org/10.1037/h0084530

Black H. C., Nolan, J. R., & Nolan-Haley, J. M. (1990). *Black's law dictionary: Definitions of the terms and phrases of American and English jurisprudence, ancient and modern* (6th ed.). West Publishing.

Campbell, N. D. (2007). *Discovering addiction: The science and politics of substance abuse research.* University of Michigan Press.

Centers for Disease Control and Prevention. (2023, December 11). *United States dispensing rate maps.* Centers for Disease Control and Prevention. https://www.cdc.gov/drugoverdose/rxrate-maps/index.html

Cicero, T. J., Ellis, M. S., Surratt, H. L., & Kurtz, S. P. (2014). The changing face of heroin use in the United States. *JAMA Psychiatry, 71*(7), 821. https://doi.org/10.1001/jamapsychiatry.2014.366

Cohen, S. (1972). *Folk devils and moral panics: The creation of the mods and rockers.* Paladin, 1973.

Courtwright, D. T. (1978). Opiate addiction as a consequence of the Civil War. *Civil War History, 24*(2), 101–11. https://doi.org/10.1353/cwh.1978.0039

Courtwright, D. T. (2001). *Forces of habit: Drugs and the making of the modern world.* Harvard University Press.

Croq, M. (2007). Historical and cultural aspects of man's relationship with addictive drugs. *Dialogues in Clinical Neuroscience, 9*(4), 355–61.

De Quincey, T. (1852). *Confessions of an English opium eater.* Boston, Ticknor, Reed, and Fields.

Drug Enforcement Administration (DEA) The Early Years. (n.d.). https://www.dea.gov/sites/default/files/2018-05/Early%20Years%20p%2012-29.pdf

Falk, G. (2001). *Stigma: How we treat outsiders.* Prometheus Books.

Gallagher, R. M. (1998). Outcomes and moral hazards in the medical culture of opioid phobia. *The Clinical Journal of Pain, 14*(3), 185–86. https://doi.org/10.1097/00002508-199809000-00001

Garza, F. (2016, March 23). *Nixon advisor: We created the war on drugs to "criminalize" black people and the anti-war left.* Quartz. https://qz.com/645990/nixon-advisor-we-created-the-war-on-drugs-to-criminalize-black-people-and-the-anti-war-left

Goffman, E. (1963). *Stigma: Notes on the management of spoiled identity.* Touchstone.

Goldstein, A. (2001). *Addiction: From biology to drug policy.* Oxford University Press.

Haider Warraich, M. (2022, August 15). *Opioid addiction and overdoses are increasingly harming black communities.* Harvard Health. https://www.health.harvard.edu/blog/opioid-addiction-and-overdoses-are-increasingly-harming-black-communities-202208152800

Hall, O. T., Bhadra-Heintz, N. M., Teater, J., Samiec, J., Moreno, J., Dixon-Shambley, K., Rood, K. M., Fiellin, D. A., & Jordan, A. (2022). Group-based medical mistrust and care expectations among black patients seeking addiction treatment. *Drug and Alcohol Dependence Reports, 2*, 100026. https://doi.org/10.1016/j.dadr.2022.100026

Hamarneh, S. (1972). Pharmacy in medieval Islam and the history of drug addiction. *Medical History, 16*(3), 226–37. https://doi.org/10.1017/s0025727300017725

Han, B., Compton, W. M., Jones, C. M., & Cai, R. (2015). Nonmedical prescription opioid use and use disorders among adults aged 18 through 64 years in the United States, 2003–2013. *JAMA, 314*(14), 1468. https://doi.org/10.1001/jama.2015.11859

Hawdon, J. E. (2001). The role of presidential rhetoric in the creation of a moral panic: Reagan, Bush, and the war on drugs. *Deviant Behavior, 22*(5), 419–45. https://doi.org/10.1080/01639620152472813

Hickman, T. A. (2007). *The secret leprosy of modern days: Narcotic addiction and cultural crisis in the United States, 1870–1920.* University of Massachusetts Press.

Jones, C. M., Paulozzi, L. J., & Mack, K. A. (2014). Sources of prescription opioid pain relievers by frequency of past-year nonmedical use. *JAMA Internal Medicine, 174*(5), 802. https://doi.org/10.1001/jamainternmed.2013.12809

Jones, J. S. (2020). Opium slavery: Civil War veterans and opiate addiction. *Journal of the Civil War Era, 10*(2), 185–212. https://doi.org/10.1353/cwe.2020.0025

Lemon, R. (2018). *Addiction and devotion in Early Modern England.* https://doi.org/10.9783 /9780812294811

Levine, H. G. (1978). The discovery of addiction. Changing conceptions of habitual drunkenness in America. *Journal of Studies on Alcohol, 39*(1), 143–74. https://doi.org/10.15288 /jsa.1978.39.143

McCracken, L. M., Hoskins, J., & Eccleston, C. (2006). Concerns about medication and medication use in chronic pain. *Journal of Pain, 7*(10), 726–34. https://doi.org/10.1016/j .jpain.2006.02.014

Mendoza, S., Hatcher, A. E., & Hansen, H. (2019). Race, stigma, and addiction. In J. Avery & J. Avery (Eds.), *The stigma of addiction* (pp. 131–53). Springer.

Merrill, J. O., Rhodes, L. A., Deyo, R. A., Marlatt, G. A., & Bradley, K. A. (2002). Mutual mistrust in the medical care of drug users. The keys to the "narc" cabinet. *Journal of General Internal Medicine, 17*(5), 327–33. https://doi.org/10.1046/j.1525-1497.2002.10625.x

Murakawa, N. (2011). Toothless: The methamphetamine "epidemic," "meth mouth," and the racial construction of drug scares. *Du Bois Review: Social Science Research on Race, 8*(1), 219–28. https://doi.org/10.1017/s1742058x11000208

Nathan, P. E., Conrad, M., & Skinstad, A. H. (2016). History of the concept of addiction. *Annual Review of Clinical Psychology, 12*(1), 29–51. https://doi.org/10.1146/annurev -clinpsy-021815-093546

Netherland, J., & Hansen, H. B. (2016). The war on drugs that wasn't: Wasted whiteness, "dirty doctors," and race in media coverage of prescription opioid misuse. *Culture, Medicine, and Psychiatry, 40*(4), 664–86. https://doi.org/10.1007/s11013-016-9496-5

Peele, S. (2012). Addiction myths. *RSA Journal, 158*(5549), 20–24.

Raymond, F. B. (1975). A sociological view of narcotics addiction. *Crime & Delinquency, 21*(1), 11–18. https://doi.org/10.1177/001112877502100102

Rosenthal, R. J., & Faris, S. B. (2019). The etymology and early history of "addiction." *Addiction Research & Theory, 27*(5), 437–49. https://doi.org/10.1080/16066359.2018.1543412

Santoro, T. N., & Santoro, J. D. (2018). Racial bias in the US opioid epidemic: A review of the history of systemic bias and implications for care. *Cureus, 10*(12), e3733. https://doi .org/10.7759/cureus.3733

Szasz, T. S. (1960). The myth of mental illness. *American Psychologist, 15*(2), 113–18. https:// doi.org/10.1037/h0046535

Szasz, T. (1974). *The myth of mental illness: Foundations of a theory of personal conduct.* Harper and Row.

Turk, D. C., Brody, M. C., & Okifuji, A. E. (1994). Physicians' attitudes and practices regarding the long-term prescribing of opioids for non-cancer pain. *Pain, 59*(2), 201–8. https://doi.org/10.1016/0304-3959(94)90072-8

U.S. Department of Health and Human Services. (n.d.). National Institutes of Health. https://nida.nih.gov/

Weinberg, D. (2011). Sociological perspectives on addiction. *Sociology Compass, 5*(4), 298–310. https://doi.org/10.1111/j.1751-9020.2011.00363.x

White, W. L. (2004). The lessons of language: Historical perspectives on the rhetoric of addiction. In S. W. Tracy & C. J. Acker (Eds.), *Altering the American consciousness: The history of alcohol and drug use in the United States, 1800–2000* (pp. 33–55). University of Massachusetts Press.

Wood, E., & Elliott, M. (2019). Opioid addiction stigma: The intersection of race, social class, and gender. *Substance Use & Misuse, 55*(5), 818–27. https://doi.org/10.1080/10826084.2019.1703750

Yang, T. Y, & Haffajee, R. L. (2016). When do opioid prescribers become criminals? *Mayo Clinic Proceedings, 91*(10), 1331–35.

2

Opioids from Abroad

The Chinese Connection

Josiah R. Baker

RISING DEATH TOLLS

Starting in the mid-1990s, the United States has endured an ongoing and growing opioid abuse epidemic. Since then, drug-related hospital emergency department visits, substance abuse treatment admissions, and overdose deaths have dramatically increased. The typical prescription opioid abuser is white, male, and between 45 and 55 years of age (Gardner et al., 2022). The hardest-hit states were in Appalachia and the Northeast (Gardner et al., 2022). Furthermore, fentanyl's potency is best illustrated by the total amount consumed. For example, in 2021, despite having many more users, only single-digit metric tons of fentanyl were consumed compared to roughly 145 tons of cocaine. Although the crisis began with legally prescribed drugs, particularly the painkiller OxyContin (Paulozzi et al., 2011), healthcare experts did not anticipate it, and medical workers were ill-prepared for the negative and alarming consequences of widespread state-sanctioned opioid use.

Key factors in the emergence of the fentanyl black market include legal and illegal drug manufacturers and distributors, liberalization of enforcement measures by the Drug Enforcement Administration (DEA), the role of the Food and Drug Administration (FDA), licensure boards and legislatures, competing interpretations of scientific and medical studies, and an abundance of misuse of prescribed medicine. Moreover, big pharma's financial influence, including its role in improperly advocating profit-seeking efforts with physician groups, and by promoting literature (considered peer-reviewed) led to the explosive use of opioid drugs going into the 21st century and beyond (Manchikanti et al., 2018).

Fentanyl's ubiquitous popularity is better explained by considering both sides of the market. From the demand-side argument, compared to heroin, fentanyl is easier to use, costs less, is less dangerous to purchase, and falsely presents itself as having fewer contaminants and impurities. From the supplier-side argument (again, compared to heroin), since fentanyl is usually a powder-based substance, it is primarily sold as cheap manufactured pills that are easier to transport, store, and retain a higher degree of potency longer (especially if their final destination is in relatively remote, lower-income rural areas).

Among an abundance of evidence that supports the seriousness and severity of the American opioid epidemic, from 1996 to 2019, the Centers for Disease Control and Prevention (CDC) estimated a total of nearly 500,000 overdose deaths (Gardner et al., 2022). According to the CDC, since the late 1990s, drug overdoses more than tripled, becoming the top cause of injury-related deaths (exceeding those from automobile accidents and homicides). From 1999 to 2006, the US average annual growth of drug-related fatalities hovered around 10%. By 2009, drug overdose deaths exceeded those involving automobiles (Gardner et al., 2022). Furthermore, between 1999 and 2017, drug-related mortality rates jumped from 6.1 to 21.7 per 100,000 people. Among these fatalities, opioids alone accounted for 67.8% of them (Hedegaard et al., 2020; Scholl et al., 2019). Consequently, between 2014 and 2017, American average life expectancy decreased from 78.8 to 78.5 (Gardner et al., 2022).

During the following year, 2010, responding to immense social and political pressure, the pharmaceutical industry finally produced abuse-deterrent formulations of OxyContin (Cicero et al., 2012; Evans et al., 2018). However, by then, millions of addicts had adjusted to using heroin or synthetic opiates (Hedegaard et al., 2020; Ho, 2017; Jones et al., 2018; Paulozzi et al., 2011). Unfortunately, the death toll continued rising with annual total fatalities increasing by 16% from 2014 to 2017 (Hedegaard et al., 2020). By 2017, among all high-income countries in the world, the United States had the highest drug overdose mortality totals (Crimmins & Zhang, 2019; Hedegaard et al., 2020; Ho, 2013; Thombs et al., 2020; Woolf & Laudan, 2013). Note that these sums did not include unreported, misreported, and accidental deaths attributed to drug abuse. These statistics demonstrate the extent of this national public medical emergency (Gomes et al., 2018; Hedegaard et al., 2020; Kariisa et al., 2022).

What caused the high number of fatal cases among illicit opioid users? Fentanyl and its analogs have a lower median lethal dose than other opioids, which makes it easier to have a fatal overdose. Other factors included a lack of awareness about synthetic opioid potency, its variability, availability, and increasing adulteration of the drug that involved mixing heroin and other potentially lethal substances. In addition, almost all the increases in overdose deaths are attributed to illicitly manufactured fentanyl, not due to misused or diverted pharmaceutical fentanyl because the total prescriptions for pharmaceutical fentanyl have remained relatively stable since 2010. Prescription fentanyl, if it were available, would be at least safer than low-quality illicit opioids (Sun & Breslin, 2021).

By 2019, a consensus among American politicians and the public was that the country had become embroiled in an ongoing drug overdose epidemic of an unprecedented magnitude. In 2022, the CDC reported an estimate of over 110,000 drug overdose deaths and, of those, more than two-thirds included fentanyl or fentanyl-related synthetic drugs (John et al., 2023; Ovalle & Hudson, 2023). In June 2022, Congress responded to the growing opioid epidemic by passing a bipartisan bill introduced by Senator Rick Scott (R-FL), called "The Eradicating Narcotic Drugs and Formulating Effective New Tools to Address National Yearly Losses of Life Act" or the "End Fentanyl Act," which focused on strengthening border enforcement to stem the flow of fentanyl into the United States. This legislation required "U.S. Customs and Border Protection to review and update, as necessary, manuals and policies related to inspections at ports of entry to ensure the uniformity of inspection practices to effectively detect illegal activity along the border, such as the smuggling of drugs and humans" (Ovalle & Hudson, 2023).

Disavowing any meaningful cooperation from China, Senator Scott later proclaimed, "No amount of weak appeasement from Joe Biden is going to change Communist China's desire to weaken the United States and kill Americans. We've seen this failed playbook before when then–Vice President Joe Biden tried to get Communist China to crack down on fentanyl during the Obama administration. They didn't keep their word then and won't now" (Ovalle & Hudson, 2023).

Given the opioid epidemic's longevity and its many complicities, will Senator Scott's legislation accurately address and solve the crisis? Or is this effort another regulatory attempt that offers a passing hope of which will soon be sidestepped, or is its impact minimized by the overwhelming effects of this social disease driven by an inelastic chemical dependency?

This chapter will explore and examine many of the opioid market's key driving factors with a special emphasis on international trafficking, particularly China's involvement, and other exogenous variables that play a vital role in perpetuating this crisis.

BACKGROUND: CULTURAL ACCEPTANCE OF CONSUMING OPIOIDS

The naturally strong human aversion toward experiencing pain is the primary desire for consuming opioids. To minimize or reduce physical and psychological discomforts in their daily life, people will resort to trying or experimenting with various chemical substances by imbibing, inhaling, ingesting, and injecting them. In the case of opioid consumption, the most common method of delivery into the human body is popping pills (rather than inhalation or injection). The lure of using prescribed pills is further legitimized because such drug usage has become normalized among people across the entire socioeconomic and political spectrum. Consider this: Young people will experience considerably more social acceptance by swallowing a few pills than by using a pipe or administering an injection in the presence of possibly judgmental, critical onlookers (many of whom likely also take prescription pills).

Illicit or not, the behavior of seeking and consuming pharmaceutical products to resolve or treat one's mental and physical ailments has become embedded and firmly accepted into a part of contemporary American life and culture. Superbowl commercials, internet advertisements, and printed ads in their promotional efforts routinely endorse the benefits of consuming pills (Ovalle & Hudson, 2023). The process of procuring prescription drugs is also a remarkable contrast to what is often experienced when obtaining the same pills in a black-market setting. Purchasing potentially lethal drugs from a socially acceptable, legitimized source is reinforced and condoned by the trustworthy image of receiving such deadly pills from a white-coated physician or pharmacist. Furthermore, conventional wisdom prods people into trusting their doctors, especially compared to anonymous sellers (online or on the street). Assurances from physicians and pharmacists, who are direct financial beneficiaries, coax consumers into making such transactions similarly as would street dealers, prompting further consumption.

An abundance of evidence indicates that this pervasive legitimized process has initiated and inflicted more mass suffering than those originating from illegal transactions (i.e., back alley drug deals). Most importantly, a persistent and excessive (even misplaced) faith in state-sanctioned medical services drives the demand for more pills. This strong predisposition is further reinforced by dispensing the products via a veneer of polished professionalism in well-lit, sanitized settings that help coax people into consuming ever-increasing volumes of prescribed pills.

Last, various authorities (political, religious, financial) have consistently given explicit or implicit consent to increasing drug usage for various reasons, and purposes, that then reinforce and support their interests. Retirement funds, institutional endowments, and key political contributors have all greatly benefited from mass pill consumption because spiking pharmaceutical sales boosted the value of their investment portfolios. Thus, a wide spectrum of American society became acclimated to the ever-increasing and overwhelming preponderance of consuming drugs in daily life. To underscore the degree of such mass-scale dependency, tens of millions (if not more) would immediately physically and psychologically be devastated if the supply of all pharmaceutical products suddenly ceased.

ORIGINS OF THE EPIDEMIC

While the United States has experienced prior drug epidemics, this current crisis has three critically distinctive elements: (1) the magnitude of the contemporary epidemic as estimated by the number of addicts and deaths because they far exceed any prior epidemic; (2) earlier epidemics were driven primarily by illicit substances (e.g., heroin in the 1970s; cocaine in the 1980s and early 1990s), but in this case legal drugs (i.e., prescribed opioids) initiated and still substantially sustain this current epidemic; and (3) drug overdose deaths were previously concentrated in major cities (e.g., San Francisco, Baltimore, New York, Philadelphia). Yet, this crisis experienced dramatic increases in drug overdose mortality in nontraditional locations, particularly in rural areas, suburbs, and smaller, more isolated towns (Paulozzi & Xi, 2008; Rigg et al., 2018).

Prior to the 1980s, regarding the use of painkillers (especially opioids), the American medical community widely believed that they were highly and hazardously addictive and should not qualify for prescriptions unless they involved terminally ill people (i.e., cancer patients). Above all, most physicians downplayed pain management and generally expected patients to live with more pain (Chiarello, 2018; Ho, 2017; Meier, 2003; Wailoo, 2014).

Beginning in the 1990s, the American medical establishment experienced a seismic shift in how to effectively address patient problems by adopting a new paradigm in believing that pain was an undertreated condition (Chiarello, 2018; Ho, 2017; Meier, 2003; Wailoo, 2014). This approach mirrored a cultural orientation that sought "quick fixes" or "magic bullets" toward healthcare and the issue of pain. Patients increasingly expected and demanded immediate pain relief and prescription painkillers from their physicians (Onishi et al., 2017). American doctors, compared to other high-income countries, more eagerly prescribe painkillers, anxiety relief, or chemical remedies to address many illnesses and maladies. The attitude and climate toward healthcare have resulted in the demand for new drugs and treatments. Thus, legally prescribed drugs played a crucial role in causing and perpetuating the epidemic.

In recent decades, via legal circumstances (i.e., an injury or illness), an exponential growth in the proportion of young people had become acquainted with using prescription pills. Early life exposure to such chemical-inducing sources of relief or pleasure fueled a growing demand for obtaining substances to sustain a feeling of well-being or comfort. Furthermore, the American healthcare system allows multiple junctures for drug seekers, meaning that they have many avenues for obtaining pills and can easily change providers. Physicians are then also strongly incentivized to placate patients by prescribing painkillers, particularly because of having heavy caseloads, and their salaries are tied to patient satisfaction (Ho, 2017).

Given America's aging demographics, more people started claiming age-related ailments to justify or rationalize using pain-killing medications. Responding to a growing belief that freedom from pain should be a universal human right and that presumably safe and nonaddictive and effective painkillers were now available, more doctors felt morally obligated to treat pain using recently developed medications. Thus, a new medical narrative emerged, claiming that millions of Americans were needlessly suffering. Physicians were encouraged to evaluate a patient's physical pain as a "fifth vital sign" (Brennan et al., 2016; Cousins et al., 2004; International Association for the Study of Pain, 2018; Lohman et al., 2010).

The recognition and treatment of physical discomfort became a top priority, resulting in the first pain management professional certificates being issued in 1993. Shortly thereafter, pain medicine training programs popped up around the country (Conrad & Muñoz, 2010; Rathmell & Brown, 2002). Given the increased focus on reducing discomfort, medical practitioners began prescribing opioids to treat many different types of noncancer-related pain. Pain medicine rapidly spread as a subspecialty, resulting in an explosive growth in the number of pain management specialists who then sharply increased the number of painkiller prescriptions to unprecedented levels (Ho, 2017). Physicians relied upon the pharmaceutical industry, which is known for the pharmaceuticalization of medical issues, rather than seek policy interventions or social reforms (Abraham, 2010; Bell & Figert, 2012).

THE AMERICAN OPIOID MARKET: AN OVERVIEW

In most cases, a lack of supply for illicit goods due to inherent risks associated with breaking laws commands an exceptionally high profit margin. The prospect of obtaining such robust profits reinforces behaviors that involve manufacturing, distributing, and selling contraband (Baker, 2004). Black markets attract organized crime because (in lawless environments) aggressive proprietors can muscle out less violent competitors and seize the profits. A nasty side effect of these circumstances is that often the most merciless criminal enterprises obtain power.

From an exporter's perspective, the sheer size of the American population, exceeding 335 million, along with its well-publicized history of mass drug consumption and very high per capita income (allowing for large profit margins) make it an irrefutable alluring, lucrative target market for profit-seeking opioid manufacturers (legal and illegal) (Norton, 2019).

As the most populous high-income per capita country that also allows and welcomes for-profit pharmaceutical products, drug manufacturers view the United States as their prime market. Drug prices are also higher because of organizational, legal, and long-standing cultural reasons (Danzon & Furukawa, 2003). Classical economic price and supply-demand theory indicate that reduced supply will cause a price increase if the quantity of demand is fixed. For opioid addicts, their demand for the product is inflexible to price changes, meaning that it is inelastic. Therefore, higher prices will not deter consumption as it would when considering purchasing more elastic goods. A lack of price sensitivity demonstrates a rigid neediness that is a hallmark characteristic of addicts. This also means that whenever law enforcement enforces stricter regulations that reduce the quantity of opioids supplied, prices will increase.

If drug abusers cannot afford higher prices, they will resort to cheaper substitute goods. Hence, policies that restrict prescription opioids that then reduce the legal supply, make illicit opioids (including synthetic opioids such as fentanyl) a desired alternative. Such restrictive efforts may briefly decrease opioid-related deaths in a specific jurisdiction, but then an inevitable increase in fatalities from black-market sources follows. Whenever users obtain lower-quality black-market opioids, they risk experiencing serious damage to their overall health compared to using prescribed opioids. Therefore, restrictive opioid policies indirectly kill consumers (Sun & Breslin, 2021).

EXPANDING CONSUMER INFORMATION
AND ACCESSIBILITY

The internet's global reach readily connects opioid users to an ever-expanding world market for illicit prescription pills. In addition, interested or potential consumers can satisfy their curiosity by accessing the abundance of information pertaining to available varieties of opioid products and their perceived beneficial features. Thus, a plethora of market information facilitates the interests of more savvy consumers while also allowing or alluring more inexperienced, younger, and less educated consumers into the black market. In the world market, prescribed opioids, heroin, and illicitly manufactured fentanyl can become interchangeable, largely substitutable goods. Thus, the pervasive availability of low-cost, knockoffs, and adulterated drugs amplifies the degree of risk and potential pitfalls of continued use.

INCENTIVIZED HEALTHCARE PROVIDERS

Because of managed care, during the 1990s, the US healthcare system underwent many structural changes that included: (1) increasing patient caseloads, (2) time constraints, and (3) financial pressures. Also, employment and income became strongly linked to patient satisfaction in the form of evaluations. The arrangement greatly incentivized physicians to prescribe pills to patients upon request. Therefore, excessive prescriptions happened because patients who received their requested prescribed painkillers effectively rewarded physicians (Quinones, 2015; Van Zee, 2009). Pills began flooding the streets.

In the 1990s, the US healthcare system was legally and communicatively fragmented, meaning that healthcare providers did not report patient information to any central system (between and within all of the states) and that physicians were often unaware of when or where patients made other attempts to obtain prescriptions. Given the lack of interconnectivity between healthcare providers, pill-seeking patients employed a common tactic known as "doctor shopping" to obtain multiple simultaneous prescriptions for opioids with minimal chance of being detected, tracked, or caught (Hall et al., 2008; McDonald & Carlson, 2013). Sometimes, doctor-shopping patients would obtain five or more simultaneous opioid prescriptions.

Soon, clinics where doctors prescribed excessive amounts of painkillers with little or no medical justification acted as "pill mills" clinics. Often clients would obtain pills onsite for cash. Notably in Florida, many owners and operators of these pill mill clinics were not part of the medical establishment. At times, people posing as "sponsors" recruited and transported users to pain clinics. In exchange for paying for their appointments, sponsors would obtain their prescribed painkillers and resell them on the black market (Macy, 2018; Quinones, 2015; Rigg, & Ibañez, 2010).

For a variety of reasons, the United States consistently approves new drugs before other higher per capita income countries (Downing et al., 2012). In the case of OxyContin, the FDA approved for sales and prescriptions about four years earlier, in 1995, than other OECD countries (Ho, 2017). In 1996, OxyContin netted 316,786 prescriptions and $45 million in revenue. By 2002, there were seven million prescriptions and $1.5 billion in revenue (General Accounting Office, 2003; Ho, 2017; Paulozzi et al., 2011). During this time, OxyContin spilled into and began harming historically geographically isolated small-town rural areas. Unfortunately, in the case of OxyContin, it took years for the public to learn of its addictive, deadly nature (Ho, 2017).

Public awareness of the deepening opioid crisis lagged because annual increases in drug-related deaths were gradual and involved a variety of drugs and mixes of drugs (e.g., morphine or weaker opioids instead of strong opioids like oxycodone). Another cause for the downplaying of the epidemic was that some drug overdoses are not recorded as a primary cause of death. For example, accidental deaths, cardiac arrests, and suicides are listed instead. Since US death logs are not nationally standardized, interpretations and recorded data vary considerably which complicates year-to-year domestic-level statistical analysis and country-to-country statistical comparisons (Ho, 2017).

Eventually, awareness of the epidemic grew to the point that regulators responded by limiting legal drug prescriptions. However, unfortunately, drug-related deaths still rose (and continued to rise) because by the time action was initiated the flood of prescribed drugs had already created a large, addicted population dependent upon cheaper, easily accessible opioids (Cicero et al., 2012; Evans et al., 2018; Jones et al., 2018; Muhuri et al., 2013; Quiñones, 2015; Rudd et al., 2016). It is important to note that by 2007, the United States consumed nearly all of the world's opium supply (83% of oxycodone and 99% of hydrocodone).

A VULNERABLE, FRAGMENTED HEALTH SYSTEM

Numerous facets of American healthcare institutional structures have unintentionally aggravated the conditions and severity of the opioid epidemic. First, the provider reimbursement system encourages physicians to write more prescriptions. Second, there is a strong linkage between patient satisfaction and compensation for physicians. Should doctors refuse patient demands for prescription painkillers, they risk incurring lower patient satisfaction scores, which can reduce their paychecks (Ho, 2017; Hoffman & Tavernise, 2016). Third, the United States, as mainly a multi-payer system, has less negotiating power for drug prices than single-payer systems. The largest single US payer, Medicare, cannot by law negotiate prescription drug prices (Kanavos et al., 2013; Morgan and Lee, 2017). It is important to note that, in 2016, President Trump campaigned to change the Medicare pricing law. When Congress failed to deliver a satisfactory bill to address this matter, in 2020, he issued multiple executive orders that partly remedied the problem. However, later, federal judges and President Biden nullified these efforts. In contrast, centralized authorities in other high-income countries regularly negotiate and set drug prices for the whole country (Cohen & Villarroel, 2015). Fourth, American physicians overwhelmingly operate in a fee-for-service (FFS) payment system, which pays for each test and service provided. The FSS payment system incentivizes providing more care regardless of medical necessity and is associated with an increase in the number of services or the overuse of services (Berenson & Rich, 2010; Davis & Guterman, 2007; Gosden et al., 2003; Ho, 2017; Zuvekas & Cohen, 2016).

America's fragmented system is a consequence of lacking a centralized healthcare administration. Patient records are often underutilized, poor quality, incomplete, and lacking critical information. Fragmentation abetted the start of the epidemic because in the 1990s abusers could use doctor shopping and obtain multiple prescriptions for the same drug. Physicians had limited access to their patient's medical history or possible other current treatments. Much of the system relied on patients self-reporting their past and current medical issues (Weisberg & Stannard, 2013). Though some reforms and interconnectivity efforts have been initiated, prescription drug monitoring in the United States remains quite limited and underutilized and varies in quality and effectiveness.

By 2017, tighter legal and regulatory enforcement and the implementation of new federal restrictions had reduced the total number of official opioid prescriptions. Yet, by then, the illicit drug market functioned as a predictable substitute in that it more than absorbed the deficit by supplying increasingly cheaper fentanyl (and heroin) and by making it more widely available. Law enforcement agencies observed that the sources of fentanyl consumed inside the United States were geographically diversified. Unlike classic narcotics (i.e., cocaine and heroin) whose production is geographically limited (because they are derived from plants) (Baker, 2004), fentanyl production and its precursor chemicals lack such limitations of scope, which means that they may originate from dozens of countries.

THREE COMMON EXPLANATIONS: MARKET DEMAND, MARKET SUPPLY, AND INADEQUATE ACCESS

Some scholars have contended that America's opioid epidemic is the "most consequential preventable public health problem" (Manchikanti et al., 2018); yet, that belief overlooks or minimizes the many market and societal forces that contributed to the pervasive presence and increasing popularity of painkillers as well as the associated predictably reckless behaviors of millions of users. When considering the confluence of commercially minded self-interested forces, who disregarded the potentially devastating consequences of expanding access to opioids and normalizing their widespread use, this epidemic may have been inevitable.

When assessing the effects of increasing drug-related deaths since the mid-1990s, experts generally cite three common explanations for the opioid epidemic (Case & Deaton, 2020; Monnat, 2018; Ruhm, 2019), which are (1) market demand factors, (2) market supply factors, and (3) inadequate access to legal medical care. All of these are intertwined with significant macroeconomic shifts that affect individual consumption at the street (or micro) level. The inadequate resources argument, often portrayed as inequalities of income or accessibility, offers a bleak narrative that focuses on "deaths of despair." In 2020, Case and Deaton cited that Americans are self-reporting higher levels of pain than ever before, yet these increases are largely derived from social and economic distress, not from physical ailments.

Such negative reports regarding less privileged people are not new. Since the 1970s, domestic and global macroeconomic shocks and shifts have strained and harmed the real income rates (purchasing power) and employment benefits of many members of the working and lower classes, contributing to the vulnerability of people in these marginalized communities. Ho (2017) and others have repeatedly verified that the subgroups who experienced the largest increases in drug overdose mortality are less educated, non-Hispanic whites. Consequential psychological and physical pains have greatly enticed despondent people to resort to using opioids. Furthermore, an overwhelming majority of these susceptible groups lack a college education and therefore may not be aware of (or care about) the short- and long-term health risks associated with consuming street-level pills (Case & Deaton, 2020).

THE DEMAND SIDE EXPLANATION
FOR THE OPIOID MARKET

As previously noted, the origins of the current drug overdose epidemic partly attributed to how some segments of the population responded to misfortunate macroeconomic structural changes, despite them beginning in the 1970s (Case & Deaton, 2015, 2017, 2020; Dasgupta et al., 2018; Monnat, 2018). In particular, middle-aged white men with a high school diploma or less education experienced the most diminished economic opportunity and had the largest increase in overall mortality. Consequential "deaths of despair," included mortality related to drugs, suicide, and alcohol. Self-destructive behavioral patterns were a response to the greatly reduced availability of well-paying jobs (especially in the manufacturing sector), which once were in abundance regardless of educational attainment (Case & Deaton, 2017; Charles et al., 2018; Thombs et al., 2020).

The demand argument points to the power of advertising and marketing pharmaceutical products. Patients, when they consult with their physicians, are routinely given pharmaceutical options. The commercially motivated push to encourage mass consumption of new medicines, compared to other high-income countries, is almost uniquely American. For example, in contrast, in Sweden, billboards, televised commercials, and printed pharmaceutical advertisements are illegal. *Only* two countries (New Zealand and Brazil) allow direct consumer advertisements (Ventola, 2011).

OxyContin (opioid oxycodone) was aggressively marketed by its manufacturer, Purdue Pharma, popularizing the narrative that treating pain had become a moral obligation and portraying opioids as a safe, effective way to address a wide range of conditions including tooth extractions, sports injuries, back pain, and headaches (Meier, 2003; Van Zee, 2009). During the 1990s, Purdue Pharma's roughly $300 million (in 2024 dollars) ambitious publicity campaign included: (1) advertisements, (2) promotional activities, (3) sponsorship of pain management conferences, and (4) funding licensure-required continuing medical education seminars. In fact, many states require continuing education for physicians to retain their medical licenses. Sales representatives encouraged prescriptions and underplayed their risks by claiming a "less than one percent" chance of addiction (Goldenheim, 2002; Ho, 2017; Meier, 2003; Van Zee, 2009). The successes of this marketing campaign were quite clear in that by 2000, millions of patients were taking opioids for pain relief (Arpa, 2017; Hamunen et al., 2009; Ruhm, 2019; Van Zee, 2009).

THE SUPPLY SIDE EXPLANATION
FOR THE OPIOID MARKET

The supply-side explanation maintains that the epidemic has been primarily driven by production changes in the licit and illicit opioid market since the 1990s (Paulozzi et al., 2014; Pezalla et al., 2017; Ruhm, 2019; Thombs et al., 2020). As previously noted, the United States was the first higher income per capita country that widely allowed OxyContin for legal prescriptions. Note that statewide regulations vary; so, it did not happen at once for all states. Drug manufacturers eagerly (to have first mover advantages) and quickly penetrated the American market with inflows of legally sanctioned opioids. Much harm happened before a palpable awareness garnered enough attention from the general public, healthcare policymakers, and experts to recognize the brevity of this crisis and its horrific consequences.

The supply-side explanation highlights the role that pharmaceutical companies play in increasing opioid access by incentivizing physicians to prescribe opioids (Hadland et al., 2018; Makary et al., 2017). Opioid manufacturers, distributors, physicians, and pharmacists were all financially incentivized by the prospects of purveying a highly profitable product. The allure of obtaining financial gains from large profit margins contributed to more widespread availability for mass consumption (Ho, 2017).

Undoubtedly, the increased accessibility of low-cost opioids (and other drugs) significantly expanded and deepened the epidemic (Thombs et al., 2020). In particular, drug-related deaths are a consequence of more readily available and affordable opioids via legal and illegal channels (Lin et al., 2020; Ruhm, 2019; Singhal et al., 2016). For example, as Ruhm points out, some more prosperous states with relatively strong economies (e.g., Massachusetts) experienced increased drug-related mortality rates after opioids became readily and conveniently available through legally prescribed drugs (Ruhm, 2019). Given the persistent large profit margins and the high degree of inelasticity of these easily addictive drugs, international and domestic suppliers eagerly flooded the American market (Thombs et al., 2020). Yet, the supply-side explanation does not delve into socioeconomic reasons for why people become drug users and why some groups are disproportionately harmed.

THE ECONOMICALLY DISADVANTAGED
EXPLANATION

Distraught individuals, who lack financial resources, are more susceptible to opioid usage and its consequential risks (Thombs et al., 2020). Harsh macroeconomic conditions negatively affect households and individuals, especially workers who become structurally unemployed, underemployed, or displaced. The economically disadvantaged explanation for the opioid consumption market emphasizes the hardships endured by population segments who are not a part of and are alienated from the economy's overall prosperity. Initially, working-class white males had the highest death rates among all groups, but over time deaths of despair increased for women and minorities without a college education (Case & Deaton, 2021; Ruhm, 2019; Thombs et al., 2020). According to Case and Deaton (2021), in recent years Blacks and other minority groups are fast catching up.

Geography is another facet of the economically disadvantaged explanation. Low-income people face portability and proximity problems. Travel is a luxury, especially if obtaining medical services would require routine trips. Regarding geographic disparities, the Bureau of Labor Statistics and Census Bureau (Thombs et al., 2020) data reveal uneven opioid consumption within different parts of individual states and differences between regions. Case and Deaton (2017) suggest that highly unequal states (e.g., California and New York), have relatively low rates of drug-related mortality. Whereas more income-equal states, like New Hampshire, have higher mortality rates (Thombs et al., 2020). Bureau of Labor Statistics and the Census Bureau (Thombs et al., 2020) data also show higher overall opioid consumption in uneven, internal regional economic conditions. Among lower income groups, due to the sheer distance from any healthcare provider, rural users will infrequently visit doctors. Also, aside from inaccessibility to good quality care, countryside populations more likely lack affordable health insurance options in proportion to their meager income levels (Kawachi and Kennedy, 1997; Truesdale & Jencks, 2016).

A third dimension to the economically disadvantaged explanation contends that in effect, drug-related deaths are a consequence of economic exploitation cultivated by opportunistic wealthy and politically powerful elites who prey upon vulnerabilities experienced by lower-income populations (Thombs et al., 2020). The attractiveness of conducting such avaricious endeavors is also amplified by the increasing numbers of monopolistic and oligopolistic market structures of industries in the United States (Piketty & Goldhammer, 2014; Saez & Zucman, 2019). For instance, there are fewer private healthcare insurance companies and fewer, but substantially larger, pharmaceutical firms. A lack of competition results in larger (or economic) profit levels, which means ever higher prices and additional hardships for modest or low-income people who struggle to afford healthcare (Saez & Zucman, 2019).

Fourth, ongoing macroeconomic shifts have included structural adjustments that brought forth a postindustrial economy and supplanted the traditional, industrialized system, further elevating a sense of hopelessness and despair (Case & Deaton, 2017, 2020). Modern economic market structure realities and devastating managerial actions have resulted in disappearing jobs, declining wages, and outsourcing (relocating production overseas). Contributing factors include weak labor unions and an increasing reliance on computer (including robotic) technologies instead of skilled workers (DeSilver, 2017; Pierce & Schott, 2020).

Fifth, many antidrug policies aimed at limiting legal prescriptions have unintentionally encouraged patients to (1) "doctor shop," (2) switch insurance coverages, (3) travel to other locations, and (4) personally demand more access using social connections, but the poor lack the resources to carry out these measures. Consequently, numerous studies have found higher opioid prescription drug mortality rates in more economically depressed counties or economically marginalized places (Thombs et al., 2020). Among the many financial obstacles that low-income people encounter when attempting to obtain legally prescribed drugs is the high cost of private health insurance (that is usually also unusable). Many "affordable" health insurance policies have such high co-pays, deductibles, and co-insurance amounts that they are unaffordable. In effect, the lowest 20% of earners (the bottom quintile) are pushed into the black market (Gross & Gordon, 2019; Thombs et al., 2020; Monnat et al., 2019). Lower-income states (i.e., West Virginia) especially experience disproportionately higher opioid use death rates.

Impoverished conditions contribute to low-income people resorting to the black market (Neumayer & Plümper, 2015; Wilkinson & Pickett, 2019). Since poverty profoundly negatively affects one's well-being, a psychological component in the form of stress, low self-esteem, and a general greater emotional distress persists. Wilkinson and Pickett (2019) stress that relative deprivation leads to risky coping behaviors (i.e., drug use). Desperate, often alienated, marginalized low-income people are vulnerable to turning to illicitly manufactured fentanyl because it is considerably cheaper.

Last, in effect, healthcare insurance especially after the Affordable Care Act of 2010 became mandatory (as ruled by the US Supreme Court) and is a tax on labor. Since it increases the effective labor tax rate, it behaves as a regressive tax that disproportionately burdens lower-income workers (Saez & Zucman, 2019). Yet, funds from this unofficial tax are channeled to industry shareholders and senior executives (Thombs et al., 2020). Other structural factors include the excessive powers of pharmaceutical companies, the overprescribing practices of physicians, and the ever-increasing costs of individual health insurance which (according to Saez & Zucman, 2019) in 2019 averaged $13,000 a year (Thombs et al., 2020).

POLYSUBSTANCE ABUSE

Since 2013, drug overdoses involving cocaine and psychostimulants have increased across all demographic groups and US census regions (Kariisa et al., 2022). Although opioids are often recognized as the major contributor to drug-related mortality, it is important to note that in 2017, cocaine and other psychostimulants were involved in one-third of the drug overdose deaths in the United States (Kariisa et al., 2022). Three-fourths of cocaine-involved deaths and one-half of the psychostimulant-involved deaths also included an opioid. Thus, the current drug overdose epidemic in the United States appears to be an evolving one that is increasingly characterized by polysubstance use (Jones et al., 2018; McCall et al., 2017; Thombs et al., 2020).

INCREASING INTERCONNECTIVITY
AIDES CONTRABAND CHANNELS

The growing influence of exogenous factors driven chiefly by modern communication and transportation technologies has greatly enabled and expanded an increasingly integrated global supply chain and has coaxed the involvement of more foreign suppliers connected to transnational organized crime (i.e., growing linkages between the Chinese and Mexican drug cartels). Access to drugs, due to increased global commercial connectivity and the widespread usage of the internet, has enabled innumerable drug transactions within the country and beyond its political borders. Modern communication technologies introduce and enhance international trade involving the US drug market. Such variables frequently undermine regulatory and law enforcement efforts aimed at stemming the flow of illicit fentanyl and related substances into communities throughout the country. In addition, legal prescription sales also have behaved as a powerful endogenous force that penetrated and then permeated America's metropolitan markets before saturating small-town rural areas via networks of legitimate and informal channels (i.e., local healthcare providers and word of mouth).

CHINA'S ROLE

Many governmental, academic, and media sources, including the *Journal of Political Risk* (*Epoch Times*, 2023) contend that China has perpetually played a key role in flooding the United States with fentanyl. Having the world's largest domestic pharmaceutical market, China possesses an enormous chemical production capacity, allowing it to easily act as a major global producer and distributor of fentanyl and related synthetic opioids. Also, among all Asian countries, China is estimated to have the most clandestine chemical laboratories.

Since the 1990s, because of its prominent role in exporting illicit opioids and related substances into the United States, China has endured considerable pressure and criticism from Democratic and Republican leaders. Embracing the more politically acceptable supply-side market argument, five presidents and many Congresses, often using bipartisan efforts, have repeatedly tried to stifle Chinese drug trafficking but have largely failed. When faced with condemning evidence that points the blame on them and considerable harsh accusations, Beijing has repeatedly echoed the demand side argument claiming that America's insatiable appetite for opioids is the true culprit. Yet, all the while, mainland Chinese organized crime has cooperated with Chinese diaspora communities in using well-established global supply chain networks to transport product to other criminal groups, particularly those in Mexico (Norton, 2019).

PRECURSOR CHEMICALS AND CHINA

Survival in the business of manufacturing illicit synthetic drugs demands constant vigilance and an alacrity of adaptability to dodge detection and prevent prosecution from law enforcement agencies. Suppliers who exhibit rapid and creative responsive behaviors have repeatedly thwarted drug control strategies. For example, during the mid-2000s, recognizing that the United States was undergoing a growing drug crisis, the federal government tried restricting access to pseudoephedrine with the intention of curbing domestic production of methamphetamine. However, Mexican cartels sidestepped these efforts and managed to gain control over a greater proportion of the growing American methamphetamine market because they began making a more potent product using a different synthesis process, without pseudoephedrine. This clever market adaptation was also famously illustrated in the popular AMC fictional TV series *Breaking Bad*.

Throughout the many years of this crisis, governmental restrictive and law enforcement efforts have faced ongoing setbacks in their quest to suppress opioid consumption. During the 2010s, in cooperation with the Mexican cartel, clever Chinese chemical makers dramatically increased the volume of exported illicit fentanyl (Suzuki & El-Haddad, 2017). For example, in 2012, although the total annual number of opioid prescriptions peaked at 255 million (with deaths exceeding 11,000 per year) (Gardner et al., 2022), the illicit suppliers of fentanyl and related opioids (i.e., heroin) filled in and exceeded the void (Ruhm, 2019).

Chinese exporters made some tactical adjustments, which included decreasing their directly exported fentanyl and fentanyl-related chemicals into the United States while it simultaneously became the principal supplier of legal chemical products (i.e., ephedrine and pseudoephedrine), to third-party countries where these substances were synthesized into illegal products (i.e., fentanyl) and then covertly transported to the United States (overwhelmingly from Mexico) for consumption. These kinds of chemicals, by which organized crime can synthesize into contraband, are known as precursor chemicals. A key difficulty in restricting this segment of the chemical goods market is that many precursor chemicals have legitimate and critical uses. Yet, according to the DEA and other sources, Chinese manufacturers have shifted parts of their overall operations to other countries, such as Mexico and India (John et al., 2023).

Restricting chemical exports, according to Jon E. Zibbell (2021) (RTI International), creates unintended problems. Attempts to suppress production of illicit drugs are sometimes described as like pressing against an air-filled balloon; in that, if law enforcement cracks down in one spot, drugs will simply be supplied somewhere else (Rogin, 2023). For example, Chinese manufacturers facing greater scrutiny from Beijing will have brokers, using well-connected individuals and larger family-based networks (albeit arguably temporary) to sell precursor chemicals to Mexico and other destinations (Sevastopulo, 2023). In Mexico's case, cartel-run secret labs will synthesize fentanyl and then export the contraband using small, easy-to-hide packages covertly into the United States (Sun & Breslin, 2021). Further evidence of Chinese complicity, according to the DEA, is best exemplified by the tendency of Chinese exporters to include step-by-step recipes on how to synthesize their products into fentanyl (Rogin, 2023).

Aside from chemical precursors, drug manufacturers extended their creativity into augmenting the chemical effects of illicit products. Their evasive tactics include manufacturing other cheap, synthetic drugs that in some cases have replaced fentanyl. For many reasons, regulatory and restrictive production efforts have continually been compromised in China. According to Zongyuan Liu, a Council on Foreign Relations researcher, China's chemical and drug sectors are fragmented, yet mammoth-sized, consisting of many small firms operating on thin margins (Ovalle & Hudson, 2023).

The highly competitive, low-profit margin chemical markets can induce and encourage legitimate producers to divert a portion of their products to financially lucrative destinations. Efforts to evade the detection of regulators include mixing chemical supplies and selling them online. According to an investigation by Elliptic, a crypto compliance analytics firm, often these diverted products are sold via small-time brokers who use English-speaking staff on messaging services (i.e., WhatsApp). While pursuing profits, producers will concoct, synthesize, and promote new hybrid products which are typically more toxic, dangerous versions of street drugs (John et al., 2023). An example of such a hybrid chemical sold on Chinese websites is a combination of fentanyl and xylazine (an animal tranquilizer), that allegedly gives the user an extended high.

THE TRANSNATIONAL ROLE: CHINESE ADAPTATION

Survival for unscrupulous, profit-seeking Chinese chemical manufacturers often requires frequent adaptations in production, distribution, and transportation—especially if these processes involve fentanyl and related drugs. Entanglements with organized crime demand applying tactics to avoid detection, confiscations, and arrests from law enforcement agencies.

Over time, China-based criminal operators and their affiliates greatly expanded their global supply chains, using new source countries and additional transit countries to traffic fentanyl and related substances. For example, according to the DEA, between 2014 and 2019, the geographical patterns of the flows of fentanyl into America became diversified. Instead of China directly shipping fentanyl into the United States, Chinese manufacturers shipped precursor chemicals to Mexico where the drug cartels synthesized fentanyl from it (Rogin, 2023). Mexican-made fentanyl then mostly entered the United States via vehicles crossing legal ports of entry (John et al., 2023). Until 2019 with the passage of the Synthetics Trafficking and Overdose Prevention Act (which will later be discussed), mail and courier services functioned as the primary suppliers of fentanyl and other synthetic drugs coming from Mexican chemical and pharmaceutical firms.

INDIA

Among the many clever production and distributive adaptations made by unscrupulous Chinese chemical manufacturers is the involvement of India as a source for finished fentanyl powder and fentanyl precursor chemicals (DEA Intelligence Report,

2020). As a recent example of geographic diversification of production, according to the DEA, India has emerged as a significant precursor chemical and fentanyl supplier since the Chinese government tightened its regulatory efforts involving fentanyl and fentanyl precursor chemical production. Indian-based operations have also cooperated with Mexican cartels in coordinating the production and transportation of fentanyl and fentanyl-containing illicit pills destined for the American market (DEA Intelligence Report, 2020).

In 2017, in response to new and allegedly newly enforced regulations from Beijing, which caused hardships in obtaining precursor chemicals inside China, Chinese chemical manufacturers shifted a portion of their production to India. The consequential intensifying cooperation between Indian and Chinese nationals helped to circumvent China's new production controls. Having successfully shifted fentanyl and precursor trafficking to India, from there it then went to Mexico or sometimes directly into the United States. However, like most strategies involving the transport of contraband goods, this arrangement soon experienced complications.

Later in 2017, the DEA alerted India's Directorate of Revenue Intelligence that Indians (with Chinese nationals) had partnered with the Mexican-based Sinaloa cartel by supplying fentanyl and fentanyl precursor chemicals (which were then synthesized into fentanyl at illicit labs in Mexico). Consequently, the Indian government swiftly announced regulations similar to those in China and imposed stricter production and exportation controls on fentanyl and precursor chemicals (DEA Intelligence Report, 2020).

In February 2018, rumors of increased involvement of Indian-based production operations were validated by the shutdown of an illicit fentanyl lab in Indore, India (DEA Intelligence Report, 2020). Later, in December 2018, India's Mumbai Anti-Narcotics Cell (ANC) seized roughly 100 kilograms of a fentanyl precursor called "NPP" and arrested four Indian nationals. The NPP was deceptively mislabeled and destined for Mexico. According to the DEA, this was the *third* significant seizure of a fentanyl-related substance or fentanyl precursor with the India-Mexico linkage in 2018. Mexican-based processors had routinely sent their finished product to the United States (DEA Intelligence Report, 2020).

In 2023, Rahul Gupta the White House Office of National Drug Control Policy director, cited the 2019 crackdown as proof that "when China wants to act, it can act, and it can be decisive in its action to yield results." He added that Beijing needs to keep enforcing regulations to ensure that Chinese-based shipments are designated for legitimate customers. Gupta acknowledged that although China is the chief supplier of precursor chemicals, "criminal elements could quickly shift to countries like India" (John et al., 2023).

MEXICO AS A CONDUIT

As previously mentioned, Chinese fentanyl producers, as a means to evade regulatory demands, shifted production (especially after 2016) to Mexico. Like the Chinese,

Mexican cartels adjusted their business practices. According to the DEA, in 2023, not only did the Mexicans diversify their sources of supply for fentanyl and precursor chemicals by opting for Indian-based ingredients—before that these pills already served as substitute goods insomuch that when the Mexican government (responding to pressure from US authorities) started eliminating opium poppy crops from which heroin is derived—the cartel switched their production efforts to manufacturing synthetic fentanyl.

Due to Mexico's proximity and lengthy land-based border with the United States along with the well-known and widely publicized lax security conditions along the border, its drug cartels became the chief recipient of diverted yet legally produced Chinese-made chemical products. The Mexican cartel easily recognized the prospective financial windfall for handling Chinese-trafficked powdered fentanyl. Cheaper ingredients meant huge profit margins. For example, at a cost of a few thousand dollars per kilogram, the Mexicans transformed the powder into hundreds of thousands of pills worth millions of dollars on the American streets.

Quite quickly, the Mexican cartel established many sophisticated secret laboratories that applied advanced processing methods (i.e., use of laboratory-grade glassware and industrial-sized tablet presses) to synthesize precursor powders into fentanyl, transforming raw materials into fentanyl-laced pills, or combining other chemicals to create fentanyl-related synthetic drugs. These Mexican clandestine labs played a pivotal role in supplying increased quantities of fentanyl that supplanted a demand deficit caused by declines in legally prescribed painkillers (due to tighter restrictions). Soon, the mass consumption of Mexican-based fentanyl overtook heroin as the leading cause of drug-related deaths in the United States.

In 2018 and 2019, evidence of advanced drug manufacturing in Mexico became clear when the DEA (with Mexican officials) seized and dismantled numerous fentanyl pill-pressing operations and fentanyl synthesis laboratories (*Epoch Times*, 2023). These efforts helped US and Mexican officials confirm the top two cartels involved in smuggling fentanyl across the border: the Sinaloa and the New Generation Jalisco (*Cártel de Jalisco Nueva Generación*). Here are two examples: in September 2018, in Mexico City, authorities raided a fentanyl pill mill linked to the Sinaloa cartel. Later, in December, another illicit pill mill in the Azcapotzalco borough of Mexico City was seized that housed fentanyl-laced oxycodone M-30 pills, fentanyl powder, precursor chemicals, and multiple other substances commonly used to produce fentanyl-laced illicit pills. To date, all significantly sized fentanyl synthesis and fentanyl pill production operations dismantled inside Mexico occurred in territories controlled by these cartels or had cartel members or associates running them (DEA Intelligence Report, 2020).

In 2023, according to the DEA, precursor Chinese-made chemicals were the source of about "99 percent of the fentanyl" processed and then smuggled by the Jalisco and Sinaloa cartels. From 2020 to 2022, the US Customs and Border Protection went from seizing 4,800 to 14,700 pounds of fentanyl originating from Mexico. Driven by high profits, Mexican traffickers use private cars, pedestrians, and commercial vehicles to illegally export fentanyl through American ports of entry.

Often the drugs are hidden with or inside of legal products (i.e., inside coconuts). Sometimes, fentanyl is smuggled across the US-Mexico border in low-concentration, high-volume loads, often containing less than a 10% concentration of fentanyl (DEA Intelligence Report, 2020).

The Chinese-Mexican partnership extended beyond production in that Mexico's drug cartels used China's financial system to launder their proceeds. For example, in November 2018, a Mexican cartel money laundering case involving $25–65 million resulted in the US authorities arresting several Chinese nationals (*Epoch Times*, 2023). Investigators reported that Chinese-based launderers leveraged encrypted mobile communications apps (i.e., WeChat) to move money from the United States into China and then back to Mexico. These efforts were executed with "great speed, discretion, and efficiency." After entering China, the drug money procured consumer goods and precursor chemicals, effectively recycling the funds into China's economy. Furthermore, the cartels reduced their risk of detection by mixing transported legal goods with illegal chemicals out of China and into Mexico. As another precautionary measure, often these transactions involved convertible virtual currencies, or cryptocurrencies (e.g., Bitcoin, Ethereum, or Monero) because they are so difficult to track.

While other countries are certainly engaged in the illegal drug trade, US law enforcement agencies have persistently complained about not receiving adequate cooperation from Mexican officials. Denial from the Mexican side is another common problem. For example, in spring 2023, Mexican President Andres Manuel Lopez Obrador claimed that no fentanyl was produced in his country—despite common knowledge that Mexico is the predominant place where fentanyl is synthesized. Later in 2023, during a meeting with US officials, the Mexican government demonstrated some cooperation by extraditing Ovidio Guzman (a Sinaloa cartel leader) to the United States. Yet, US law enforcement agents still cannot currently operate in the field with Mexican counterparts because the Mexican government is unwilling to confront the cartel (Rogin, 2023).

Addressing Supply: Endogenous and Exogenous Factors

So far, five presidential administrations, which include Presidents Clinton (1993–2001), G. W. Bush (2001–2009), Obama (2009–2017), Trump (2017–2021), and Biden (2021–2025), have attempted to address the opioid drug epidemic by fighting two fronts: first, at the domestic level, to quash production of illicit opioids; second, at the international level, to reduce the volume of imported fentanyl. Within the executive branch, two administrative tactics have continually been applied: first, pressuring law enforcement agencies to conduct more raids, make more arrests, and launch more investigations; second, by intensifying State Department and federal agencies' efforts to obtain international cooperation.

Within the legislative realm, presidents have used their "bully pulpit" in mass media to publicly demand Congressional action which has routinely yielded bipartisan bills aimed at reducing opioid addiction. For example, in October 2018, President Trump signed the $6 billion Substance Use-Disorder Prevention

That Promotes Opioid Recovery and Treatment Act (SUPPORT Act) and proclaimed it as "the single largest bill to combat the drug crisis in the history of our country." The legislation addressed opioid addiction prevention and emphasized more funding for individual treatment (most notably for mothers and incarcerated people). Also included was the Synthetics Trafficking and Overdose Prevention Act (STOP Act), which intended to curb the flow of opioids sent through the mail system by improving coordination between the US Postal Service (USPS) and the US Customs and Border Protection (*Epoch Times*, 2023). In doing so, the STOP Act required that package-level detail and accurate advanced electronic data (AED) must accompany all incoming international mail. Consequently, by May 2019, the USPS reported that 85% of the volume of inbound shipments from China had AED compared to 32% in October 2017, which significantly improved the government's ability to confiscate illicit drugs within the mail system (*Epoch Times*, 2023).

INTERNATIONAL COOPERATION: NEGOTIATING WITH BEIJING

Ongoing efforts to curb the flow of illicit drugs into the United States have included increased international engagement and cooperation, especially as a means to improve intelligence abroad. Unfortunately, Chinese-based fentanyl products continue to be widely available throughout America's black market. Regarding matters involving money laundering investigations, criminal prosecution, and legal assistance in ongoing cases, Beijing's cooperation has persistently lagged (US-China Economic and Security Review Commission, 2021). For example, requests to inspect and investigate suspected sites of illegal chemical production for precursors have been continually delayed. In many situations, postponements lasted long enough to allow operators to vacate or clean up the premises.

In December 2018, Ben Westhoff, an award-winning investigative journalist, who had visited a Chinese fentanyl lab, told National Public Radio that China has no real intention to follow through and warned, "doing that on paper is one thing, but the enforcement is the part where China has really lagged. They don't have enough people on the ground to enforce the laws they have on the book. And often, there are competing layers of government that are at odds with each other. So you might have a provincial official who wants to let these companies keep doing what they're doing because it brings in more revenue for the area" (*Epoch Times*, 2023). Westhoff then further claimed that the Communist Party of China encouraged chemical exports to the United States as part of their economic growth plan by offering "a series of tax breaks, subsidies, and other grants" (*Epoch Times*, 2023).

Westhoff also observed, "The big problem in China is that a lot of these drugs, which are banned in the U.S., are still legal in China . . . Chinese companies can make them with the full support of the government and have them basically smuggled into the U.S." (*Epoch Times*, 2023). He added that manufacturers only need to slightly tweak the chemical formula of fentanyl to make it legal (*Epoch Times*, 2023).

At best, meaningful cooperation from the Chinese government has been inconsistent. For example, on May 1, 2019, President Xi fulfilled a pledge at the G-20 Summit (responding to pressure from the Trump administration), by officially implementing a measure that classified fentanyl and all of its known analogs as scheduled substances. This effort did the following: (1) criminalized producing and exporting precursors (if they lacked proper permits), (2) launched investigations in known fentanyl manufacturing areas, (3) applied stricter control of internet sites advertising fentanyl, (4) pressed for stricter enforcement of shipping regulations by requiring more international package data, and (5) created special teams to investigate fentanyl trafficking leads (DEA Intelligence Report, 2020). Also, in 2019, after receiving tips from the DEA, Chinese authorities arrested and sentenced nine fentanyl suppliers (John et al., 2023).

Despite Xi's proclamation, during 2020–2023 significant tensions between the United States and China persisted, resulting in little cooperation in the war on drugs (Rogin, 2023). In January 2020, the US DEA reported that Wuhan, China, effectively functioned as the world's fentanyl capital and that the coronavirus outbreak invoked Chinese governmental restrictions that caused "substantial disruptions to fentanyl production and its supply." These hardships hampered fentanyl and methamphetamine production in Mexico, which skyrocketed street drug prices in the United States. Later in May 2020, after the United States imposed sanctions against China's Public Security Ministry's Institute of Forensic Science for violating the human rights of Uyghurs (and other predominantly Muslim ethnic groups in the Xinjiang region), China ceased further cooperation (Ovalle & Hudson, 2023; US Department of Commerce, 2020).

As Westhoff and others predicted, Beijing's classification of fentanyl and its related analogs, as a controlled substance, failed. In August 2021, the US-China Economic and Security Review Commission reported that Chinese chemical manufacturers had repeatedly modified synthetic fentanyl chemical compounds; thereby, creating a new, not yet regulated fentanyl-related product. In 2022, China suspended all cooperation involving drug trafficking and production after US House Speaker Nancy Pelosi visited Taiwan (Ovalle & Hudson, 2023). Nonetheless, American law enforcement increasingly targeted Chinese companies and brokers suspected of supplying precursors sent by ship and through parcels to Mexico.

After Sinaloa cartel leaders were arrested and extradited to the United States, federal prosecutors linked them to Chinese-affiliated companies, who then were issued sanctions by the Treasury Department (John et al., 2023). Also, in June 2023, the Justice Department unveiled indictments against companies that had advertised illicit drugs online and then shipped them overseas using fake labeling and deceptive delivery procedures. In Fiji, they announced the arrests of two Chinese nationals—a rare circumstance by which Chinese suspects ended up in US custody. In response, a Chinese diplomat called the indictments "entrapment" and again shifted blame to the United States for not addressing their "own drug problems."

Later in October 2023, the Justice Department unsealed indictments against more Chinese companies and their executives (John et al., 2023), and the US Treasury (as an effort to disrupt an alleged fentanyl, methamphetamines, and ecstasy production network) imposed sanctions on 25 Chinese individuals and entities who supplied chemicals used in the illicit fentanyl trade. Also, a crackdown on clandestine labs was announced and some companies were shut down (Sevastopulo, 2023).

After quietly agreeing to lift sanctions on China's Institute of Forensic Science, on November 15, 2023, US officials met with Chinese delegates at the Asia-Pacific Economic Cooperation Conference near San Francisco. According to a White House summary, for the first time in over three years, China began sharing drug trafficking intelligence and blocked some "international payment accounts" (John et al., 2023). However, many analysts claim that restricting the chemical trade is not a priority and that President Xi is aiming to stabilize Sino-American relations. Note that before Biden and Xi met, senators from both parties drafted letters urging Beijing to cut off the precursor supply and spur "a drastic drop in illicit fentanyl being trafficked across our southern border and killing vulnerable Americans" (Ovalle & Hudson, 2023). Considering that the demand for illegal drugs rages onward, some experts believe that an ebb in precursor chemicals from China will lead to a rise in the development of synthetic narcotics elsewhere (John et al., 2023). For example, Jonathan Caulkins, a criminal drug trade expert at Carnegie Mellon, stated, "I have a hard time believing this is a permanent game-changing scenario because somebody else can step in and provide the chemicals. The Chinese are not the only ones who know how to manufacture these chemicals" (Ovalle & Hudson, 2023).

Finally, on January 30, 2024, China again agreed to cooperate "to stem the flow of fentanyl into the U.S." (Ovalle & Hudson, 2023). Despite creating and a renewal of enforcing older regulations, Vanda Felbab-Brown at the Brookings Institute doubted that Chinese enforcement efforts will be "robust" or have a "lasting cooperation" (as cited in Ovalle & Hudson, 2023). Since it is commonly believed that Chinese authorities lack adequate resources for meaningful enforcement and regulation of chemical production, many other experts also doubt that President Xi's promises will be impactful on the overall global supply chain of illicit drugs. Furthermore, key Congressional Republicans perceive Xi's recent pledges as hollow (John et al., 2023).

CONCLUSION

Abstinence-only policies favored by the United States have contributed to riskier drug use, less access to treatment, and higher drug overdose mortality (Ho, 2017). Stringent and quite costly legal entanglements, including ominous criminal charges, dissuade many American drug addicts from obtaining substance abuse treatment (i.e., using buprenorphine to reduce the physical dependency on opioids). The death toll persists because so many users are purposefully avoiding detection due to fears of brutal legal consequences.

The US government's continual engagement to fight the supply of fentanyl while largely ignoring the demand and inadequate individual resources arguments does not bode well for obtaining meaningful and positive changes as the opioid epidemic rolls on, year after year. Even when considering the limited successes of controlling the supply of opioids, none of these actions has quelled the American appetite to dull itself from pain. Until the demand for such hazardous products is addressed in ways that will reduce the need for such substances, the epidemic will continue.

This conclusion is no secret. Special interests in Washington represent those who thrive from the ongoing "war" and would rather sustain the status quo. As long as the American public supports and believes that attacking the supply side of the drug market will work, senators, congressmen, and presidents will perpetuate these efforts. Addressing the demand side would greatly diminish legal cases, criminal and civil, employment in the incarceration business (i.e., jails, prisons, hospitals, rehab centers), and harm the financial prospects of medical interests (i.e., pharmaceutical firms, doctors, therapists). Consequently, Chinese involvement, like that from India, Mexico, and other supplying countries, is a response to satisfying the American appetite for dulling pain. Thus, the epidemic is a self-inflicted, self-destructive, self-serving toll on the economy, society, and many millions of American households stuck in a state of despair.

REFERENCES

Abraham, J. (2010). Pharmaceuticalization of society in context: Theoretical, empirical and health dimensions. *Sociology*, 44(4), 603–22. https://doi.org/10.1177/0038038510369368

Arpa, S. (2017). *Women who use drugs: Issues, needs, responses, challenges and implications for policy and practice*. Background paper commissioned by the European Monitoring Centre for Drugs and Drug Addiction for Health.

Baker, J. R. (2004, November 28). Coca leaf crop transforms destitute nation. *Orlando Sentinel*. http://articles.orlandosentinel.com/2004-11-28/news/0411270106_1_coca-boliviagrowing

Bell, S. E., & Figert, A. E. (2012, September). Medicalization and pharmaceuticalization at the intersections: Looking backward, sideways and forward. *Social Science & Medicine*, 75(5), 775–83. doi: 10.1016/j.socscimed.2012.04.002

Berenson, R. A., & Rich, E. C. (2010). US approaches to physician payment: The econstruction of primary care. *Journal of General Internal Medicine*, 25, 613–18.

Brennan, F., Carr, D., & Cousins, M. (2016). Access to pain management—Still very much a human right. *Pain Medicine*, 17, 1785–89.

Case, A., & Deaton, A. (2015). Rising morbidity and mortality in midlife among white non-Hispanic Americans in the 21st century. *Proceedings of the National Academy of Sciences of the United States of America*, 112(49), 15078–83. https://doi.org/10.1073/pnas.1518393112

Case, A., & Deaton, A. (2017). Mortality and morbidity in the 21st century. *Brookings Papers on Economic Activity*, 2017, 397–476. https://doi.org/10.1353/eca.2017.0005

Case, A., & Deaton, A. (2020). *Deaths of despair and the future of capitalism.* Princeton University Press.

Case, A., & Deaton, A. (2021). Life expectancy in adulthood is falling for those without a BA degree, but as educational gaps have widened, racial gaps have narrowed. *Proceedings of the National Academy of Sciences of the United States of America, 118*(11), e2024777118. https://doi.org/10.1073/pnas.2024777118

Charles, K. K., Hurst, E., & Notowidigdo, M. J. (2018). Housing booms and busts, labor market opportunities, and college attendance. *American Economic Review, 108*(10), 2947–94.

Chiarello, E. (2018). Where movements matter: Examining unintended consequences of the pain management movement in medical, criminal justice, and public health fields. *Law & Policy, 40,* 79–109. https://doi.org/10.1111/lapo.12098

Cicero, T. J., Surratt, H. L., Kurtz, S., Ellis, M. S., & Inciardi, J. A. (2012, January). Patterns of prescription opioid abuse and comorbidity in an aging treatment population. *Journal of Substance Abuse Treatment, 42*(1), 87–94. doi: 10.1016/j.jsat.2011.07.003

Cohen, R. A., & Villarroel, M. A. (2015). *Strategies used by adults to reduce their prescription drug costs: United States, 2013.* US Department of Health and Human Services, Centers for Disease Control and Prevention, National Center for Health Statistics.

Conrad, P., & Muñoz, V. (2010). The medicalization of chronic pain. *Tidsskrift for Forskning i Sygdom og Samfund, 7,* 13–24.

Cousins, M. J., Brennan, F., & Carr, D. B. (2004, November). Pain relief: A universal human right. *Pain, 112*(1–2), 1–4. doi: 10.1016/j.pain.2004.09.002. PMID: 15494176

Crimmins, E. M., & Zhang, Y. S. (2019). Aging populations, mortality, and life expectancy. *Annual Review of Sociology, 45,* 69–89.

Danzon, P. M., & Furukawa, M. F. (2003). Prices and availability of pharmaceuticals: Evidence from nine countries: The US market structure, with its higher prices for on-patent products and strong generic competition, appears more favorable to innovation than markets elsewhere. *Health Affairs, 22,* W3–521.

Dasgupta, N., Beletsky, L., & Ciccarone, D. (2018). Opioid crisis: No easy fix to its social and economic determinants. *American Journal of Public Health, 108*(2), 182–86.

Davis, K., & Guterman, S. (2007). Rewarding excellence and efficiency in Medicare payments. *The Milbank Quarterly, 85*(3), 449–68.

DEA Intelligence Report. (2020, January). Fentanyl flow to the United States. DEA-DCT-DIR-008-20.

DeSilver, D. (2017). The Pew Center. U.S. students' academic achievement still lags that of their peers in many other countries. https://www.pewresearch.org/short-reads/2017/02/15/u-s-students-internationally-math-science/

Downing, N. S., Aminawung, J. A., Shah, N. D., Braunstein, J. B., Krumholz, H. M., & Ross, J. S. (2012). Regulatory review of novel therapeutics—comparison of three regulatory agencies. *New England Journal of Medicine, 366*(24), 2284–93.

Epoch Times. (2023, January 8). China's role in illicit fentanyl running rampant on US streets. https://trone.house.gov/2023/01/08/chinas-role-in-illicit-fentanyl-running-rampant-on-us-streets

Evans, T. M., Bira, L., Gastelum, J. B., Weiss, L. T., & Vanderford, N. L. (2018). Evidence for a mental health crisis in graduate education. *Nature Biotechnology, 36*(3), 282–84. https://doi.org/10.1038/nbt.4089

Gardner, E. A., McGrath, S. A., Dowling, D., & Bai, D. (2022). The opioid crisis: Prevalence and markets of opioids. *Forensic Science Review, 34*(1), 43–70.

General Accounting Office. (2003). *Prescription drugs: OxyContin abuse and diversion and efforts to address the problem.* Publication GAO-04–110.

Goldenheim, P. (2002, February 12). *OxyContin: Balancing risks and benefits.* Testimony in Hearing of the Committee on Health, Education, Labor, and Pensions, United States Senate.

Gomes, T., Tadrous, M., Mamdani, M. M., Paterson, J. M., & Juurlink, D. N. (2018). The burden of opioid-related mortality in the United States. *JAMA, 1*(2), e180217. https://doi.org/10.1001/jamanetworkopen.2018.0217

Gosden, T., Sibbald, B., Williams, J., Petchey, R., & Leese, B. (2003). Paying doctors by salary: A controlled study of general practitioner behaviour in England. *Health Policy, 64*(3), 415–23.

Gross, J., & Gordon, D. B. (2019). The strengths and weaknesses of current US policy to address pain. *American Journal of Public Health, 109*(1), 66–72.

Hadland, S. E., Bagley, S. M., Rodean, J., Silverstein, M., Levy, S., Larochelle, M. R., Samet, J. H., & Zima, B. T. (2018). Receipt of timely addiction treatment and association of early medication treatment with retention in care among youths with opioid use disorder. *JAMA Pediatrics, 172*(11), 1029–37. https://doi.org/10.1001/jamapediatrics.2018.2143

Hall, A. J., Logan, J. E., Toblin, R. L., Kaplan, J. A., Kraner, J. C., Bixler, D., . . . Paulozzi, L. J. (2008). Patterns of abuse among unintentional pharmaceutical overdose fatalities. *JAMA, 300*(22), 2613–20.

Hamunen, K., Paakkari, P., & Kalso, E. (2009). Trends in opioid consumption in the Nordic countries 2002–2006. *European Journal of Pain, 13*(9), 954–62.

Hedegaard, H., Curtin, S. C., & Warner, M. (2020). *Increase in suicide mortality in the United States, 1999–2018.* NCHS Data Brief, no 362. National Center for Health Statistics.

Ho, J. Y. (2013). Mortality under age 50 accounts for much of the fact that US life expectancy lags that of other high-income countries. *Health Affairs* (Project Hope), *32*, 459–67. 10.1377/hlthaff.2012.0574

Ho, J. Y. (2017). The contribution of drug overdose to educational gradients in life expectancy in the United States, 1992–2011. *Demography,* 54(3), 1175–202.3.

Hoffman J., & Tavernise, S. (2016, August 4). Vexing question on patient surveys: Did we ease your pain? *New York Times,* http://www.nytimes.com/2016/08/05/health/pain-treatment-hospitals-emergency-rooms-surveys.html

International Association for the Study of Pain. (2018). *Declaration of Montréal.* Retrieved January 2, 2019, from https://www.iasp-pain.org/DeclarationofMontreal

John, T., Xiong, Y., Culver, D., Rappard, A. M., & Joseph, E. (2023, March 30). *The US sanctioned Chinese companies to fight illicit fentanyl. But the drug's ingredients keep coming.* CNN. https://www.cnn.com/2023/03/30/americas/fentanyl-us-china-mexico-precursor-intl/index.html

Jones, A., Pierce, M., Sutton, M., Mason, T., & Millar, T. (2018). Does paying service providers by results improve recovery outcomes for drug misusers in treatment in England? *Addiction, 113*(2), 279–86.

Kanavos, P., Ferrario, A., Vandoros, S., & Anderson, G. F. (2013). Higher US branded drug prices and spending compared to other countries may stem partly from quick uptake of new drugs. *Health Affairs, 32*(4), 753–61.

Kariisa, M., Davis, N. L., Kumar, S., et al. (2022, July 22). Vital signs: Drug overdose deaths, by selected sociodemographic and social determinants of health characteristics—25 states and the District of Columbia, 2019–2020. *Morbidity and Mortality Weekly Report, 71,* 940–47. DOI: http://dx.doi.org/10.15585/mmwr.mm7129e2

Kawachi, I., & Kennedy, B. P. (1997). Socioeconomic determinants of health: Health and social cohesion: Why care about income inequality? *BMJ, 314*(7086), 1037.

Lin, L., Brummett, C. M., Waljee, J. F., Englesbe, M. J., Gunaseelan, V., & Bohnert, A. S. (2020). Association of opioid overdose risk factors and naloxone prescribing in US adults. *Journal of General Internal Medicine, 35,* 420–27.

Lohman, D., Schleifer, R., & Amon, J. (2010). Access to pain treatment as a human right. *BMC Medicine, 8,* 8.

Macy, B. (2018). "I am going to die if I keep living the way I am." She was right. *New York Times.*

Makary, M. A., Overton, H. N., & Wang, P. (2017). Overprescribing is major contributor to opioid crisis. *BMJ* (Clinical research ed.), *359,* j4792. https://doi.org/10.1136/bmj.j4792

Manchikanti, L., Sanapati, J., Benyamin, R. M., Atluri, S., Kaye, A. D., & Hirsch, J. A. (2018). Reframing the prevention strategies of the opioid crisis: Focusing on prescription opioids, fentanyl, and heroin epidemic. *Pain Physician, 21*(4), 309–26.

McCall, L., Burk, D., Laperrière, M., & Richeson, J. A. (2017). Exposure to rising inequality shapes Americans' opportunity beliefs and policy support. *Proceedings of the National Academy of Sciences, 114*(36), 9593–98.

McDonald, D. C., & Carlson, K. E. (2013). Estimating the prevalence of opioid diversion by "doctor shoppers" in the United States. *PLOS One* 8, e69241.

Meier, B. (2003). *Pain killer: A wonder drug's trail of addiction and death.* Rodale Press, Emmaus.

Monnat, S. M. (2018). The contributions of socioeconomic and opioid supply factors to US drug mortality rates: Urban-rural and within-rural differences. *Journal of Rural Studies, 68,* 319–35.

Monnat, S. M., Peters, D. J., Berg, M. T., & Hochstetler, A. (2019). Using census data to understand county-level differences in overall drug mortality and opioid-related mortality by opioid type. *American Journal of Public Health, 109*(8), 1084–91. https://doi.org/10.2105/AJPH.2019.305136

Morgan, S. G., & Lee, A. (2017). Cost-related non-adherence to prescribed medicines among older adults: A cross-sectional analysis of a survey in 11 developed countries. *BMJ, 7*(1), e014287.

Muhuri, P. K., Gfroerer, J. C., & Davies, M. C. (2013). Substance Abuse and Mental Health Services Administration. Associations of nonmedical pain reliever use and initiation of heroin use in the United States. http://www.samhsa.gov/data/2k13/DataReview/DR006/nonmedical-pain-reliever-use-2013.pdf. August 2013

Neumayer, E., & Plümper, T. (2015). *W. Political science research and methods.* Cambridge University Press.

Norton, S. (2019). *Australia—China law enforcement cooperation. Australian Strategic Policy Institute.* Australian Strategic Policy Institute. http://www.jstor.com/stable/resrep23112.4

Onishi, E., Kobayashi, T., Dexter, E., Marino, M., Maeno, T., & Deyo, R. A. (2017). Comparison of opioid prescribing patterns in the United States and Japan: Primary care physicians' attitudes and perceptions. *Journal of the American Board of Family Medicine, 30*(2), 248–54. https://doi.org/10.3122/jabfm.2017.02.160299

Ovalle, D., & Hudson, J. (2023, November 19). China vows to crack down on fentanyl chemicals. The impact is unclear. *Washington Post.* https://www.washingtonpost.com/health/2023/11/19/china-fentanyl-crackdown/

Paulozzi, L. J., Kilbourne, E. M., & Desai, H. A. (2011). Prescription drug monitoring programs and death rates from drug overdose. *Pain Medicine, 12,* 747–54. https://doi.org/10.1111/j.1526-4637.2011.01062.x

Paulozzi, L. J., Mack, K. A., & Hockenberry, J. M. (2014). Vital signs: Variation among states in prescribing of opioid pain relievers and benzodiazepines—United States, 2012. *Morbidity and Mortality Weekly Report, 63*(26), 563–68.

Paulozzi, L. J., & Xi, Y. (2008). Recent changes in drug poisoning mortality in the United States by urban–rural status and by drug type. *Pharmacoepidemiology and Drug Safety, 17*(10), 997–1005.

Pezalla, E. J., Rosen, D., Erensen, J. G., Haddox, J. D., & Mayne, T. J. (2017). Secular trends in opioid prescribing in the USA. *Journal of Pain Research,* 383–87.

Pierce, J. R., & Schott, P. K. (2020). Trade liberalization and mortality: Evidence from US counties. *American Economic Review: Insights, 2*(1), 47–63.

Piketty, T., & Goldhammer, A. (2014). *Capital in the twenty-first century.* Harvard University Press. http://www.jstor.org/stable/j.ctt6wpqbc

Quinones, S. (2015). *Dreamland: The true tale of America's opiate epidemic.* Bloomsbury Publishing USA.

Rathmell, J., & Brown, D. (2002). Evolution of pain medicine training in the United States. *American Society of Anesthesiologists Newsletter, 66*(10).

Rigg, K. K., & Ibañez, G. E. (2010). Motivations for non-medical prescription drug use: A mixed methods analysis. *Journal of Substance Abuse Treatment, 39*(3), 236–47.

Rigg, K. K., Monnat, S. M., & Chavez, M. N. (2018). Opioid-related mortality in rural America: Geographic heterogeneity and intervention strategies. *International Journal of Drug Policy, 57,* 119–29.

Rogin, A. (2023, October 8). *Why the US is pressuring China amid a global crackdown on the global fentanyl trade.* Interview with Vanda Felbab-Brown, The Brookings Institute. PBS NewsHour. https://www.pbs.org/newshour/show/why-the-u-s-is-pressuring-china-amid-a-crackdown-on-the-global-fentanyl-trade#transcript

Rudd, R. A., Puja, S., Felicita, D., & Scholl, L. (2016). Increases in drug and opioid-involved overdose deaths—United States, 2010–2015. *Morbidity and Mortality Weekly Report 65*(50–51), 1445–52.

Ruhm, C. J. (2019). Drivers of the fatal drug epidemic. *Journal of Health Economics, 64,* 25–42. https://doi.org/10.1016/j.jhealeco.2019.01.001

Saez, E., & Zucman, G. (2019). Progressive wealth taxation. *Brookings Papers on Economic Activity,* 437–533.

Scholl, L., Seth, P., Kariisa, M., Wilson, N., & Baldwin, G. (2019). Drug and opioid-involved overdose deaths—United States, 2013–2017. *Morbidity and Mortality Weekly Report, 67,* 1419–27. DOI: http://dx.doi.org/10.15585/mmwr.mm675152e1

Sevastopulo, D. (2023, November 14). China and US to agree crackdown on fentanyl trade in Washington. *Financial Times.*

Singhal, A., Tien, Y. Y., & Hsia, R. Y. (2016). Racial-ethnic disparities in opioid prescriptions at emergency department visits for conditions commonly associated with prescription drug abuse. *PLOS One, 11*(8), e0159224.

Sun, W., & Breslin, T. (2021). A new trade war with an opium component: Can the U.S. opioids crisis be solved by banning fentanyl in China? *Iranian Journal of Public Health, 50*(11), 2347–48. https://doi.org/10.18502/ijph.v50i11.7595

Suzuki, J., & El-Haddad, S. (2017). A review: Fentanyl and non-pharmaceutical fentanyls. *Drug and Alcohol Dependence, 171,* 107–16.

Thombs, R. P., Thombs, D. L., Jorgenson, A. K., & Harris Braswell, T. (2020). What is driving the drug overdose epidemic in the United States? *Journal of Health and Social Behavior, 61*(3), 275–89.

Truesdale, B. C., & Jencks, C. (2016). The health effects of income inequality: Averages and disparities. *Annual Review of Public Health, 37*, 413–30.

U.S.-China Economic and Security Review Commission. (2021). https://www.uscc.gov/annual-report/2021-annual-report-congress

U.S. Department of Commerce. (2020). *Commerce Department to add nine Chinese entities related to human rights abuses in the Xinjiang Uighur autonomous region to the entity list.* https://2017-2021.commerce.gov/news/press-releases/2020/05/commerce-department-add-nine-chinese-entities-related-human-rights.html

Van Zee, A. (2009). The promotion and marketing of oxycontin: Commercial triumph, public health tragedy. *American Journal of Public Health, 99*(2), 221–27.

Ventola, C. L. (2011). Direct-to-consumer pharmaceutical advertising: Therapeutic or toxic? *Pharmacy and Therapeutics, 36*(10), 669.

Wailoo, K. (2014). *Pain: A political history.* Johns Hopkins University Press. https://doi.org/10.1353/book.30085

Weisberg, D., & Stannard, C. (2013). Lost in translation? Learning from the opioid epidemic in the USA. *Anaesthesia, 68*(12).

Wilkinson, R., & Pickett, K. (2019). *The inner level: How more equal societies reduce stress, restore sanity and improve everyone's well-being.* Penguin Press.

Woolf, S. H., & Laudan, A. (Eds.). (2013). *US health in international perspective: Shorter lives, poorer health.* National Academies Press.

Zibbell, J. E., Peiper, N. C., Duhart Clarke, S. E., Salazar, Z. R., Vincent, L. B., Kral, A. H., & Feinberg, J. (2021). Consumer discernment of fentanyl in illicit opioids confirmed by fentanyl test strips: Lessons from a syringe services program in North Carolina. *International Journal of Drug Policy, 93*, 103128. https://doi.org/10.1016/j.drugpo.2021.103128

Zuvekas, S. H., & Cohen, J. W. (2016). Fee-for-service, while much maligned, remains the dominant payment method for physician visits. *Health Affairs* (Project Hope), *35*(3), 411–14. https://doi.org/10.1377/hlthaff.2015.1291

3

The International Dimension of America's Opioid Epidemic

Robert Gmeiner

The opioid epidemic in the United States is nothing new, and neither is its international dimension. Morphine was widely used for pain relief during the Civil War and also relief of coughs and diarrhea in children, but its recreational abuse quickly became a problem. German pharmaceutical manufacturer Bayer introduced Heroin, which was a brand name before it was genericized, as an alternative for morphine addicts. Addiction was a factor in the passage of the Pure Food and Drug Act of 1906 and the 1909 prohibition on importing opium for the purpose of smoking (Realuyo, 2019).

Since that time, various opioid epidemics have risen and fallen in the United States, each with some international implications. Prescription opioids are still abused, but this has declined considerably in recent years. As that happened, epidemics of benzodiazepines and heroin (no longer a brand name) ensued. Recently fentanyl and other synthetic opioids have become more widely used (Zoorob, 2019). These epidemics are related but they are distinct both in the nature and origin of the drug and in their geographic concentrations. The fentanyl epidemic was initially concentrated in the eastern United States, including but not limited to Appalachia, but is only weakly linked to prior patterns of abuse of other opioids. Fentanyl has become a major national problem, and it has since spread to the western states, where it is often found in heroin samples (Shover et al., 2020).

Although internationally sourced opioids are nothing new for the United States, a few aspects of the current epidemic are. Global economic conditions affect Americans' demand for opioids, and this is a recent phenomenon. There are new techniques for facilitating illicit international transactions. Last, geopolitical intrigue, although also not new to opioid problems in general, plays a major role in facilitating the current epidemic.

Both the supply of and demand for opioids are affected by international trade. On the demand side, a more globalized economy has caused economic hardship due to job losses in some parts of the United States despite net benefits globally to producers and consumers throughout the economy. This hardship has induced despondency that has led to illicit opioid use. Legitimate medicinal use of opioids is a source of opioid demand that has international reach. As high costs and increasing hesitancy among prescribers make medicinal use of branded opioids more difficult, patients look to foreign sources. On the supply side, overseas production is often more convenient and less susceptible to American enforcement. The current geo-political environment impedes international cooperation on drug enforcement as a matter of governmental objectives, not just capabilities, making foreign production especially lucrative.

This chapter begins with an overview of relevant economic principles and models as a framework for understanding the international dimension of America's opioid epidemic. From there, it discusses international trade and demand for opioids. Because international supply is a matter of foreign governments' incentives, some historical background is presented next, specifically an overview of the Opium Wars. This overview is imperative because these events still influence opioid policy today. After the historical discussion, this chapter describes the international flows of opi-oids and drug money. Following that, a more detailed overview of the complications of international trade completes the chapter.

RELEVANT ECONOMIC PRINCIPLES AND MODELS

A few economic principles are needed to understand the international flow of opi-oids. Any drug policy manipulates the incentive to produce and consume in predict-able ways for the same reason that economic policies of all kinds manipulate markets. This section discusses several economic principles as well as a few models of global trade to explain the incentives for international trade in opioids.

The Profit Motive

As the difference between sale prices and production costs rises for any good, including opioids, more will be produced because producers stand to make more money. As of 2019, accidental overdose deaths for most drugs had stabilized, but they were rising for opioids, and much of this is attributable to fentanyl and similar substances, which are often called fentanyl analogs. Fentanyl is approximately 100 times stronger than morphine, but these analogs may be even more potent, and with potency comes lethality. Very little fentanyl is needed in a pill compared to other substances for a similar clinical effect, and production is inexpensive, making fentanyl and other synthetic opioids especially lucrative. The US Drug Enforcement Administration estimates that, in 2019, one kilogram of fentanyl purchased in China or $3,000 to $5,000 could have a street value in excess of $1.5 million (Donahue,

2019). Because of the illegal nature of the trade and the number of traffickers and producers involved, no individual will receive this entire difference as profit, but there is still much wealth to be had from the opioid trade.

Substitutes and Complements

Most goods have substitutes and complements. Substitutes replace others to varying degrees, like fentanyl and heroin. Complements must be consumed together, like crack cocaine and a crack pipe. No drug exists in isolation. Attempts to curtail the illicit drug trade need to take account of markets for substitutes and complements, and these markets may be international in scope. Successful interdiction of one drug may not solve the problem of illicit drug use and trafficking in general. A succession of epidemics of different opioids has enveloped the United States, often because enforcement of one drug leads to production of another.

Drug policies create an incentive to develop new drugs and to evade enforcement. The development of new drugs is not only a matter of finding a clinical equivalent of a scheduled substance but also of finding one that is easier to disguise. Some drugs, like cocaine, must be produced in large volumes that are more detectable and can be sniffed by trained dogs. "Traditional" opioids (i.e., not synthetic or chemically compounded) are derived from poppies that require large swaths of land for cultivation. Fentanyl, in contrast, is easily produced in a lab and is potent enough to be shipped in small volumes that are harder for law enforcement to intercept. Fentanyl is often hidden inside other products that may not attract inspectors' attention (US Customs and Border Protection, 2023).

Secondary Effects

Any government policy can have far-reaching effects that policymakers may not foresee. Changes in price can be driven by drug enforcement. As authorities successfully interdict more of one specific drug, the reduced supply makes it more expensive on the street. At the same time, interdiction raises producers' and traffickers' costs because they must evade enforcement. Drug dealers, not wanting to lose customers over affordability, look for substitutes that attract less attention from authorities. This is why heroin became popular, then fentanyl, and then other synthetic opioids. Successful enforcement decreases opioid trafficking, but it raises addicts' costs and encourages producers and traffickers to lace pills with other drugs or find new drugs. This is a problem in its own right as users may not know what they are consuming, posing a problem for well-intentioned doctors.

Prices can rise because of decreases in supply (caused by interdiction) or because of increases in demand. Decreases in supply result from increases in producers' and traffickers' and may not improve their bottom line, even as it encourages them to seek substitutes. Increased demand, in contrast, leads to higher prices that line producers' pockets and encourage more production of the same drugs. An increase in demand for drugs in one country makes production more lucrative *anywhere*, if transport costs are low enough, which they evidently are.

Even well-intentioned efforts to curb opioid addiction can have the unforeseen consequence of making opioid production more lucrative. Naloxone, a drug that reverses opioid overdoses, lowers the total cost of consuming opioids. Death by overdose is a serious cost that an addicted user might face, although addiction impairs decision-making. A drug that can reverse opioid overdose reduces the cost (lowers the risk of death) and may make current or prospective users less cautious. If users want to buy more, producers logically make more. A lifesaving remedy can thus encourage more production of the life-destroying opioids. Compounding this issue is the fact that many users and their families may not be aware that naloxone has less efficacy against fentanyl overdoses than those caused by less potent opioids (Volkow, 2021).

Models of International Trade

Several models of international trade have been devised to explain trade in goods and services. Heckscher-Ohlin models are among the most classic, and they have distant roots in theories of absolute and comparative advantage developed by Adam Smith and David Ricardo. Heckscher-Ohlin models rely on differences in endowments of production factors between countries as the source of comparative advantage. For example, a country with a large population and low wages will attract labor-intensive industries and export labor-intensive products. This explains China's rapid growth as a manufacturing center. Because Heckscher-Ohlin models could not explain everything, New trade theory (NTT) was developed in the 1970s and 1980s. NTT focused on increasing returns to scale, which gave countries with similar factor endowments the ability to gain a competitive advantage by specializing in niche industries. Gravity models were developed to explain the fact that trade tends to fall as distances grow between partners and increase as their economic sizes increase. Recent advances in freight transportation, especially the advent of the shipping container, have made long-distance trade cheaper, which is monetarily equivalent to reduced distance. All of these models have some relevance for international trade, although the specifics are beyond the scope of this chapter. More pertinent is that all of these models have assumptions that may not be met but are relevant for current patterns of international opioid trade.

Augmenting Trade Models with Political Intrigue

Economic models can be criticized for being amoral and focused only on efficiency and profits. This criticism is misguided, though, because an unrealistically high degree of morality exists under their surface. Without stating it explicitly, these models assume perfect enforcement of contracts, full knowledge of the buyer and seller of all transaction terms, and absolutely no theft or deception. These trade models also imply similar laws in both countries, similar levels of legal enforcement, and the absence of any geopolitical intrigue that may affect a government's choices of what to legalize or proscribe. Trade models thus have relevance for the opioid trade, but they must be understood in light of different legal regimes and the varied incentives of political actors. Not all governments share the same ability or resolve to fight opioid trade and consumption.

Comparative advantage is a major reason for producing and exporting any good, opioids included, but this comparative advantage need not come from technical know-how or the availability of source materials. Legal differences may matter even more. China can produce many export products at a lower cost than the importers can because it has less stringent environmental rules. Greater tolerance for opioid production in one country gives its producers a comparative advantage. The choice of whether to crack down on opioid production may be made to stop the trade of a harmful drug, or to curry favor with or retaliate against another country. The issue is deeper than just each government's attitude toward drugs or geopolitical ambitions; other laws can interact with drug policy to create a favorable environment for money laundering and other crimes. The drug industry can thus become intertwined with other industries and international political situations.

Legal Technicalities and Chemical Properties

The chemical properties of opioids, including fentanyl and its analogs, pose challenges for enforcement and make these substances uniquely susceptible to international trafficking. Opioids are hard to outlaw in many legal regimes because of the vast number of substances that can be artificially compounded and have similar clinical effects. Creating new opioids with slight chemical differences from a scheduled substance is not difficult with the right equipment and knowledge of chemistry. As a result, any legal regime requiring that scheduled substances be clearly defined is not equipped to classify all opioids, a seemingly infinite quantity of which have not yet been "discovered" (US Drug Enforcement Administration, 2023b, 2023c).

Schedule I substances in the United States, as defined by the Controlled Substances Act, are those with a high potential for abuse and no medicinal value. Fentanyl is not a Schedule I substance because it does have medicinal uses. Substances chemically similar to fentanyl, which are easily developed and produced but narrowly defined, are only placed on Schedule I on a case-by-case basis, although their nonmedicinal use may still be prosecutable if they are not scheduled (US Drug Enforcement Administration, 2023c). Avoiding Schedule I classification in the United States is a specific goal of many opioid producers in foreign countries. However, these substances may vary in potency (and thus lethality) and, because they are illicit, are not subject to the same stringent standards as controlled substances used in medicine. The availability of substitutes complicates efforts to curb the opioid epidemic, and the ease of international trade expands the scope of the problem.

International Trade and Demand for Opioids

Demand for opioids in the United States is largely a domestic problem that is matched by international sources. However, two aspects of opioid demand do have an international dimension. The first is domestic demand that is created by circumstances that result from international trade, such as when trade-related job losses lead to despondency and drug abuse. The second is high costs and prescriber hesitancy, which leads patients to international sources for legitimate medical uses.

Areas Affected by Trade-Related Job Losses

Dean and Kimmel (2019) link job losses from global outsourcing to increased opioid abuse and overdose deaths. The link is stronger in places where fentanyl is mingled with the heroin supply, and these same places have higher trade-related job losses. Pierce and Schott (2020) complement this finding, and they also observe lower rates of other causes of death in these areas.

These findings have attracted much attention, but they are not universally accepted (Ruhm, 2019). Areas with high opioid overdose deaths, such as Appalachia, have long been economically depressed areas even before the expansion of international trade that characterized the final decades of the 20th century. Opioids, and illicit drugs more generally, are often cheaper in urban centers where there is greater supply, but eventually spread to very rural areas where sellers' monopoly power makes them more expensive. Areas where drugs are more expensive are naturally more attractive to drug cartels, and this has been observed in extremely remote areas in the western states, not just Appalachia (Cavazuti et al., 2024). Appalachia is especially vulnerable in that it feels rural, has been affected by international trade, and many of its residents lack good mobility, yet at the same time, it is close enough to urban centers to be easily accessible by cartels. Addiction may start more easily in rural areas, though, because prescribing rates are higher (García et al., 2019). If adverse economic circumstances affect demand for opioids, the causes of the opioid epidemic in Appalachia are likely multifaceted. Trade-related job losses contribute to the epidemic, but they are likely not the only or perhaps even primary cause.

Medical Tourism

American demand for illicit opioids is not limited to recreational use and addiction. The legitimate use of opioids is increasingly controlled in the United States as a response to abuse, yet patients with chronic pain still need them (Owens, 2019). Some patients who need powerful pain relief turn to the illicit market. Others, innocently attempting to get opioids for legitimate use, look to international sources without realizing the danger. The high cost of medical care in the United States has encouraged Americans to go abroad for drugs and services more generally. Medical tourism has been normalized, and this explains why many Americans suffering from chronic pain may not foresee a problem with buying painkillers in foreign countries.

Medical tourism historically had been used to get procedures performed at a lower cost; traveling for opioid availability is a more recent phenomenon. Americans can get genuine, name-branded opioid painkillers from Mexican pharmacies. Enterprising purveyors of illicit opioids sensed a profit opportunity, though, and they have set up their own pharmacies to target American medical tourists. The "branded" painkillers in these pharmacies like oxycodone and Adderall are counterfeits. They are known to contain heroin, methamphetamine, and fentanyl. Labels and boxes are easy to forge, but counterfeit pills are produced well enough to be indistinguishable from genuine products without specialized equipment, and this is compounded by nearby pharmacies selling authentic drugs (Friedman et al., 2023).

THE OPIUM WARS AND A HISTORY OF INTERNATIONAL OPIOID CONFLICT

The current American opioid epidemic is not the first opioid problem to be tightly linked to international trade. Before discussing the international supply of opioids, some background on geopolitical intrigue is in order, specifically involving China. Current significant differences in willingness to combat the drug trade, not just the ability to do so, have their roots in conflicts more than a century old. China has a unique economic system, a complicated and worsening relationship with the United States, and a fraught history with opium that has left it broadly unwilling to help actual or perceived adversaries combat opioid problems. This is compounded by China's status as a major supplier of precursor chemicals and supplies needed to produce the illicit opioids that fuel America's current problem. The international supply of opioids and any potential solutions cannot readily be understood without some knowledge of this history.

During the 19th century, at the height of European colonization, China produced many goods, especially tea, desired by Europeans. Other than silver, which the Chinese demanded as payment, European countries were of little interest to the Chinese. The state-owned British East India Company developed a multicountry operation of shipping both cotton from India and silver from Britain to China in exchange for porcelain, tea, silk, and other Chinese products that were wanted in Britain. The result was a trade deficit and net outflow of silver from Britain. Hoping to improve the balance of trade, British merchants began shipping opium, which was highly addictive, to China in exchange for silver. The plan worked and opium addiction became more widespread in China. The Chinese government attempted to crack down on it in 1838, but the British East India Company enlisted the help of local smugglers (Shapiro, 2019). Despite the prohibition, opium abuse did not materially diminish (Feige & Miron, 2008). To understand current international issues surrounding the opioid epidemic, it is essential to remember that the British East India Company deliberately tried to create and worsen an opioid epidemic for the sake of pecuniary gain, and the British public was aware of opium's addictive nature (Caquet, 2015). China's government was not blameless, however, as the smugglers were local Chinese, and China's government had made serious threats against British civilians in Canton, which later became Hong Kong, so British authorities felt justified in military action (Gelber, 2006).

The British East India Company had a state-granted monopoly on trade with China, which was abolished in 1834, after its monopoly on trade with India ended in 1813 under pressure from pro-market forces in rapidly industrializing Britain (Power, 1929). With the demise of the monopoly, prices subsequently tumbled, enabling more addictions in China, even among soldiers and government officials. Tensions boiled over and the First Opium War broke out in 1839, which the British won easily by 1842. Following the war, they imposed the Treaty of Nanjing on China, the terms of which favored Britain at China's expense, and forced China to permit continued opium importation. The Second Opium War broke out in 1856 and ended with a Western victory in 1860. The weakened Chinese state subsequently endured the Boxer Rebellion and imperial expansion by Russia and Japan.

The Opium Wars have left a lasting impression on China, where they are viewed as a smug victory by foreign powers that had taken advantage of China by causing widespread opium addiction, which led to further devastation. The "unequal treaties," as they are known in China, were indeed very unequal and harmful to China. These treaties demonstrated the economic and geopolitical harm that came from an opium epidemic, which epidemic was started as a response to a trade imbalance. China is closely involved in the American opioid epidemic, which involves synthetic opioids as opposed to natural opioids derived from poppies, and China's 19th-century history of humiliation informs its attitude to a rival country's similar problem; China's leaders show little interest in assisting to solve America's opioid problem (Shapiro, 2019). Geopolitical intrigue is every bit as important as relative prices and comparative advantage in understanding trade flows and decisions of the governments involved, especially the Chinese government. Just as the opium trade helped improve Britain's trade balance, China's involvement in America's opioid epidemic is a source of domestic income and also a source of dollars for independently wealthy Chinese to use and invest for their gain in Western countries.

International Trade and the Supply of Opioids

Many legitimate industries have lengthy supply chains that cross many international borders. There is no reason to expect drugs to be any different, and drugs may be even more likely to be sourced internationally because of their illegal nature, especially opioids. Production operations are difficult to move, so they are an easier target for authorities. Traffickers and especially consumers are far more mobile and harder to catch.

China is a major source of fentanyl in the United States, so American efforts to stop importation likely require Chinese assistance. Prior to the COVID-19 pandemic, which further strained relations between the United States and China, much fentanyl was smuggled by air or sea directly from China to the United States. In 2019, China cracked down on fentanyl production and shipments under pressure from the Trump administration, though this does not reflect goodwill toward the United States as much as opposition to the drug trade in general and a desire to avoid more American economic pressure.

Despite cracking down on finished fentanyl, China did not control many precursor chemicals, aside from the few that it controlled in 2018 (US Drug Enforcement Administration, 2018, 2020). This left open the possibility that Chinese manufacturers could profit from drugs by supplying precursors to Mexican cartels, which were able and willing to finish the manufacturing process. Even if more precursor chemicals were controlled, developing new fentanyl analogs is simple enough that one crackdown will not have long-lasting effects. Moreover, fentanyl precursor chemicals can be compounded with masking molecules to evade detection. China has remained a source for ingredients to produce fentanyl, but the supply chain and trafficking process to the United States has become routed through Mexico (Doherty, 2023; US Department of Justice, 2023; US Drug Enforcement Administration, 2020, 2023d).

Chinese Money Laundering Networks and the US Fentanyl Trade

The change in fentanyl trafficking routes arose from the confluence of China's capital controls and the near-cashless nature of its economy. Capital controls impede international transfers of money, and smartphone apps have enabled money launders to develop a shadow system of banking and bookkeeping. This system facilitates an international drug trade that relies on informal accounting of international transactions that move currency between persons within a country on behalf of people in other countries while never sending money internationally through the legitimate banking system. To understand how this is possible, suppose person A in the United States wants to send US$200 to person B in Europe, who can only use that sum if it is converted into euros. This may be done through an international transfer and currency exchange, but this may not be necessary if person X in Europe wants to send person Y in the United States the euro equivalent of $200. An informal accounting system can have person A send person Y the dollars, and person X send person B the euros. If a centralized operation handles the transactions, persons A and Y need not be acquainted, nor persons X and B. Neither currency ever moves between American and European banks, and both transactions avoid foreign exchange fees.

Most transactions in China take place via smartphone apps like WeChat, which are ubiquitous among China's population; cash is almost nonexistent. Payments to and from drug manufacturers can be made via WeChat. These apps, controlled by Chinese firms and thus connected to the Chinese Communist Party, are largely impervious to American efforts to intercept communications. As a result, they became more reliable than earlier, less secure methods of communication, which made transactions with Chinese money launderers very attractive to Mexican cartels and American consumers.

American consumers provided dollars, but Mexican cartels needed Mexican pesos for their operations in Mexico, and Chinese manufacturers needed Chinese renminbi. China's capital controls augmented these circumstances by making the drug trade more lucrative specifically for Chinese money launderers. Exchanging renminbi for dollars and moving any country's currency in and out of China is tightly restricted when done through legitimate financial institutions. Wealthy Chinese, of whom there are many because of China's recent economic success, wanted to convert renminbi into dollars and move it outside of China but they often encountered difficulty. The Chinese money launderers' task was to get dollars from American consumers to wealthy Chinese and somehow compensate the precursor manufacturers and Mexican cartels.

The best sources of information on the international flows of money and resources in the drug trade are journalistic exposés and government reports. These paragraphs are based on the money laundering ring operated by Li Xizhi, a naturalized US citizen, which was ultimately broken up by American authorities. Li's operation dovetails so well with the geopolitical and economic circumstances of the fentanyl trade that other flows of money likely operate in a similar fashion, even if specifics differ (Rotella & Berg, 2022). These techniques, which did not originate with Li, are now well-known to the US Drug Enforcement Administration (Jorgic, 2020). Li is not the only Chinese money launderer whom American authorities have caught. In 2021, Xianbing Gan, a Chinese national, was sentenced to 14 years by a US federal judge for drug-related money laundering in a scheme similar to Li's. These money laundering techniques are commonplace enough that they were featured in the National Money Laundering Risk Assessment from the US Department of the Treasury (2022). There are few such networks, but they deal in large quantities of cash (US Department of Justice, 2021). The volume of cash is large enough that the Treasury Department's Office of Foreign Asset Control has taken notice and imposed sanctions (US Department of the Treasury, 2023a).

Li's money laundering operation began at the point of consumption when an American consumer buys drugs from a dealer linked to a Mexican cartel using dollars, always in cash. Often, the cartels front the drugs to American dealers and expect payment upon sale. The American dealers then contract with Chinese couriers to convey payment to the cartel. The Chinese couriers do not physically take the dollars to Mexico. Instead, they control safe houses in Mexico that are stocked with Mexican pesos. With mobile communications, the Chinese ring provides an equivalent sum in pesos to the Mexican cartel kingpins without the transit delays that characterize physical transfers of cash. Moreover, the Chinese money launderers charge a lower fee for the service than what Latin American money launderers historically charged, but the transaction is completed faster and with lower risk.

After providing the pesos to the cartel, the Chinese ring takes the dollars to major American cities. From there, the money launderers sell the dollars at a profit to Chinese immigrants or persons with wealthy contacts in China who want to convert their wealth into dollars but cannot easily move money out of China. These transactions may involve elaborate schemes. These Chinese citizens use WeChat to pay the Chinese couriers in Chinese renminbi from their Chinese accounts. Once the courier network receives renminbi, it sells them to the Mexican cartels in exchange for pesos, although the transfer of renminbi is a bookkeeping exercise that does not involve international bank transfers. The Mexican cartels then use the renminbi to buy drug ingredients, and the couriers return the pesos to the safe houses for the next round of drug transactions (Rotella & Berg, 2022). Because access to the Chinese banking system is very limited for noncitizens, Chinese money launderers are uniquely positioned to facilitate the illicit opioid trade in the United States because of the chemicals' Chinese origin and China's capital controls regime. Persons with other nationalities lack the comparative advantage of access to the Chinese banking system.

The system is advantageous to the drug dealers because they can pay the cartel in a low-risk way, and the cartels get paid right away. The couriers are reliable enough and deal in sufficiently high volumes to guarantee payment to the cartels even if the dollars are sometimes interdicted during subsequent money laundering efforts to get them to wealthy Chinese citizens. Chinese money launderers can correct imbalances in currency holdings through legitimate channels because those transactions, like acquiring more pesos for the safe houses, were at least one step removed from the drug trade and thus less suspicious. If volumes were large enough, the money launderers could alter their internal exchange rates to correct imbalances.

International flows become a bookkeeping matter for the money launderers to handle amongst themselves. American drug dealers owe money to the cartels that fronted the drugs as soon as they sell them. Rather than trying to get stacks of cash to the cartel, the dealer could pay a Chinese courier to take the dollars and sell them to Chinese interests in the United States. When the courier sells the dollars to Chinese interests in the United States, those interests use WeChat to pay the renminbi to the courier. The renminbi stayed in the China-controlled WeChat ecosystem and thus did not appear to leave China. The courier then used the renminbi to buy pesos from the Mexican cartel, but this was more of a bookkeeping transfer and the pesos just went back to the safe house, and the renminbi went to manufacturers of precursor chemicals on behalf of the cartel. The renminbi, never having left the Chinese system, were legally owned by the couriers, who made no effort to conceal themselves on WeChat, yet tacitly owned by the cartel, which could use them to pay for precursor chemicals to make fentanyl. Thus, the renminbi never really left China and, although such transactions should raise a red flag, the Chinese government has turned a blind eye.

Besides precursor chemicals, fentanyl production also requires tablet presses to make pills. Tablet presses are unregulated in China and subject to limited regulation in the United States, where possession is legal, although possession of counterfeit dies to produce proprietary designs on pills is not. Importation of a tablet press into the United States is legal, but it must be declared to Customs and Border Protection, which often does not happen (DEA Strategic Intelligence Section, 2016). Although some compounding does happen in the United States, most of it happens in Mexico, where producers are known to use Chinese tablet presses beyond the reach of American law (Lassi, 2023). The US Office of Foreign Asset Control has imposed sanctions on Chinese producers of tablet presses alongside some Mexican businesses linked to the drug trade (US Department of the Treasury, 2023b).

Unlike fentanyl with its small volumes, tablet presses are large and easier to control. Despite their larger size, much international freight is not inspected. It is nearly impossible for customs inspectors to verify the contents of more than a small minority of shipping containers (Levinson, 2016). US Customs and Border Protection has intercepted them, mostly but not exclusively from China (US Customs and Border Protection, 2023). As with so many other aspects of the opioid epidemic, preventing the flow of tablet presses from China to Mexico may not solve the problem if Mexican producers can find other sources for tablet presses or improvise other ways of making tablets, which they almost certainly can.

Internationally Sourced Substitutes for Opioids

Preventing the illegal importation of synthetic opioids, if possible, does not get rid of the homegrown domestic demand for the effects of opioids. Higher prices for fentanyl and related substances, which interdiction naturally causes, push traffickers and addicts toward substitutes. These substitutes may or may not meet the chemical definition of opioids but may produce similar physiological effects. At present, xylazine has become a noteworthy, attractive drug because of logistical difficulties in obtaining opioids due to greater drug enforcement. It will not be the only one, and another drug will fill the void should the authorities devote greater attention to xylazine.

In 2022, 23% of fentanyl powder and 7% of fentanyl pills seized by the DEA contained xylazine (US Drug Enforcement Administration, 2023a). Prevalence varies sharply from one area to another, with some areas in Maryland reporting that around 80% of illicit opioids contain xylazine. Federal authorities first detected it in the United States in 2006, but it became widespread only recently (Centers for Disease Control, 2023).

Like fentanyl, xylazine is also sourced from China, often at low cost (US Drug Enforcement Administration, 2022). Xylazine is a veterinary sedative for large animals with dangerous side effects that include seizures and deep flesh wounds with necrosis that can require amputations, and naloxone cannot reverse an overdose. Currently, xylazine attracts less attention from authorities than fentanyl precursors because it has legitimate uses, although this could change.

Authorities have not definitively said that xylazine's growing use is because opioids are harder and more expensive to obtain on the black market, but the timing of its appearance implies as much. If this is indeed what is happening, it is a tragic example of well-intentioned drug enforcement leading to the abuse of more dangerous drugs. Increasing interdiction of cocaine, methamphetamine, and heroin led to the abuse of the more dangerous fentanyl and then to the development of its analogs. Xylazine is yet another example of the dangerous, secondary effects of drug enforcement. Any time the American demand for drugs is met with stronger enforcement, another drug will take its place, and international supply is often ready to meet the demand. Legitimate American vendors may know that it is only appropriate to dispense xylazine to veterinary clinics for veterinary use. However, if the drug is not sufficiently controlled, international suppliers will likely be willing to continue shipping it. For this reason, veterinary associations have been skeptical that scheduling xylazine will be of much value in combating its abuse.

Unlike fentanyl analogs, which must be compounded clandestinely and trafficked illegally, xylazine is readily available from foreign pharmacies. NBC reporters were able to quickly procure it from multiple suppliers in India without a prescription. One of the suppliers responded to a reporter's concerns about interdiction by US authorities by offering dexmedetomidine, another legal sedative for humans and animals, as an alternative (Strickler, 2023).

When making policy around opioids, it is essential to keep in mind that the problem is not solely to interrupt the supply. Foreign suppliers have shown that they can stay one step ahead of American authorities by developing new drugs or finding potentially more dangerous substitutes. The international dimension of America's opioid epidemic is largely a matter of foreign supply satisfying domestic demand, the same as with any other class of imported goods. It will only stop when demand decreases, and that necessarily requires treating and preventing addictions. Intercepting all illegal drugs entering the United States is nearly impossible, but any increasing success in enforcement raises street prices and leads to these secondary effects, which are often international in scope.

Complications of International Politics

Concerning the fentanyl trade that is facilitated by Chinese money laundering, the activity spans three countries at a minimum—the United States, Mexico, and China. Little money crosses international borders, even as bookkeeping transfers are orchestrated to serve financial interests in all three countries. The incentives and capabilities of the authorities in these countries do not align to stop the activity. Despite drug enforcement, the United States has not been able to stop drug abuse. For China, it is an issue of political will, but it may also involve capabilities to some extent. The Mexican government has repeatedly demonstrated its inability to defeat the cartels. Although China may be able to stop these money laundering networks, many of its wealthy citizens benefit from being able to move money out of the country under the radar. Many wealthy Chinese are connected to the ruling Chinese Communist Party, so giving them a tacit end-run around the capital controls mitigates possible discontent. China can plausibly claim to fight the drug trade by cracking down on fentanyl production yet antagonize the United States by tacitly permitting the manufacture of precursor chemicals.

Recent tensions between the United States and China do not encourage its leaders to cooperate in combating the drug trade, and they even offer China's leaders a bargaining chip. If the American authorities want help in combating the drug trade, they may need to offer concessions on geopolitical objectives or trade policy, which may harm American interests more than opioid abuse. To complicate the matter, China has a history of cracking down selectively, by prohibiting the manufacture of some precursor chemicals but ignoring those which are newly developed. This strategy preserves the bargaining chip. The key takeaway from this section is that geopolitical strategy toward China may affect the opioid problem in the United States.

The Asia-Pacific Economic Cooperation summit near San Francisco in 2023 brought some agreements between US President Joe Biden and Chinese President Xi Jinping. Official US government sources have few details, leaving most information to be gleaned from what reporters claim to have heard from American officials (White House, 2023). Xi agreed to crack down on fentanyl precursor chemicals by targeting specific Chinese manufacturers, and Biden vowed to "trust but verify" (Hunnicutt et al., 2023). In exchange, Biden agreed to remove China's Institute of Forensic Science from the Commerce Department's entity list, which prohibited it from receiving exports from the United States. The institute was on the entity list because of abuses of the Uyghur minority in western China (Martina, 2023). If these reports are true, it shows the extent to which the United States must go to win assurances on fentanyl. The usefulness of this exchange depends on whether China will abide by its commitments, which is very uncertain. The simple fact that China was only willing to crack down on fentanyl precursors after negotiations with the United States shows that this is not one of Beijing's domestic priorities.

The supply chain of opioids flows through Mexico, whose diplomatic relations with the United States and government enforcement capabilities differ sharply from China's. The simplest positive statement that can be made about the Mexican government and the opioid problem is that the Mexican government has not prevented the Mexican cartels from engaging in this trade. Whether they are unwilling or unable to do so is a more normative question. It may be more of a matter of ability, in contrast to China's intransigence which seems more a matter of willingness.

In March 2023, Mexican President Andres Manuel Lopez-Obrador sent a letter to Chinese President Xi Jinping to request help for humanitarian reasons to combat the opioid problem. He asked Xi specifically for information about when and where fentanyl was being sent. Lopez-Obrador claimed that fentanyl production had been occurring in Mexico, but that his government had destroyed more than 1,400 labs, although Reuters found that most of those were inactive. Lopez-Obrador said that Mexico was not producing fentanyl anymore and that only 30% of American consumption entered through Mexico, which is contrary to the assessment of American officials. The Chinese embassy in Mexico did not comment on the letter (Reuters, 2023). Despite differences over whether fentanyl enters the United States through Mexico, the American and Mexican sides do agree that China is a major source of the problem.

CONCLUSION

The opioid epidemic in the United States cannot be fully understood as a purely domestic problem. Economic hardship in some areas has been exacerbated by international trade, and this is correlated with opioid abuse, showing some domestic demand induced by international causes. American patients with a valid need for pain relief have looked to international sources for opioids, showing homegrown domestic demand deliberately searching for foreign supply. In the illicit market, internationally sourced supply is the norm. Fentanyl precursor chemicals are produced in China and shipped to Mexico, where they are compounded into a marketable form and trafficked into the United States. The ratio of potency to physical volume aids in evading enforcement. China's leaders, partly due to lingering animosity over the Opium Wars but also due to current geopolitical goals that conflict with the United States, have demonstrated an unwillingness to crack down on its own manufacturers of fentanyl precursors. Complex networks of Chinese money launderers have developed to coordinate international transfers of wealth ownership outside the legitimate banking system of international transfers. Despite some American enforcement success, these networks are widespread and have enjoyed remarkable success. As American efforts to combat the opioid epidemic have been somewhat successful at times, traffickers and producers have found other drugs that attract less attention from authorities. These drugs are also frequently sourced internationally, often but not always from China. The key takeaways of this chapter are that demand for opioids exists, some of which are caused by international circumstances, and that an international supply chain has developed to meet this demand, and any successful enforcement depends on multiple countries whose cooperation is exceedingly unlikely. Should enforcement against any single drug succeed, experience has shown that, as long as demand for illicit drugs exists, a new drug will take its place, often sourced internationally.

REFERENCES

Caquet, P. (2015). Notions of addiction in the time of the first opium war. *The Historical Journal*, *58*(4), 1009–29. doi:10.1017/S0018246X14000739

Cavazuti, L., McFadden, C., & Schapiro, R. (2024, February 10). Mexican drug cartels are targeting America's "last best place." *NBC News*. Retrieved February 13, 2024, from https://www.nbcnews.com/news/mexican-drug-cartels-are-targeting-americas-last-great-place-rcna130822

Centers for Disease Control. (2023). *What you should know about xylazine.* Retrieved January 16, 2024, from https://www.cdc.gov/drugoverdose/deaths/other-drugs/xylazine/faq.html

DEA Strategic Intelligence Section. (2016). *Counterfeit prescription pills containing fentanyl: A global threat.* US Drug Enforcement Administration. Retrieved February 2, 2024, from https://www.dea.gov/sites/default/files/docs/Counterfeit%2520Prescription%2520Pills.pdf

Dean, A., & Kimmel, S. (2019, August). Free trade and opioid overdose death in the United States. *SSM Population Health*, *8*, 100409. doi:https://doi.org/10.1016/j.ssmph.2019.100409

Doherty, J. (2023, May 18). The China-Mexico fentanyl pipeline: Increasingly sophisticated and deadly. *The Guardian*. Retrieved February 7, 2024, from https://www.theguardian.com/us-news/2023/may/18/china-mexico-opioid-traficking-us-sanctions

Donahue, M. (2019). *Statement before the House Energy and Commerce Committee Subcommittee on Oversight Investigations for a Hearing Entitled "Oversight of Federal Efforts to Combat the Spread of Illicit Fentanyl."* US Drug Enforcement Administration. Retrieved October 17, 2023, from https://www.dea.gov/sites/default/files/2019-07/DEA%20Testimony%20fentanyl%20071619%20HENC%20OI%20_Cleared_1.pdf

Feige, C., & Miron, J. A. (2008). The opium wars, opium legalization, and opium consumption in China. *Applied Economics Letters, 15*(12), 911–13. doi:10.1080/13504850600972295

Friedman, J., Godvin, M., Molina, C., Romero, R., Borquez, A., Avra, T., . . . Shover, C. L. (2023, August). Fentanyl, heroin, and methamphetamine-based counterfeit pills sold at tourist-oriented pharmacies in Mexico: An ethnographic and drug checking study. *Drug and Alcohol Dependence, 249*, 110819.

García, M. C., Heilig, C. M., Lee, S. H., Faul, M., Guy, G., Iademarco, M. F., . . . Gray, J. (2019, January 18). Opioid prescribing rates in nonmetropolitan and metropolitan counties among primary care providers using an electronic health record system—United States, 2014–2017. *Morbidity and Mortality Weekly Report.* Retrieved February 13, 2024, from https://www.cdc.gov/mmwr/volumes/68/wr/mm6802a1.htm

Gelber, H. G. (2006). *China as "victim"? The opium war that wasn't.* Center for European Studies Working Paper Series. Retrieved February 5, 2024, from https://ces.fas.harvard.edu/uploads/files/Working-Papers-Archives/CES_WP136.pdf

Hunnicutt, T., Mason, J., & Holland, S. (2023, November 16). Biden, Xi's "blunt" talks yield deals on military, fentanyl. *Reuters.* Retrieved February 7, 2024, from https://www.reuters.com/world/biden-xi-meet-us-china-military-economic-tensions-grind-2023-11-15/

Jorgic, D. (2020, December 3). Special Report. Burner phones and banking apps: Meet the Chinese "brokers" laundering Mexican drug money. *Reuters.* Retrieved October 4, 2023, from https://www.reuters.com/article/mexico-china-cartels-idLTAL8N2I34RV

Lassi, N. (2023). Strengthening pill press control to combat fentanyl: Legislative and law enforcement imperatives. *Exploratory Research in Clinical and Social Pharmacy, 11*, 100321. doi:https://doi.org/10.1016%2Fj.rcsop.2023.100321

Levinson, M. (2016). *The box: How the shipping container made the world smaller and the world economy bigger.* Princeton University Press.

Martina, M. (2023, November 14). US set to take action to win China's cooperation on fentanyl. *Reuters.* Retrieved February 7, 2024, from https://www.reuters.com/world/us-set-take-action-win-chinas-cooperation-fentanyl-2023-11-14/

Owens, B. (2019, May). Opioid prescriptions down but some patients fear doctors now too strict. *Canadian Medical Association Journal, 191*(19), E546–E547. doi:https://doi.org/10.1503%2Fcmaj.109-5748

Pierce, J. R., & Schott, P. K. (2020, March). Trade liberalization and mortality: Evidence from US counties. *American Economic Review: Insights, 2*(1), 47–64. doi:10.1257/aeri.20180396

Power, E. (1929). Book review: The East India Company Trading to China, 1635–1834, by H. B. Morse. *The Economic History Review, 2*(1), 157–61.

Realuyo, C. B. (2019). The new opium war: A national emergency. *PRISM, 8*(1), 132–42.

Reuters. (2023). *Mexico asks China for help on fentanyl, slams US critics.* Reuters. Retrieved January 9, 2024, from https://www.reuters.com/world/americas/mexico-asks-china-help-control-fentanyl-shipments-2023-04-04/

Rotella, S., & Berg, K. (2022, October 11). How a Chinese American gangster transformed money laundering for drug cartels. *ProPublica.* Retrieved February 7, 2024, from https://www.propublica.org/article/china-cartels-xizhi-li-money-laundering

Ruhm, C. J. (2019, March). Drivers of the fatal drug epidemic. *Journal of Health Economics, 64*, 25–42. doi:https://doi.org/10.1016/j.jhealeco.2019.01.001

Shapiro, J. L. (2019). The third opium war? Understanding China through history. *Horizons: Journal of International Relations and Sustainable Development, 13*, 52–65.

Shover, C. L., Falasinnu, T. O., Dwyer, C. L., Benitez Santos, N., Cunningham, N. J., Freedman, R. B., . . . Humphreys, K. (2020, November). Steep increases in fentanyl-related mortality west of the Mississippi River: Recent evidence from county and state surveillance. *Drug and Alcohol Dependence, 216*, 108314. doi:https://doi.org/10.1016%2Fj.drugalcdep.2020.108314

Strickler, L. (2023, December 10). First came fentanyl. Now this state is counting the casualties from another deadly drug. *NBC News*. Retrieved January 16, 2024, from https://www.nbcnews.com/health/health-news/fentanyl-xylazine-west-virginia-rcna128327

US Customs and Border Protection. (2023). *22 Pill presses, 257 pill press parts; fentanyl, and xylazine: Cincinnati CBP targets deadly imports.* Retrieved January 16, 2024, from https://www.cbp.gov/newsroom/local-media-release/22-pill-presses-257-pill-press-parts-fentanyl-and-xylazine-cincinnati

US Department of Justice. (2021). *Chinese national sentenced to 14 years in prison for laundering drug proceeds on behalf of traffickers in Mexico.* Retrieved January 16, 2024, from https://www.justice.gov/usao-ndil/pr/chinese-national-sentenced-14-years-prison-laundering-drug-proceeds-behalf-traffickers

US Department of Justice. (2023). *Justice Department Announces Eight Indictments Against China-based chemical manufacturing companies and employees.* Retrieved February 6, 2024, from Office of Public Affairs: https://www.justice.gov/opa/pr/justice-department-announces-eight-indictments-against-china-based-chemical-manufacturing

US Department of the Treasury. (2022). *National money laundering risk assessment.* Retrieved February 6, 2024, from https://home.treasury.gov/system/files/136/2022-National-Money-Laundering-Risk-Assessment.pdf

US Department of the Treasury. (2023a). *Treasury sanctions China- and Mexico-based enablers of counterfeit, fentanyl-laced pill production.* Retrieved February 2, 2024, from https://home.treasury.gov/news/press-releases/jy1507

US Department of the Treasury. (2023b). *Treasury targets large Chinese network of illicit drug producers.* Retrieved January 16, 2024, from https://home.treasury.gov/news/press-releases/jy1779

US Drug Enforcement Administration. (2018). *China announces scheduling controls on two fentanyl precursor chemicals.* Retrieved October 4, 2023, from https://www.dea.gov/press-releases/2018/01/05/china-announces-scheduling-controls-two-fentanyl-precursor-chemicals

US Drug Enforcement Administration. (2020). *Fentanyl flow to the United States.* Retrieved October 4, 2023, from https://www.dea.gov/sites/default/files/2020-03/DEA_GOV_DIR-008-20%20Fentanyl%20Flow%20in%20the%20United%20States_0.pdf

US Drug Enforcement Administration. (2022). *The growing threat of xylazine.* Retrieved January 16, 2024, from https://www.dea.gov/sites/default/files/2022-12/The%20Growing%20Threat%20of%20Xylazine%20and%20its%20Mixture%20with%20Illicit%20Drugs.pdf

US Drug Enforcement Administration. (2023a). *DEA reports widespread threat of fentanyl mixed with xylazine.* Retrieved February 7, 2024, from https://www.dea.gov/alert/dea-reports-widespread-threat-fentanyl-mixed-xylazine

US Drug Enforcement Administration. (2023b). *Drug scheduling.* Retrieved January 26, 2024, from https://www.dea.gov/drug-information/drug-scheduling

US Drug Enforcement Administration. (2023c). *Fentanyl-related substances.* Retrieved January 26, 2024, from https://www.deadiversion.usdoj.gov/drug_chem_info/frs.pdf

US Drug Enforcement Administration. (2023d). *Three Chinese chemical manufacturing companies and five employees charged with conspiring to manufacture fentanyl.* Retrieved February 6, 2024, from https://www.dea.gov/press-releases/2023/06/23/three-chinese-chemical-manufacturing-companies-and-five-employees-charged

Volkow, N. D. (2021). *The overdose crisis: Interagency proposal to combat illicit fentanyl-related substances.* National Institute on Drug Abuse. Retrieved January 26, 2024, from https://nida.nih.gov/about-nida/legislative-activities/testimony-to-congress/2021/the-overdose-crisis-proposal-to-combat-illicit-fentanyl

White House. (2023). *Readout of President Joe Biden's meeting with President Xi Jinping of the People's Republic of China.* Retrieved February 7, 2024, from https://www.whitehouse.gov/briefing-room/statements-releases/2023/11/15/readout-of-president-joe-bidens-meeting-with-president-xi-jinping-of-the-peoples-republic-of-china-2/

Zoorob, M. (2019, August). Fentanyl shock: The changing geography of overdose in the United States. *International Journal of Drug Policy, 70,* 40–46. doi:https://doi.org/10.1016/j.drugpo.2019.04.010

4

Regulating into Crisis

The Government's Role in the Opioid Epidemic

Josiah R. Baker and Matthew L. Dobra

The opioid crisis in the United States, marked by widespread addiction and escalating overdose deaths, has deep roots in governmental policy (Spencer et al., 2022). While the dominant theory tends to posit that the escalation in addiction and overdose deaths stems from over-prescription of opioids, this chapter articulates an alternative thesis: the primary catalyst for the opioid epidemic is the legal and regulatory framework imposed by the US government on opioids. Despite having good intentions, these policies, rather than mitigating the crisis, have had the unintended consequence of driving consumers toward more dangerous alternatives on the black market.

The linkage between stringent federal and state regulations of opioids and the subsequent rise in black market dependency underscores not merely a policy failure but a profound misalignment with the societal trend toward self-medication. As regulations tightened around prescription opioids in a bid to reduce abuse, the unintended consequence was a significant migration to the black market. These government interventions did not account for the entrenched cultural practice of seeking out pharmaceuticals for mental and physical relief, and overlooked the persistent demand, fueled by a society accustomed to pharmacological solutions (Patel & Rushefsky, 2021). This shift to illicit sources demonstrates the complex challenge of addressing opioid abuse through regulation alone, highlighting the inadequacy and ineffectiveness of these government interventions. It underscores the complexity of the drug market, which is too multifaceted for the government to effectively address, particularly concerning policies primarily focused on curbing legitimate supply since the 1990s (Sarpatwari et al., 2017).

BACKGROUND

In contemporary American culture, there is an increasing tendency to seek pharmaceutical solutions for mental and physical discomfort, no matter how small. Not feeling good? There's a pill for that. Feeling too good? There's a pill for that too. *Overmedicalization* (sometimes called *overdiagnosis*) refers to the tendency to describe and treat nonmedical issues as though they are medical problems, often leading to excessive use of medical services and overprescription of pharmaceutical products.

The trend toward overmedicalization in the United States has been noted since at least the 1970s (see, for example, Szasz, 2007) for some early works on overmedicalization in psychiatry) and underscores a broader shift toward medication as a universal remedy, be it in the form of over-the-counter medicine, prescription medicine, or illicit drugs. As overmedicalization accelerated, federal and state legislative and law enforcement have attempted to put in measures that would subdue the persistent and ravenous demand for opioids and related hazardous substances, but for the most part governmental initiatives have been ineffective because they have primarily focused on curtailing supply of legal products.

These efforts were also stymied by contradicting efforts, often from commercial interests and special interest groups (i.e., the pharmaceutical industry, physicians, and lawyers who stand to profit from overmedicalization) (Sarpatwari et al., 2017), but often simply from consumers seeking comfort, have further aggravated the negative consequences of this crisis by finding ways to circumvent, and thereby undermine, governmental policies. Furthermore, the pervasive geographic prevalence of mass opioid consumption throughout rural America (after having thoroughly saturated the major metropolitan areas) reflects the degree to which drug consumption has become normalized in the national consciousness (Monnat, 2019). Given the extent and complexity of America's opioid consumption crisis, addressing it effectively requires an examination not just of social attitudes but of the economic and political economy aspects driving this phenomenon (Thombs et al., 2020). Effort to resolve the crisis must accurately assess the interplay between market demand, regulatory environments, and the vested interests that shape the opioid landscape, underscoring the need for policies that engage with these economic and political realities to stem the tide of opioid misuse.

The escalating reliance on pharmaceuticals for dealing with mental and physical discomfort has led the United States into a persistent, deepening opioid crisis. Although the government made numerous attempts to address both the direct causes and broader contributing factors, it has not stemmed the tide of opioid consumption. Disappointing restrictive policies have aggravated an exasperated public who increasingly demand action against the ongoing issue of substance misuse (Manchikanti et al., 2018). Interestingly, there's a persistent naïve optimism that "this time," government interventions will yield different results, despite a track record suggesting otherwise. These efforts often fail to address the complex socioeconomic factors driving the crisis or to align with the underlying market dynamics that are crucial for understanding and resolving the issue effectively.

During the early years of overmedicalization in the latter third of the 20th century, most of the public focus on drug abuse was concerned with the use of illicit drugs in America. In particular, narcotics and cannabis received the lion's share of political and societal attention. Mass media portrayals of the ills of drug usage in printed news stories, films, songs, theatrical performances, and television shows were persistently imbued and illuminated into the greater consciousness of contemporary American culture. Although cannabis and cocaine became illegal during President Franklin Roosevelt's administration in the 1930s, it wasn't until the early 1970s with President Nixon's "war on drugs" that concerted and well-publicized federal efforts to combat drug use began. These efforts continued with President Reagan's 1980s antidrug education campaigns (most notably "Just Say No"), followed by President George H. Bush's public pleas focused on curbing illegal drug use and its associated criminal elements through increasing enforcement efforts and by imprisoning suppliers of such substances. In the early 2000s, the anti-supply side agenda expanded into disrupting narcotics production and trafficking operations in many parts of Latin America (Baker, 2004). By all accounts, these initiatives have failed. The war on drugs has been lost; the drugs have won.

Drug abuse as a major public policy issue persisted and morphed over the past half-century, as the nature of the issue has changed, and continues to persist today (Patel & Rushefsky, 2021). Whereas the focus in the 1980s and 1990s was primarily on restricting street drugs, notably crack cocaine and marijuana, the current focus is on opioids and the abuse of prescription medicine.

At the root of the conventional wisdom, surrounding the root of the opioid epidemic, is the belief that it is fueled by a dramatic uptick in drug prescriptions, perhaps an unintended consequence of the over-medicalization trend discussed previously. This perspective is supported by data showing a marked demand for prescription drugs between the 20th and 21st centuries; the overall and proportional use of prescription pills among virtually all segments of the population has dramatically increased.

Encouraged by physicians, bombarded with advertisements in mass media, and incentivized by healthcare insurance policies, Americans of all ages and socioeconomic backgrounds have increasingly relied upon prescriptions to address or treat more kinds of illnesses and maladies. Prior research points to the exploitive practices of pharmaceutical companies, which include hundreds of millions of dollars spent on advertising and marketing that made opioids more appealing to the general public (Arpa, 2017; Hamunen et al., 2009; Ruhm, 2019; Van Zee, 2009). Such efforts motivated more patients to seek prescriptions. Furthermore, *only* two other countries (Brazil and New Zealand) allow direct-to-consumer advertising. All other countries have banned such practices (Ventola, 2011). In Sweden, for example, it is illegal to use billboards, televised commercials, and many forms of printed pharmaceutical advertisements. Patients must consult with their physicians who then are primarily tasked with revealing possible pharmaceutical options.

Opioids, in particular, began their meteoric rise as America's most abused drug in the mid-1990s as pain management emerged as a primary healthcare focus. Many trace these roots to James Campbell's "Pain as the 5th Vital Sign" presidential address to the American Pain Society, ushering in an age where physicians would treat pain with the same urgency as the traditional vital signs of temperature, blood pressure, pulse, and respiration. With this enhanced focus on pain, opioids were often prescribed as a drug for pain management. Thus, opioids became engrained in the overmedicalization of American culture, and quickly gained traction among the general populace as a normal (or at least normalized) consumption behavior (Sarpatwari et al., 2017).

In the dominant narrative, the increased frequency and widespread social acceptance of consuming an ever-increasing quantity of medications and drugs is only half of the story; this bias is exacerbated by the extent to which pharmaceutical firms incentivize many physicians to write prescriptions by offering substantial kickbacks in the form of bonuses or extra payments (Sarpatwari et al., 2017). Such mercantile relationships further strengthen and tacitly support the positive bias or perception that most consumers exhibit toward medications, as when they are authorized by a professional healthcare provider it reinforces a greater sense of legitimacy and deepens its widespread acceptance.

Filling a prescription within the safe confines of a well-lit, clean pharmacy, unlike obtaining drugs in a back-alley black market setting from shady street peddlers, is perceived as considerably safer and lacks obvious social stigmas. This process legitimizes its market environment (Sarpatwari et al., 2017) since there is a perceived reduction of all kinds of risks (in contrast to logistical hardships and overt risks when dealing with street-level criminals) which consequently gives most buyers a false sense of safety. Although many warnings and list of potential negative side effects were made available via Food and Drug Administration (FDA) mandates (i.e., via printed material accompanying filled prescriptions), American consumers focused on resolving or coping with their personal ailments persistently exercise a form of rational ignorance and, thus, have purposefully overlooked, minimized, or disregarded specific warnings. Again, the perceived safe and sanitized confines of a modern pharmacy quash many concerns.

At the surface, such widespread consumer behavior became normalized, pervasive, and most importantly, overtly legitimate. It took years for the general public to become aware of the subtle but very real dangers of using and abusing legally obtained drugs (Sarpatwari et al., 2017). Nonetheless, a wide swath of the American populace became particularly enraptured by taking an increasing number of pills under the guise of improving or sustaining one's physical and psychological well-being. Furthermore, social institutions such as public schools, private therapists, and even many religious leaders encouraged legalized prescription drug consumption.

At some point, due to such conducive and enabling market mechanisms, for many Americans, chemical needs began to trump considerations of potential negative consequences. Drug overdoses soared. Since shady drug dealers were often not involved or played a reduced role, such horror stories were not as articulately or vividly portrayed in the media with many hundreds of thousands of people quietly and privately dying from such misadventures of consumption. Blaming the authorities and professionals also proved to be less achievable and positive biases made them less culpable than maligned images of street-level drug dealers. Financial and political connections and incentives also undoubtedly aided and perpetuated the legalized mechanisms and channels of prescribing potential drugs to the populace.

AN ALTERNATIVE THEORY

The preceding section broadly sketches the dominant rhetoric surrounding America's opioid epidemic. We believe that this story is at best a reasonable story for the beginnings of the crisis, but closer scrutiny of the data suggests that to gain a true understanding of the opioid crisis, we need to construct a theory that can explain the coexistence of several important stylized facts that seem to contradict this narrative:

- Between 2001 and 2021, on a per capita basis, drug overdoses increased by roughly 400% (Spencer et al., 2022).
- The rate of increase in drug overdoses was not constant over this period; overdose deaths grew steadily between 2001 and 2006, remained relatively constant between 2006 and 2013, but then accelerated rapidly between 2013 and 2021 (Spencer et al., 2022).
- Between 1999 and 2010, opioid prescriptions in the United States roughly quadrupled (Paulozzi et al., 2011).
- From 2010 to 2022, opioid prescriptions *fell* by roughly 50% (American Medical Association, 2023).
- Also, between 2010 and 2022, prescription opioid overdose deaths remained roughly constant, meaning that the massive escalation of overdose deaths in the United States was primarily associated with illegal drugs, especially fentanyl, heroin, cocaine, and methamphetamines (National Institute on Drug Abuse, 2023).

Reconciling the fact that the opioid epidemic accelerated as opioid prescriptions were falling and the majority of overdoses stem from the use of illicit narcotics suggests that the relatively mainstream theory of overprescription is incomplete.

The push in recent years to curb prescription drug abuse has brought the opioid crisis toward the forefront of policymaking at the state and federal levels. For example, in 2016, the United States officially had 42,000 opioid overdose deaths. Many of these deaths were from the use of fentanyl; between 2009 and 2016 fentanyl deaths increased 520%. Of that figure, there was an increase of 87.7% annually between 2013 and 2016. Meanwhile, heroin deaths from 2000 to 2016 increased 533%. Note that the primary source of the increase in overdose deaths came from illegal drugs, as the rate of prescription opioid deaths increased by only 18% overall between 2009 and 2016. By 2016, there were also over 20,000 synthetic opioid deaths (excluding methadone) and over 15,000 heroin overdose deaths (Manchikanti et al., 2018). Given these statistics, it's crucial to recognize that the significant loss of human lives extends beyond overprescription or mere cultural trends. As the focus broadens to the dangers of consuming excessive non-illicit prescription drugs and the rising potency of newly developed chemical mixtures, our understanding must also evolve to grasp the true root of the crisis.

The incredible persistence of demand for opioids is evident from the many previous policies that have largely failed to adequately reduce deaths and its widespread consumption. Thus, a reframing of preventive strategies is needed to address the ongoing pervasive use of fentanyl and heroin. For example, by 2013, prescriptions for opioids reached 252 million (Sarpatwari et al., 2017). Efforts to curb excessive prescriptions pressured physicians by 2017 into reducing the total number to 196 million which was below the 2006 total. Additionally, the proportion of patients receiving high-dose opioid prescriptions between 2013 and 2017 fell by 16.1% of the total. This is more precisely measured by the decrease of average milligram equivalents of morphine prescriptions from 2013–2017 dropping 12.2% (Manchikanti et al., 2018). The reduction in prescriptions, in conjunction with Drug Enforcement Administration (DEA) mandates to reduce opioid manufacturing, resulted in official opioid manufacturing (which of course excludes black market manufacturing and illicit imports) with a 25% drop in 2017 and another 20% drop in 2018 (Manchikanti et al., 2018). Yet, these regulatory "achievements" in diminishing legal opioid distribution have inadvertently fueled an increase in illicit consumption and overdoses (Sarpatwari et al., 2017), underscoring a grave miscalculation by the government in addressing the true nature of the opioid crisis (Monnat, 2019).

MARKET DYNAMICS AND REGULATORY FAILURES

The crux of the government's regulatory failures lies in a fundamental misunderstanding of the drug market's dynamics and the motivations of those involved—suppliers, consumers, and the regulatory bodies themselves. By overlooking the complex interplay of supply and demand, as well as the adaptability of both the market and its participants, policies have inadvertently propelled the shift toward drug users resorting to more hazardous, unregulated alternatives (Thombs et al., 2020). This misalignment suggests that effective intervention requires a nuanced appreciation of the economic incentives at play, a factor that has been conspicuously absent in the formulation of past strategies.

Following this critical assessment of legal and regulatory shortcomings, it becomes apparent that the opioid crisis is perpetuated not just by market forces, but also by the intricate roles and motivations of key players within this ecosystem. This includes pharmaceutical companies, whose aggressive marketing has been criticized as being geared more toward profit maximization than patient health (Sarpatwari et al., 2017), but also regulatory agencies like the DEA and FDA. These bodies, ostensibly guardians of public safety and health, face a complex set of incentives that might not always align with the public's best interests (Ciccarone, 2019). Their regulatory actions, including drug approvals and crackdowns on illicit substances, are influenced by a mix of political, economic, and bureaucratic pressures. This complex scenario underlines the unintended consequences of well-meaning policies: rather than curbing the epidemic, they have redirected consumers from tightly regulated prescription opioids to the perilous uncertainties of the black market.

Governmental efforts to curb opioid addiction through stringent regulation of prescriptions have not only failed to reduce opioid misuse but have exacerbated the problem, as the reduction in legally available opioids has not diminished demand but has simply shifted it to illicit channels. This transition is a direct consequence of regulatory actions that fail to consider the persistence of demand among individuals previously dependent on these medications for pain management.

The role of economic factors in the opioid crisis is nuanced. While lower-income individuals may be more susceptible to the lure of cheaper, illicit opioids, the issue transcends simple economic inequality. The broader problem involves accessibility and the regulatory environment's impact on legitimate opioid use. As regulations tightened around the prescription of opioids, aiming to curb abuse, they inadvertently made it more difficult for patients with legitimate needs to obtain these drugs legally. This regulatory squeeze pushed a sizable segment of opioid users toward illicit markets, where drugs like heroin and fentanyl are more readily available but are also more dangerous.

The shift to the black market has had significant implications for drug safety and quality. In a regulated market, companies are motivated by the need to maintain reputational capital, incentivizing the production of high-quality, safe products. This mechanism collapses in the black market, where anonymity is paramount. The lack of transparency and accountability means that illicit drug producers have little incentive to ensure the quality or safety of their products. This dynamic has filled the market with drugs that are not only inconsistent but often dangerously potent.

The potency of drugs in the illicit market is partly a strategic response to evade law enforcement detection, as noted by Thornton (1998). By concentrating active ingredients, manufacturers produce smaller, more concealable quantities, facilitating transport and reducing detection risks. However, this concentration significantly elevates overdose risks for consumers, as precisely dosing such potent drugs becomes challenging. Compounding this issue, black market distributors, lacking access to professional-grade facilities, resort to using everyday items found in kitchens and basements for drug preparation. This makeshift approach results in products with inconsistent quality and potency, further exacerbating the dangers faced by end-users.

The legal and regulatory environment pertaining to opioids, particularly the government's crackdown on legitimate prescriptions, has played a significant role in exacerbating the opioid crisis. Indeed, tightening restrictions and intensified scrutiny from law enforcement operations have continually tried to quash domestic demand. Yet, these stringent and strong-arm tactics have not only disrupted the supply chain of legitimate opioids but also drove individuals toward black market alternatives, effectively criminalizing its use (Thombs et al., 2020).

The criminalization of opioid use following this shift significantly stigmatizes addiction. Such stigma acts as a formidable obstacle for those grappling with dependency, discouraging them from seeking treatment due to fears of legal consequences and social rejection. Consequently, this stigma perpetuates addiction cycles, with affected individuals more inclined to continue their illicit drug use in secrecy, further isolating themselves from potential support and treatment options. This sequence of events underscores a critical flaw in current opioid policies, emphasizing the need for a revised approach that mitigates the unintended consequences of criminalization.

The current regulatory regime surrounding opioids inadvertently acts as a catalyst for organized crime, exacerbating the opioid crisis and placing additional strains on public safety. By restricting access to legal opioids and criminalizing their use, these policies have inadvertently created a lucrative opportunity for cartels and organized crime syndicates. Such groups thrive in the resultant black market, where the demand for opioids remains high despite, or perhaps because of, governmental restrictions. This illicit trade not only fuels these criminal enterprises, providing them with substantial revenue streams but also unintentionally introduces a host of dangers to communities, ranging from violence associated with drug trafficking to the broader societal impacts of increased drug addiction rates. The strength and influence of these cartels are directly empowered by the regulatory landscape, underscoring the dire need for policy reevaluation to undermine the economic foundations of organized crime within the opioid sector.

Compounding the issue, these very cartels play a central role in the manufacture and distribution of counterfeit opioids, bridging the gap between organized crime's influence and the public health crisis. In a landscape where legitimate pharmaceuticals are heavily regulated, the production of counterfeit drugs by crime syndicates flourishes, with these illicit products often being indistinguishable from their legitimate counterparts. These counterfeits, often laden with lethal doses of fentanyl and lacking quality control, are a direct consequence of the cartels' exploitation of the market created by regulatory constraints. The result is a dangerous undermining of trust in legitimate pharmaceutical companies, as the market is flooded with these hazardous substitutes. Consumers are left without assurances of safety, contributing to the significant rise in overdose incidents and deaths (Spencer et al., 2022). This unfortunate circumstance underscores the perverse outcomes of current drug policies, where the attempt to control opioid distribution not only fuels organized crime but also deteriorates the standards of drug quality and safety, eroding public trust in the process and in the pharmaceutical industry.

Moreover, this illegal marketplace has a cascading effect on public health and safety, straining law enforcement agencies and healthcare systems. The resources required to combat the distribution of illicit drugs, treat overdoses, and address the broader societal impacts of addiction are immense. At the same time, the criminalization approach to drug policy fails to address the root causes of opioid dependency (i.e., pain management, mental health issues, and socioeconomic factors). By focusing primarily on punitive measures rather than comprehensive public health strategies, the current legal and regulatory environment inadvertently exacerbates the opioid crisis, highlighting the need for a reassessment of drug policy that considers addiction as a health issue rather than solely a criminal matter.

The transition from prescribed opioids to illicit substances is a direct consequence of these tightened regulations. The DEA's and FDA's efforts to clamp down on opioid prescriptions, while well-intentioned, created these outcomes as unintended consequences of their policies. These actions have not only failed to stem the tide of opioid addiction but have also reshaped the market, driving demand for unregulated, more dangerous, and often more potent alternatives. This shift underscores the need for a reevaluation of current strategies, recognizing that the dynamics of supply and demand are influenced by both regulatory actions and the broader socioeconomic context.

In this scenario, the consideration of deregulation emerges as a potential strategy to address the crisis. By adjusting the regulatory framework to allow for safer, more open access to opioids, the government could mitigate the push toward the black market (Spencer et al., 2022). This approach would not eliminate the opioid crisis but could represent a more nuanced way of managing the complex interplay of factors contributing to the epidemic. It suggests a path forward that includes better quality control, reduced influence of illicit markets, improved access to medical care, and more informed decision-making by consumers.

CONCLUSION: DEREGULATION

Our analysis of the consequences of governmental regulation involving the opioid crisis makes it clear that policies since at least the 1970s have not only failed to stem the tide of addiction but have also contributed to creating a more perilous landscape for drug users. The reliance on regulation and criminalization has diverted attention from the root causes of addiction and ignored the adaptability of both the supply and demand sides of the market.

In conclusion, the evidence in this chapter suggests that a reevaluation of governmental policies on opioids is necessary. A renewed focus should shift from regulation and criminalization to deregulation and reduction of the government's involvement in the opioid market. Such an approach would entail relaxing prescription restrictions, thus addressing the demand for opioids through legal channels and diminishing the reliance on the black market. This strategy would not only mitigate the risks associated with unregulated drugs but also offer a more effective framework for addressing the opioid crisis by recognizing and adapting to the complexities of drug demand and addiction. Academic and policy discussions should consider the potential benefits of deregulation as a means to alleviate the opioid epidemic and focus on practical and evidence-based interventions that prioritize public health and safety instead of ineffective punitive measures.

REFERENCES

American Medical Association. (2023). *Overdose Epidemic Report 2023*.

Arpa, S. (2017). *Women who use drugs: Issues, needs, responses, challenges and implications for policy and practice*. Background paper commissioned by the European Monitoring Centre for Drugs and Drug Addiction for Health and social responses to drug problems: A European guide.

Baker, J. R. (2004, November 18). Coca leaf crop transforms destitute nation. *Orlando Sentinel*. http://articles.orlandosentinel.com/2004-11-28/news/0411270106_1_coca-boliviagrowing

Ciccarone, D. (2019). The triple wave epidemic: Supply and demand drivers of the US opioid overdose crisis. *International Journal of Drug Policy, 71*, 183–88.

Hamunen, K., Paakkari, P., & Kalso, E. (2009). Trends in opioid consumption in the Nordic countries 2002–2006. *European Journal of Pain, 13*(9), 954–62.

Manchikanti, L., Sanapati, J., Benyamin, R. M., Atluri, S., Kaye, A. D., & Hirsch, J. A. (2018). Reframing the prevention strategies of the opioid crisis: Focusing on prescription opioids, fentanyl, and heroin epidemic. *Pain Physician, 21*(4), 309–26.

Monnat, S. M. (2019). The contributions of socioeconomic and opioid supply factors to US drug mortality rates: Urban-rural and within-rural differences. *Journal of Rural Studies, 68*, 319–35.

National Institute on Drug Abuse. (2023). *Drug overdose death rates*. Retrieved March 13, 2024, from https://nida.nih.gov/research-topics/trends-statistics/overdose-death-rates

Patel, K. B., & Rushefsky, M. E. (2021). *The opioid epidemic in the United States: Missed opportunities and policy failures*. Routledge.

Paulozzi, L. J., Jones, C. M., Mack, K. A., & Rudd, R. A. (2011). Vital signs: Overdoses of prescription opioid pain relievers—United States, 1999–2008. *Morbidity & Mortality Weekly Report, 60*(43).

Ruhm C. J. (2019). Drivers of the fatal drug epidemic. *Journal of Health Economics, 64*, 25–42. https://doi.org/10.1016/j.jhealeco.2019.01.001

Sarpatwari, A., Sinha, M. S., & Kesselheim, A. S. (2017). The opioid epidemic: Fixing a broken pharmaceutical market. *Harvard Law & Policy Review, 11*, 463.

Spencer, M. R., Minino, A. M., & Warner, M. (2022). *Drug overdose deaths in the United States, 2001–2021. NCHS Data Brief No. 457, December 2022*. Centers for Disease Control and Prevention. https://www.cdc.gov/nchs/products/databriefs/db457.htm

Szasz, T. (2007). *The medicalization of everyday life: Selected essays*. Syracuse University Press.

Thombs, R. P., Thombs, D. L., Jorgenson, A. K., & Harris Braswell, T. (2020). What is driving the drug overdose epidemic in the United States? *Journal of Health and Social Behavior, 61*(3), 275–89.

Thornton, M. (1998). The potency of illegal drugs. *Journal of Drug Issues, 28*(3), 725–40.

Van Zee, A. (2009). The promotion and marketing of oxycontin: Commercial triumph, public health tragedy. *American Journal of Public Health, 99*(2), 221–27.

Ventola, C. L. (2011). Direct-to-consumer pharmaceutical advertising: Therapeutic or toxic? *Pharmacy and Therapeutics, 36*(10), 669.

5

The News Media's Role in Reporting the Opioid Crisis

Kevin Swift

And so it is to the printing press—to the recorder of man's deeds, the keeper of his conscience, the courier of his news—that we look for strength and assistance, confident that with your help man will be what he was born to be: free and independent. —John F. Kennedy (JFK Library.org)

On a Friday night, in 2009, ABC's *20/20* aired a one-hour special called "A Hidden America: Children of the Mountains" (Sawyer et al., 2009). Hosted by Diane Sawyer, the special focused on the troubles faced by families living in central Appalachia. The show is broken into six segments, each focusing on a different person, group, or family. Sawyer circles back at the end to give updates on each of them before concluding the program.

The aftermath of the report was swift and diverse. By the following Monday, ABC's website received over 1,600 comments from viewers around the country (Christians et al., 2017). Offers of assistance are extensive. Other news outlets pick up the story and the governor of Kentucky announces that his state will receive $3 billion under the Economic Recovery Act. The struggle of families in the Appalachians became a hot topic and, for a while, it remained a point of discussion. The following year, ABC News won a Peabody Award for "A Hidden America" (Christians et al., 2017).

While this may sound like solid, in-depth reporting with a positive outcome, reactions were mixed. Critics argued that the show didn't go far enough. Perhaps an entire series was in order? Some argued that there were several underlying issues of the problems faced by those in Appalachia and that Sawyer and ABC failed to mention them. While others saw it as repetitive and reinforcing stereotypes. "The same load of crap they've been doing for forty years," said Mayor Bill Gorman of Hazard, Kentucky (Meehan & Copley, 2015, para. 5). However, the biggest criticism was that Sawyer and the producers of the special offered no suggestions for solutions. It is here that parallels between the ABC special and the reporting of the opioid crisis can be found.

Debate continues publicly, in media ethics courses and in communication theory. The question remains the same: Is the news media a beacon of light that lets the public know what is happening in their communities and around the world? Should news organizations deliver straightforward information and nothing more? Or, is the news media responsible for much more, such as follow-ups, debates, and potential solutions? This decades-long debate continues to this day. Throughout this chapter, we will examine the theories, responsibilities, criticisms, and current movements aimed at making journalism more robust in an ever-changing landscape of information in the 21st century.

THE OPIOID EPIDEMIC

"By getting the story out there and reporting, we can instigate change, but I don't know that it's the journalists job to be the change maker. I think we put the information out there to the public, the politicians, civic groups, to start thinking about the change. I don't know that it is our role to actually make the change, but it's our role to examine an issue extensively" (D. Natale, personal communication, 3/11/2024).

When commentators mention that news organizations were late to the coverage of the opioid epidemic, they are often met with agreement. Research shows the epidemic is actually quite spread out and has taken place over more than two decades. However, the realization that deaths from opioid use were rising and much of it being related to overprescribing took time. As a former news professional and veteran of local broadcast news, I can attest that the news media has a very full plate in terms of covering stories, especially on the local level. The daily routine of reporting road closures, accidents, school closings, food recalls, weather, and traffic can easily fill a 30-minute newscast. An in-depth study of something like a local rise in overdoses requires quite a bit of time and energy. Some newsrooms have the workforce while others do not. National news coverage has an even bigger task of researching problem areas and determining whether or not any rise in overdose statistics is isolated or widespread. These are just some of the reasons why it is often the case that a professional news organization is behind the curve on a major story that impacts a large portion of its audience.

The opioid epidemic is clearly explained as hitting America in three waves. Howard Koh, a Public Health Leadership professor at Harvard University, describes it succinctly, "It started in the mid-1990's when the powerful agent OxyContin, promoted by Purdue Pharma and approved by the Food and Drug Administration (FDA), triggered the first wave of deaths linked to use of legal prescription opioids. Then came a second wave of deaths from a heroin market that expanded to attract already addicted people. More recently, a third wave of deaths has arisen from illegal synthetic opioids like Fentanyl" (Feldscher, 2022, para. 3).

A study from the Centers for Disease Control and Prevention (CDC) shows a rise in prescription opioid overdose deaths starting in the 1990s and showing a significant increase around 1999. This was followed by a second wave of overdoses attributed to heroin in 2010. Finally, there was a massive spike in overdose deaths beginning in 2013 from synthetic opioid use (CDC, 2024). This three-pronged spike may have been what led to a delay in coverage and the public being informed at a faster rate. While the CDC themselves describe part of their work as "monitoring trends," this is a tall task for news professionals. Many issues, locally and nationally, need to be monitored and require a very large team of researchers over an extended period.

CRITICISM OF COVERAGE

Should the news media in the United States go beyond the reporting of facts and information?

Criticism of the news coverage of the opioid epidemic is far-reaching, but largely isolated to three areas. The first is language use. Journalists often use very straightforward language. In recent years, however, the news industry has been encouraged to remove language thought to stigmatize certain individuals. In the case of the opioid epidemic, the Associated Press (AP) has updated its stylebook to address these issues. The noun "addict" should be replaced with the phrase "person with addiction." Terms such as "drug abuse" and "dependence" should be replaced by "misuse," which the AP describes as more accurate and less moralistic. Finally, words like "druggie" and "junkie" should be avoided altogether (Szalavitz, 2018). A study by the National Library of Medicine, from 2008 to 2018, viewed over 6,000 news stories of all formats. The study revealed that 49% of those stories about the opioid epidemic used terms deemed stigmatizing while 2% used the less-stigmatizing alternative. Over the 10 years, the use of stigmatizing terms increased from 37% to 45% (McGinty et al., 2019). The overall concern is that the stigmatizing language may reinforce stigma toward those with use disorders and prevent treatment.

The framing of stories, in this case, what journalists call using a "vehicle," has been described as a failure. A vehicle is a member of the public who is dealing with the issues being mentioned in the story. This member of the public often helps the audience understand the situation better. For example, a story about a tax increase, offering numbers and data, might be seen as boring or dry and not connecting with the audience. Therefore, a reporter might tell the story of a tax increase through the eyes of a local family and explain how the increase will affect their lives. The idea is that the audience will see someone with similar challenges as themselves and relate better to the story. This style of reporting is taught in journalism schools across the country and practiced as one of the many ways to frame and deliver a story in professional newsrooms.

In the case of stories about the opioid epidemic, researchers argue that thematically framed coverage was overused. A study of network news stories on the topic from 2000 to 2020 concluded that the emphasis on "personal stories" failed to show the complexity of the issue and hurt public understanding. Second, the research concludes, news did not show a much-needed representation of minorities and older adults, who already face additional stigmas (Jay et al., 2022). "The 'relatable' story journalists and editors tend to seek—of a good girl or guy (usually, in this crisis, white) gone bad because pharma greed led to overprescribing—does not accurately characterize the most common story of opioid addiction" (Szalavitz, 2018, p. 2). The author further explains that 80% of those who misuse opioids and develop dependency started by using drugs not prescribed to them, while 70% have previously used cocaine or methamphetamine (Szalavitz, 2018). This is seen by many as changing perception to the point that it led to cutting prescriptions in cases where it was not necessary.

The third, and perhaps most talked about, criticism of the news media coverage involves solutions-based reporting and a lack of suggested solutions altogether. Whether or not suggesting solutions is the job of the American news media is a topic of great debate and will be discussed at length later in this chapter. Here, we take a look at specific examples of the effectiveness of solutions that were discussed.

A five-year, 600 story, study published in *Preventative Medicine* showed that the news coverage was lacking in the area of solutions. Treatment (33% of news stories), reduction (30%), and prevention (24%) were the most often discussed solutions. The researchers conclude that several evidence-based public health solutions were largely ignored (the biggest being medication-based treatment) and that journalists, editors, and producers need to be educated on the effectiveness of these solutions (McGinty et al., 2019).

Another study concluded that news media reporting of medication-based solutions for opioid use disorder (OUD) increased in 2015–2016 compared to the previous eight years. Furthermore, while most addiction experts conclude that the underuse of medication-based solutions is a barrier to combating the crisis, stories from the news media mentioned this less than 40% of the time when discussing medication-based solutions. Where this research differs is that it does not conclude that the news media is solely to blame for this lack of information. "Given that the opioid crisis has produced reversals in life expectancy trends, the public health and addiction communities need to develop more effective strategies to communicate with the news media and public about the value of medication treatment for reducing morbidity and mortality associated with OUD" (Kennedy-Hendricks et al., 2019, para. 34).

THEORY

Much of the debate surrounding the American news media is theoretical in nature. Often, the criticisms stem from differing mindsets about how the media *should* operate. This is referred to as normative theory in the world of mass communication. Many normative theories exist, each with the idea that it most perfectly reflects the values and norms of our societal structure and constitution. With that in mind, a normative theory cannot be applied to societal expectations of another country, with its own set of values, laws, and expectations. A system of news media that works well in the United States cannot be expected to work the same way in Saudi Arabia, for example. These normative theories can be found in our "laws, regulations, media policies, codes of ethics, and the substance of public debate" (McQuail, 2000, p. 8).

Media theorist Denis McQuail (2000) breaks down the role and expectation of the American of the news media into four main goals:

1. Maintaining a constant surveillance of events, ideas, and persons active in public life, leading both to a flow of information to the public and exposing violations of the moral and social order.
2. Providing an independent and radical critique of the society and its institutions.
3. Encouraging and providing the means for access, expression, and participation by as many different actors and voices as is necessary or appropriate.
4. Contributing to shared consciousness and identity and real coherence of the community as a whole as well as its component groups. (p. 161)

The theory that applies most directly to the debate over the opioid crisis is social responsibility theory. While deregulation of certain laws and coverage rules has expanded corporate control and ownership of network affiliates, social responsibility represents somewhat of a compromise between government control and press freedom. Dating back to the 1940s, this concept saw ownership as more of a stewardship of news media outlets while the practitioners had a responsibility of their own. In this model the American press should "provide a full, truthful, comprehensive and intelligent account of the day's events in a context which gives them meaning. And should serve as a forum for the exchange of comment and criticism" (McQuail, 2000, p. 8).

However, with ownership laws loosening since the early 1980s, many practitioners have argued that a more market-oriented, bottom-line approach has changed their daily routines and interest in serving the public. While researching this subject, I studied and interviewed experienced practitioners of news in three major media markets. The results reflected their frustration with ownership. While experienced newsroom practitioners held firmly to the practice of social responsibility, they argued that management categorically did not. Philosophical differences in what needs to be emphasized daily were voiced and outright rebellion against the market-minded practices of management were frequently discussed by the participants.

Most practitioners described frustrations with maintaining the daily production of news with smaller staff and working in combined roles. All but one of the practitioners interviewed said that they still feel a sense of responsibility to serve the public. Often referred to as a "mission," this sense of responsibility includes tasks such as getting as many stories, with as much depth, as possible. Demands on their time and story turnaround were given as obstacles to completing this work.

Further questioning about this subject nearly always led to discussions about a great divide seen between practitioners and management. The concern and frustration are that practitioners still see their role as serving the public with important, accurate information that keeps them informed on as many levels as possible. The research showed that practitioners, by and large, see management as an extension of ownership that is much more concerned with earning advertising revenue than serving the public (Swift, 2013).

In a recent interview, former dean of the Philip Merrill College of Journalism at the University of Maryland, Lucy Dalglish, echoed some of these journalistic concerns, calling some of the current challenges with news coverage a bandwidth issue. "You used to have 150 people in your newsroom, now you've got 25. So, what are you going to do? Let's assign somebody to cover the schools. Three people to cover sports. Let's assign some folks to talk about elections. Then, we're going to try to keep our nose above water and cover science and technology, global warming and guns. It's a big agenda. A really big agenda. And there's not enough experienced, educated trained people available, to really give it the attention it deserves" (L. Dalglish, personal communication, 3/18/2024).

Similar discussions and arguments regarding the possibility of holding on to social responsibility theory have led many to question whether or not it is a viable concept in the 21st century. The question being the strength of ownership and the attention toward financial interests.

A popular theory of communications is Agenda Setting. This theory, introduced by Maxwell McCombs and Donald Shaw, is the concept that "the media" (often news oriented) are not telling people what to think, but what to think about (McQuail, 2000). By "stacking" news rundowns, placing stories in a specific order and offering extended words or time to a specific story, they are increasing its importance. Therefore, news professionals are, in turn, setting the agenda for what the audience should think about, debate over and see as a point of concern.

Indeed, journalists have been trained for years to look for certain elements that make for a good news story:

Timelines—This has always been the case, even with limited outlets many decades ago. What happened recently is the most important. Updates can be given about past or ongoing stories, but recent events will always go first.

Prominence—What happens to someone of notoriety will take precedence over an average person. An example I share with students is then President George W. Bush (2002) choking on a pretzel and passing out in the White House and quickly regaining consciousness. This is not a story, if it happens to an average person. In this case, nearly every major news outlet covered it.

Proximity—What happens close by is more important than what happens far away. This has to do with coverage areas and the audience the outlet is trying to reach. However, nearly every newsroom follows this concept as what is important to their audience.

Drama—This may seem quite obvious, but journalists are reminded of it often. Dramatic video, of any kind, is seen as important and of interest to the audience.

Conflict—This can be between two people, management and union, or opposing teams. Conflict, of any kind, is seen as valuable to drive viewers and readers.

Significance—What is important to the most people? A common example is an increase in the price of gasoline, compared to an increase in the price of caviar. Clearly, the price of gasoline affects more people and would be considered more important.

Uniqueness—A snake with three heads, a five-foot-tall basketball player winning a dunk contest, an animal born in captivity for the first time . . . all unique and considered by traditional news organizations to be newsworthy (Harrower, 2012).

Clearly, all of these elements can make for a good news story in the right situation. Furthermore, news organizations can make good use of guidelines of use that have proven to be effective. However, when looking at agenda setting, it must be considered that standard practices themselves may be leading the news industry to set an agenda. In her 1972 piece (often still cited and discussed), "Objectivity as Strategic Ritual: An Examination of Newsmen's Notions of Objectivity," Gaye Tuchman (1972) discussed an objectivity ritual bias, in which the ritualistic practices of news, performed in an effort to be objective can actually create bias.

As we look at coverage of the opioid epidemic, agenda-setting must be considered. As we have seen, criticisms of the news media coverage persist from many angles. Often the press is accused of having a "narrative" to fulfill, drawing direct comparisons to agenda setting. As we continue to see a polarized voting public, far-left consumers of media might accuse the news media of setting the agenda (or narrative) to protect the large pharmaceutical companies that dominate the prescription drug business, while far-right consumers might accuse the news media of attacking big business or protecting tort laws that allowed so many lawsuits to be filed. As we will see, however, many elements in play may warrant a rethinking of this long-studied theory.

Social Media

This description of agenda setting and the difficulties surrounding it stood strong for decades. However, the growing power and consumption of social media in the last twenty years must be considered. A Pew research study revealed that at least half of Americans get some of their news from social media. Among those sites most often used for news consumption are Facebook, YouTube, TikTok, and Reddit. Those statistics held steady over the three-year period of the study from 2019–2022 (Pew Research, 2023).

Another Pew study, this one focusing on journalists themselves, found both positive and negative results. The study found that journalists find social media helpful in promoting stories, connecting with their audiences, and finding story ideas. Despite these advantages, 67% of journalists responded that social media has had a negative impact on journalism in America. The main concern is harassment in the workplace. About four in ten of those surveyed said they had experienced some form of harassment or threats in the past year, with most of them occurring online. The most common forms of harassment were threats of personal, physical harm (Pew Research, 2022a).

Northwestern University's Medill School of Journalism found further concerns among journalists regarding social media. Nearly eight of ten journalists responded that harassment of journalists on social media was a "very big" or "moderately big" problem. The findings revealed that just over 90% of respondents said the role social media companies play in delivering the news results in a worse mix of news, while 86.5% said social media companies have too much control over the mix of news people see. Nearly 80% said social media has a mostly negative impact on the journalism industry, and more than 94% of respondents said that social media is responsible for spreading inaccurate news. Also cited in the article was that journalists are more critical of social media than the general public when it comes to news. Journalists polled 25 percentage points higher in the Medill survey, than a 2019 Pew study asking the general public if social media companies have too much control over the mix of news they see (Burns, 2022).

With agenda-setting theory dating back to the mid-20th century, the effects of social media on news organizations telling people what to think about are in the early stages of research. However, studies show a profound effect. An early, longitudinal experiment found that those exposed to political issues on Facebook exhibited raised levels of issue salience compared with participants who were not shown the same information. The effects were strongest among those with low political interest (Feezell, 2018).

A more recent study tested the power of the public in setting the agenda through social media. The study tested the influence of the individual compared to that of the professional news media in shaping the public discussion. The results were highly comparable with the professional news media showing a correlation of 30.3% and the individual "opinion leader" showing a correlation of 31.3% (Yi & Wang, 2022). Opinion leaders are described as people who act as gatekeepers to information and pass that information along to "opinion followers," thus eliminating the news media as the agent driving the agenda (Baran & Davis, 2015). These results make very clear the power of social media in that individuals can compete directly with professional news organizations when looking at agenda setting. In a recent interview, journalist and educator Jay Rosen commented on the changing landscape of social media and the ability of the professional news media to set an agenda. "I think it's kind of an outmoded phrase in a way. I don't think that power is there in the same way that it was during the height of agenda setting which would have been the 1950s and 1960s" (J. Rosen, personal communication, 3/14/2024). This comment is in reference to what would be considered limited information, by today's standards. The public received news and information from newspapers (usually with a very high public penetration rate), radio, and television news operations, which consisted of ABC, NBC, CBS, and their local affiliates.

With this in mind, one must question the mere possibility of the news media setting the agenda. Often, the news media is playing catch-up with social media, and many professionals don't think agenda-setting is even possible. One of the founders of agenda-setting theory, Maxwell McCombs, has even questioned the theory, calling for new theories that can explain the different influences in the modern age. Terms like "micro-agenda setters" are being used to describe opinion leaders who speak on social media. The theory is that certain individuals or groups have a belief in the reality of their chosen social network (Wohn & Bowe, 2016).

Solutions-Based Journalism

As we have seen, journalism about the opioid epidemic and other major stories (Children of the Mountains) falls under criticism for not offering solutions to the issues that have been revealed or discussed. There does, however, exist a movement within the world of journalism aimed at making solutions a part of journalistic practice. The Solutions Journalism Network describes the practice as follows, "Solutions journalism investigates and explains, in a critical and clear-eyed way, how people try to solve widely shared problems" (solutionsjournalism.org, "Mission"). The site further explains that they don't aim to replace but add to the already existing coverage of problematic situations to further tell the full story. Essentially, researching similar situations and finding working solutions that may be applicable elsewhere.

"It's not like a solutions box, where you can press a button and get a solution," says journalist Jay Rosen, who currently teaches a course at New York University about solutions journalism. "Where you might be able to make some progress is if you understand what solutions journalism is. It's very related to something I call knowledge transfer. Meaning, if there is a community that really figured out how to keep this drug from spreading, and through experiment, trial and error, or maybe just luck and determination, or great leadership, came up with a way to control the flow of fentanyl into their communities, then that's something that other communities should know about" (J. Rosen, personal communication, 3/14/24).

Solutions journalism is nothing new. The Solutions Journalism Network celebrated 10 years in December 2023. They have trained over 47,000 journalists, partnered with over 100 journalism schools, and have trainers in 40 countries. What is now often referred to as a movement can be traced back more than 15 years as journalists began looking for solutions to social problems that may be applicable elsewhere.

Considering the longevity of the solutions movement, one must consider the current state of journalism and the criticism newsrooms face, when examining its effectiveness. One study cites the enthusiasm of journalists for the solutions style of reporting and likens it to investigative reporting but with an extra step. Challenges cited are, as always, objectivity and a commitment to the practice from management and ownership (Lough & McIntyre, 2021).

When researching solutions-based journalism, the topic of hierarchical structure comes up often. Pamela Shoemaker and Stephen Reese's extensive research on organizational structure and its effects on practitioners is often applied to the news industry. When it comes to newsrooms, each practitioner answers to a higher authority within the organization. Managers answer to higher-ranking managers up through the hierarchy and finally to ownership (Swift, 2013). Shoemaker and Reese (1996) assert that the ultimate power of the organization lies in ownership. Therefore, it stands to reason that the long-term success and application of solutions-based journalism would require a great deal of commitment from ownership. One long-time journalist and former journalism school Dean adds that outside funding for such programs may be running out; "to me, solutions journalism is journalism that you should be doing along the way anyway, and it was a thing created to attract funders to keep some newsrooms going. Part of solutions journalism is a philanthropy tool. The solutions journalism money as far as I know is gone" (L. Dalglish, personal communication, 3/18/2024).

If it is true that most of the funding from outside organizations who like to fund journalism projects is largely gone, then the decision to fund these projects would fall on a financial commitment from ownership. This brings to mind public or civic journalism; a movement started in the late 1980s that involved citizens in the challenges faced by communities. Civic journalism seeks to help people participate in an effective public life (Charity, 1995). This process involved teams of reporters holding town meetings and working with the public to discover what issues they thought needed to be addressed and investigated while including them in the democratic process (in local, state, and national politics) in every way possible. Ultimately, despite a great deal of early enthusiasm, civic journalism enjoyed only modest success, mostly in the 1990s (Overholser, 2016). It was expensive and required teams of reporters with time to spend on a story or topic, therefore cutting into profits. Furthermore, when the internet took hold and deregulation expanded ownership in the 1990s, many newsrooms suffered large staff cuts.

More recently, however, it has been noted that many of the elements of civic journalism have resurfaced due to technology and a hyperconnected audience (Overholser, 2016). Despite concerns over funding, those who support more in-depth forms of reporting such as solutions-based journalism or civic journalism remain optimistic. "I think it's possible that if we had more recognition for what solutions journalism is, and if we had more practitioners of it, maybe the news media would have made a bigger contribution" (J. Rosen, personal communication, 3/14/2024). It would stand to reason that with audiences becoming increasingly more connected with information of all forms, the possibility of a revisit (even if that means a slight shift in focus) is a possibility.

QUESTIONS AND DISCUSSION

Should the news media in the United States go beyond the reporting of facts and information?

Perhaps a better question is, could they? Certainly, there is room for many different types of journalism and the public can choose between styles. We have local, national, and cable news (largely talk show format), hyperkinetic (fast-paced, commercial style), and National Public Radio–style radio news, newspapers of every kind, in print and online. Why not have traditional, fast-paced, facts-only news, with some solutions-based or civic journalism mixed in? Unfortunately, the answer isn't simple.

As this chapter shows, there are staffing issues with newsrooms. Research shows that the staffs of newspapers have fallen steadily since 2008 (Pew Research, 2021). Adding responsibility and more tasks to these newsrooms could be difficult, if not impossible. "I think it's very hard now, because newsrooms have been cut. You're doing your daily job. How many stories do you have to have done by noon? When do you get time to work on those big stories? Some newsrooms have one or two reporters to do everything" (D. Natale, personal communication, 3/11/2024). While conducting research, the reality of smaller newsrooms was mentioned by every person interviewed and is seen as a widely known fact. "Of course, you still have the problem of leaner newsrooms, empty desks, newsrooms/newspapers that can't even do basic things, let alone more creative work" (J. Rosen, personal communication, 3/14/2024). This issue adds difficulty at every level. The job of a news organization is, first and foremost, to inform its audience and immediacy takes precedence.

As for the news media setting the agenda, I would suggest that those who really think so and want to write or comment on it, spend some time in an actual newsroom. There have always been limitations to this theory. Newsrooms, on the whole, have staffing issues. Broadcast newsrooms have technical challenges that could force producers to change the order of rundowns, therefore, making one story appear more important than another. In 2024, we have social media and its opinion leaders challenging newsrooms for the lead on what stories get attention. Social media will only get bigger and more a part of American lives in the future. There is certainly no turning back on social media applications and their use in our daily lives. For that reason alone, it seems that the ability of the professional news media to set an agenda is limited at best. Only strict new rules on information spread by users or a complete rethink on how to approach using social media by reporters themselves could possibly change this.

In terms of the news media serving the public and moving back to a social responsibility mindset, this is in the hands of ownership. This chapter has shown that news practitioners would like to serve in that role and see their jobs as a mission. However, since the deregulation of ownership laws allowed corporations to expand their operations and station count, news has been operating in a market model. This system expects that the newsrooms will create a better product due to competitive forces and the fight for advertising dollars (McManus, 1994). In reality, news operations are often seen by owners ownership as money-making operations. If it can be done cheaply and advertisers are still buying commercial time, it is a victory. Having multiple (or in most cases many) news operations turning a profit is clearly a model that ownership seeks.

Solutions-based journalism is something that most media critics seem to think is a good idea or expect. However, as a movement, it will likely remain a niche practice. Budgets and staffing issues are a formidable hurdle for most newsrooms.

Putting teams together to conduct considerable research and present those findings in a way that the public will follow is a time-consuming and very expensive task. Considering the market model that is now a daily reality of shrunken newsrooms, multitasking and doing more with less, is the norm. Could newsrooms incorporate solutions into their daily routines? This has been suggested and is likely to be the outcome if managers, producers, and reporters decide to follow this practice. Still, it is a difficult task. Training everyone involved in writing and reporting a story to do additional research and present the material will involve a financial commitment as well as a philosophical one. It is a possibility, but a difficult one.

Finally, we must consider audiences. The public, largely unaware of the changes newsrooms faced after new ownership laws were put in place (many of whom voted for them unknowingly), should consider their expectations. The ask (especially in broadcasting) is for news that is free, fast, transparent, and obviously correct. If the public wants more than that, perhaps news that is paid for, or paid for at an increased rate is in order. This would allow news operations to engage in solutions-based journalism or even civic journalism in some form. This raises the question, would the public pay for it? News was once released twice daily in print form and paid for. Broadcast news was once early morning, late afternoon, and at the end of prime time, before late night shows. Many newsrooms are now doing more than 10 shows per day. Clearly, ownership is trying to drive advertising dollars by adding shows. However, some of it is public demand as well. The expectation that newsrooms would do even more without a considerable increase in revenue through subscriptions is highly unlikely.

CONCLUSION

News is capable of changing. Watch a newscast or read a paper from a decade or two ago and you will see that it has changed in style and approach. Can it take on a bigger role and go beyond fact-finding into solutions? That will take a commitment from everyone. Ownership must commit to larger budgets, news practitioners (including management) must agree to further training and the public will likely have to pay something for it. This happens in smaller forms. Some independent reporters, such as Pittsburgh's Dejan Kovacevic, offer a low-cost subscription service for exclusive content. Fans of teams subscribe to services like these for exclusive content. The question then becomes how willing is the public to pay for news, especially when statistics show that many Americans take opinion leaders on social media just as seriously. The public's trust in news is fading (Pew Research, 2022b). Combine this with shrinking newsrooms, exhausted and overextended practitioners, and budgets that are often shrinking rather than increasing major change is not likely to happen soon. Should the American news media go beyond the reporting of facts and information? Perhaps. The commitment to do so, however, will have to come from everyone.

REFERENCES

Baran, S. J., & Davis, D. K. (2015). *Mass communication theory: Foundations ferment and future* (7th ed.). Cengage Learning.

Burns, G. (2022). *Journalists give thumbs down to social media.* Retrieved February 9, 2024, from https://localnewsinitiative.northwestern.edu/posts/2022/02/09/medill-social -mediasurvey/

CDC. (2024). *Understanding the opioid overdose epidemic.* Retrieved April 4, 2024, from https://www.cdc.gov/overdose-prevention/about/understanding-the-opioid-overdose -epidemic.html

Charity, A. (1995). *Doing public journalism.* Guilford Press.

Christians, C., Fackler, M., Brittain Richardson, K., Kreshel, P., & Woods Jr., R. (2017). *Media ethics: Cases and moral reasoning* (10th ed.). Routledge.

Feezell, J. (2018). *Agenda setting through social media: The importance of incidental news exposure and social filtering in the digital era.* Retrieved January 18, 2024, from https://www .jstor.org/stable/26600486

Feldscher, K. (2022). *What led to the opioid crisis and how to fix it.* Retrieved December 10, 2023, from https://www.hsph.harvard.edu/news/features/what-led-to-the-opioid-crisis -and-how-to-fix-it/

Harrower, T. (2012). *Inside reporting: A practical guide to the craft of journalism* (3rd ed.). McGraw-Hill.

Jay, J., Chan, A., Gayed, G., & Patterson, J. (2022). Coverage of the opioid crisis in national network television news from 2000–2020: A content analysis. Retrieved from https://www .tandfonline.com/doi/full/10.1080/08897077.2022.2074594.

JFK Library. The President and the Press: Address before the American Newspaper Publishers Association, April 27, 1961. Retrieved February 3, 2024, from https://www.jfklibrary.org /archives/other-resources/johnf-kennedyspeeches/americannewspaper-publishers -association-19610427

Kennedy-Hendricks, A., Levin, J., Stone, E., McGinty, E., Gollust, S., & Barry, C. (2019). *News media reporting on medication treatment for opioid use disorder amid the opioid epidemic.* Retrieved December 10, 2023, from https://www.healthaffairs.org/doi/10.1377/ hlthaff.2018.05075

Lough, K., & McIntyre, K. (2021). *Transitioning to solutions journalism: One newsroom's shift to solutions-focused reporting.* Retrieved February 19, 2024, from https://www.tandfonline .com/doi/full/10.1080/1461670X.2020.1843065

McGinty, E., Stone, E., Kennedy-Hendricks, A., & Barry, C. (2019). *Stigmatizing language in news media coverage of the opioid epidemic: Implications for public health.* Retrieved October 23, 2023, from https://pubmed.ncbi.nlm.nih.gov/31122614/

McManus, J. H. (1994). *Market driven journalism: Let the citizen beware?* Sage.

McQuail, D. (2000). *McQuail's mass communication theory* (4th ed.). Sage.

Meehan, M., & Copley, R. (2015). *Eastern Kentuckians mixed on 20/20 Report.* Retrieved November 2, 2023, from https://www.kentucky.com/entertainment/tv-movies/article 43991139.html

Overholser, G. (2016). *How to best serve communities: Reflections on civic journalism.* Retrieved February 28, 2023, from https://democracyfund.org/wpcontent/uploads/2020 /06/REPORT_Reflections-on-Civic-Journalism_Overholser_2017july7.pdf

Pew Research Center. (2021). *The number of newsroom employees at U.S. newspapers declined by 47% between 2008 and 2018*. Retrieved January 11, 2024, from https://www.pewresearch .org/short-reads/2021/07/13/u-s-newsroom-employment-has-fallen-26-since-2008/

Pew Research Center. (2022a). *Many journalists say social media helps at work, but most decry its impact on journalism*. Retrieved January 11, 2024, from https://www.pewresearch.org/ journalism/2022/06/14/many-journalists-say-social-media-helps-at-work-but-most-decry -its-impact-on-journalism/

Pew Research Center. (2022b). *U.S. adults under 30 now trust information from social media almost as much as from national news outlets*. Retrieved March 9, 2024, from https://www .pewresearch.org/short-reads/2022/10/27/u-s-adults-under-30-now-trustinformation-from -social-media-almost-as-much-as-from-national-news-outlets/

Pew Research Center. (2023). *Social media and news factsheet*. Retrieved from January 6, 2024, from https://www.pewresearch.org/journalism/fact-sheet/social-media-andnews-fact-sheet/

Sawyer, D., Diaz, J., Gray, K., Weinraub, C., & Harris, S. (2009). *A hidden America: Children of the mountains*. ABC News.

Shoemaker, P. J., & Reese, S. D. (1996). *Mediating the message: Theories of influences on mass media content*. Longman Publishers USA.

Swift, K. (2013). *The changing landscape of television news at a time of deregulation: A case study of practitioners in three major markets*. ProQuest.

Szalavitz, M. (2018). What the media gets wrong about opioids. Retrieved November 9, 2023, from https://www.cjr.org/covering_the_health_care_fight/what-the-media-gets -wrong-aboutopioids.php

Tuchman, G. (1972, January). Objectivity as strategic ritual: An examination of newsmen's notions of objectivity. *American Journal of Sociology, 77*(4), 660–79.

Wohn, D. Y., & Bowe, B. (2016). Micro agenda setters: The effect of social media on young adults' exposure to and attitude toward news. Retrieved February 16, 2024, from https:// journals.sagepub.com/doi/10.1177/2056305115626750

Yi, H., & Wang, Y. (2022). Who is affecting who: The new changes of personal influence in the social media era. Retrieved February 3, 2024, from https://www.frontiersin.org/ journals/psychology/articles/10.3389/fpsyg.2022.899778/full

6

Bringing Suit Against Big Pharma

State and Local Government's
Response to the Opioid Crisis

Paul Knudson

For over a century the United States enjoyed rising life expectancies thanks to a number of factors including scientific medical advancements, public health measures, vaccines, and decreases in rates of tobacco use. This all came to a halt in 2014–2015 when life expectancy leveled off and even reversed itself preceding a dramatic decline during the COVID-19 pandemic. Although numerous factors have contributed to this, including rising automobile and gun deaths and growing obesity-related morbidity, opioid overdose deaths have been a central cause of declining US life expectancy. What is more is that the American decline in life expectancy is unique among high-income and even middle-income countries around the world (Shmerling, 2022). The United States' comparatively unregulated opioid-based prescription pharmaceutical market contributed to this critical state of affairs. Beyond the human lives damaged and lost due to the opioid epidemic have been substantial fiscal costs imposed on governments at all levels. This chapter, therefore, focuses on the costs assumed by local and state governments and the subsequent lawsuits these jurisdictions have brought against the companies that played a dominant role in the epidemic's inception.

In this chapter, in addition to providing an overview and introduction to the opioid crisis, I examine some of the major court cases that have compelled corporations that enabled the epidemic to pay substantial settlements to states and municipalities. The lawsuits and subsequent settlements are important in that they have held responsible parties at least partially accountable, while seemingly acting as a deterrent to future corporate misbehavior and criminal acts. Cities and states have also been able to recoup some monetary resources, although the settlements do not come close to offsetting the hundreds of billions of dollars in fiscal costs imposed by the epidemic. At the end of the chapter, I highlight some of the limitations of the settlements and discuss how European countries mostly avoided a similar drug epidemic. Finally, this chapter provides a cautionary note given the drug companies' continuing promotion of powerful synthetic opioids around the world and the future damage this may unleash on societies both large and small.

BACKGROUND OF THE PUBLIC HEALTH CRISIS AND CONCEPTUAL FRAMEWORK

Over roughly the last two decades the opioid epidemic has resulted in at least 645,000 deaths in the United States. Opioid-related deaths first appeared in substantial numbers at the end of the 1990s. This rise coincided with the increased use of prescription-based opioids such as oxycodone, methadone, and hydrocodone. These drugs had initially been prescribed predominantly for cancer patients, specifically palliative care for terminal patients to ease severe pain at the end of life. As time went by, however, more physicians would write prescriptions for noncancer-related care, particularly for back pain and osteoarthritis even though these drugs posed severe risks, while offering little evidence of their long-term efficacy. Medical prescriptions varied tremendously by state and had no correlation to the respective state's preexisting health status of the population. For comparative purposes, Alabama had the highest rate of opioid prescriptions in the country, which stood at three times the rate of Hawaii, the state with the lowest rate of prescriptions in the country (Centers for Disease Control and Prevention, 2017).

The Sackler family's Purdue Pharma has arguably been the largest player in the ongoing opioid public health crisis. Beginning in the early 1990s the Sacklers sought to dramatically increase sales by targeting its new product OxyContin (the trademarked name of oxycodone) to noncancer patients with chronic pain. Purdue organized clinical trials with 133 elderly patients with osteoarthritis to examine the safety and efficacy of OxyContin. Only 63 patients, however, completed the trials and 82% of them experienced adverse effects from the drug (Chakradhar & Ross, 2019). This information, however, along with data from further trials, was hidden from the Food and Drug Administration (FDA), and Purdue routinely misled the FDA with fraudulent data that showed the drug as less addictive than other opioids. The FDA's approval of the drug in 1995 came as the result of a multisystem failure of regulation and oversight in the United States (Feldscher, 2022).

In addition, Purdue and other companies did not merely mislead the FDA and other regulators, but in myriad ways, industry and government are so intertwined that proper public oversight in the United States faces an ongoing and existential crisis. Beyond the political donations from opioid manufacturers to politicians, a revolving door exists between corporate America and Washington, in that former executives of industry regularly come to lead important agencies like the FDA and Drug Enforcement Agency (DEA), and vice versa (Feldscher, 2022). Various conflicts of interest can arise from this, most notably government officials engaging in actions that promote corporate profits instead of the public interest.

The noted sociologist C. Wright Mills (1956) warned of this political-corporate combine/complex between corporate leaders and government officials in his seminal work *The Power Elite*, in which the people leading industry and those at the top of government were in fact often the same people. Mills warned that elite control of institutions and the revolving door between industry and government would pose a grave threat to democracy, not only by undermining the ability of government to protect the public interest but by merely serving the public in its most basic sense and duties. Rather than representing the broad interests of the citizenry, the government would act in the interest of corporate power and of securing powerful positions for its top leaders. This chapter uses the conceptual framework of Mills to assist in the analysis of what happened in the United States, and why the opioid crisis was patently and demonstrably worse in the United States than in any other country on earth.

With government agencies being both misled and compromised by corporate interests, by the mid-aughts (2005–2006) prescription sales of OxyContin had been turbocharged through new marketing campaigns to physicians and pharmacists. McKinsey & Company, the United States' flagship business consulting firm, played a central role in developing a new marketing campaign for Purdue Pharma. By 2009 physicians were prescribing OxyContin for routine surgeries like joint replacements and plastic surgeries, and millions of prescriptions were written with very little oversight and evaluation of how they were affecting patients. Research suggests that 21–29% of American patients misuse prescribed opioids (Childers, 2019), and by 2016 11 million Americans had stated that they misused opioids (Centers for Disease Control and Prevention, 2023). Later in this chapter I will discuss major lawsuits brought against McKinsey & Company by 47 states (Hamby & Forsythe, 2022).

Once their prescriptions for OxyContin expired, a significant minority of patients turned to street drugs, particularly heroin, to achieve a similar sensation or "fix" that their OxyContin had once provided. The situation grew even grimmer by 2013 with a third wave of overdoses primarily caused by the rise of other synthetic opioids such as fentanyl. Fentanyl was developed in 1959 and introduced in the early 1960s as a powerful anesthetic used in surgeries (Department of Justice, Drug Enforcement Administration, 2020). It was developed by Belgian chemist Paul Janssen, who founded Janssen Pharmaceutica (Millar, 2018). The FDA did not approve fentanyl for use until 1968 due to its exceptional potency and potential for abuse. To put this into perspective, fentanyl is 100 times more potent than morphine. American physicians increasingly began prescribing fentanyl in its different forms in the early aughts for surgeries and nonsurgeries alike. In 2005, after a rise in overdoses and deaths, the FDA began to focus more on the misuse of one type of fentanyl, Duragesic, a commonly prescribed pain medication that came in the form of a patch. The FDA noted that too many physicians were improperly prescribing the medication and that patients were misusing the medication (Millar, 2018).

In 2013 street use of illicit fentanyl manufactured in black market labs rose to record levels. Illicit fentanyl like carfentanil can be up to 100 times more potent than prescription fentanyl. Carfentanil has been used as an elephant tranquilizer and has even been assessed to be a substance for potential use in chemical warfare (Caves, 2019). These potent substances have been responsible for the significant rise in overdose deaths in the United States. In 1999 the United States recorded about 20,000 deaths from drug overdoses. By 2016 that number had reached 64,000. Remarkably, by 2021 overdose deaths had reached more than 106,000, with opioid-related overdoses specifically totaling more than 80,000 (National Institute on Drug Abuse, 2023). Although the United States is not alone in the rise in drug overdose deaths during this 25-year period, the sheer number of deaths is unparalleled in any other country.

NATURE OF THE LAWSUITS AND SETBACKS AGAINST INDUSTRY

After providing a brief introduction to the opioid crisis, this chapter now turns to more closely examining some of the major court cases brought against corporations that enabled and facilitated the epidemic. States and municipalities have sought to recover at least a portion of the costs imposed on them by the fallout from the epidemic. A seemingly singular problem ultimately cascaded to form a multitude of dilemmas for state and local governments. Costs imposed on governments included not merely those directly related to police, fire department, and ambulatory responses, as high as those were. Additional costs consisted of financial and personnel burdens placed on public health agencies, hospitals, medical clinics, public schools, prisons, and other correctional facilities, the courts, child welfare agencies and social services, and employers or workplaces. Potent opioids sickened or killed multitudes of parents and members of local labor forces, and therefore this is why the costs imposed on the latter three institutions cannot be ignored. Overall, conservative estimates place the cost burden of the opioid epidemic at approximately $500 billion per year (Ausness, 2020).

State and local governments who decided to pursue litigation against major players in the epidemic, including pharmaceutical companies, corporate retailers, and consulting firms, used a variety of legal mechanisms in their suits. One major angle utilized various "public nuisance" ordinances. Based on legal precedent and common legal understandings, for an activity to be considered a public nuisance, it must extensively and materially interfere with a right held in common by the public, be unreasonable, be within the oversight of the defendant who subsequently has the ability to control and abate the nuisance, and proximately cause injury to the plaintiff. It is also the requirement of myriad jurisdictions that the nuisance cause damage to real property or violate criminal statutes. Public nuisance theories were one of the most commonly used approaches to bringing litigation against the parties tied to the opioid crisis. A large part of this was due to local and state governments' successful litigation of tobacco companies using this framework in the 1990s (Monea, 2019). In 2018, the Attorney General's Office of the State of Rhode Island used the public nuisance framework as part of their suit against companies involved in the epidemic. By 2019 Rhode Island had the ninth-highest rate of opioid-related deaths in the country (State of Rhode Island Superior Court, 2022). The state argued that numerous companies had knowingly created a public health crisis in Rhode Island of which the public at large bore innumerable costs. The Attorney General brought suit against Purdue Pharma and Insys, both manufacturers of prescription opioids, as well as Cardinal, McKesson, and AmerisourceBergen, distributors of opioids (*State v. Purdue Pharma*, 2019).

Rhode Island's initial lawsuit was unsuccessful and represented a common outcome in many states until various attorneys general discovered that they had to narrow down their specific charges. Nevertheless, even with narrower claims, governments at all levels struggled to go up against corporate giants like Purdue and McKinsey & Company and their well-heeled legal counsels. Numerous and varied courts dismissed initial lawsuits or transferred them to other jurisdictions. Even when plaintiffs achieved favorable outcomes, corporations' legal counsels would issue appeal after appeal. By the end of the 2010s, however, thousands of separate lawsuits against various corporate players would ultimately end in large national settlements. For example, although Rhode Island lost in various courts initially, it eventually secured $45 million from Purdue Pharma. The $45 million was that state's share of a $6 billion national settlement from Purdue that will be discussed in greater detail later in this chapter. In Rhode Island, the $45 million will help pay for opioid medical treatment and prevention activities (State of Rhode Island Office of the Attorney General, 2022).

Beyond the public nuisance framework, other legal strategies that states and municipalities used to bring litigation against corporate players have been the unjust enrichment, fraud, and civil conspiracy frameworks. Various plaintiffs argued that until the 1990s, the medical community widely viewed potent opioids like oxycodone as suitable only to treat short-term pain, notably pain among terminal cancer patients, and not chronic pain. Indeed, well into the mid-1980s the World Health Organization warned of the dangers posed by powerful opioids in the treatment of chronic pain (Ausness, 2020). Plaintiffs argued that Purdue Pharma and other entities engaged in deceitful and fraudulent marketing campaigns, including *hidden* marketing campaigns to physicians, hospitals, and pharmacists. Purdue Pharma notably reassured physicians through in-person visits by sales representatives that OxyContin posed little risk for addiction, making it suitable for the treatment of nonmalignant chronic pain. Sales representatives told physicians that Purdue had designed their new product to be safer than older opioids because of OxyContin's purported "slow-release" and "extended-release" design, in which the drug would be absorbed in the blood gradually throughout the day.

Plaintiffs also pointed out that Purdue operated a hidden and misleading marketing campaign by seemingly independent bodies, where such organizations and individuals, including prominent opinion leaders, recited the same talking points that the corporation parroted. These entities, which included prominent medical and scientific journals as well as medical education programs, all alleged that this new drug was safe (Ausness, 2020). Two major organizations Purdue funded were the now-defunct American Pain Foundation and the American Academy of Pain Medication (Berger, 2015). This stealth campaign used the same tactics and strategies that Exxon Mobil, Koch Industries, and other large corporations in the oil and gas industry employed in the 1990s to mislead the public and cast doubt on human-caused climate change. Like Purdue Pharma, the petroleum industry funded seemingly independent think tanks and the extremely small percentage of environmental scientists who held unorthodox climate science views to parrot industry propaganda in op-eds in major newspapers and magazines (Hall, 2015).

Moreover, Purdue Pharma and other manufacturers of opioids worked to convince physicians that addiction symptoms they witnessed in their patients were not authentic but what they termed "pseudo addiction." Pseudo addiction allegedly was a manifestation of further, untreated pain, and therefore more pain medication was necessary, and not a discontinuation of the treatment. Industry representatives also assured physicians that prescribing their products to patients thought to be at high risk for addiction would not be a cause for concern because they claimed that non-opioid-based drugs such as nonsteroidal anti-inflammatory medications were actually *more* addictive than their product. In addition, industry representatives falsely claimed that patients with addictive tendencies could safely take opioids because physicians simply had to engage in screening, patient counseling, and drug testing to identify nascent addiction prior to it becoming dangerous or significant (Ausness, 2020).

Furthermore, plaintiffs claimed that manufacturers' marketing efforts deliberately targeted general practitioners, rather than specialists who likely possessed greater knowledge of the addictive tendencies of opioid-based pain medications. Finally, those bringing lawsuits alleged that manufacturers broke numerous laws tied to the Controlled Substance Act. This law requires distributors of pharmaceuticals to flag and report suspicious orders to the DEA. Manufacturers' and distributors' failure to comply with these stipulations allowed an immense amount of opioids to be channeled to other parties for illicit use or distribution instead of going to a pharmacy or an individual who was prescribed the medication (Ausness, 2020).

In their lawsuit against industry players, Orange County, California, used many of these examples to illustrate a pattern of fraud, civil conspiracies, and unjust enrichment. The lawsuit brought by Orange County did not seek to ban the prescribing and use of opioids but to end the false and deceptive marketing campaigns of the industry and hold the industry accountable for that alleged deception. Orange County District Attorney Tony Rackauckas stated, "It is imperative for prescription drugs to be taken to promote health, not endanger lives, and that those responsible for producing these drugs not engage in deception" (Berger, 2015, PA15). Rackauckas went along to further state that he wants "to require these companies to change their conduct and to tell people—to tell the doctors, to tell the patients—tell them that these drugs are dangerous. Tell them they are addictive, and you could overdose on them, and you could die" (Schwartz, 2014, p. 9).

Rackauckas brought the lawsuit against Purdue Pharma (OxyContin), but also Actavis (maker of Kadian), Endo Health Solutions (maker of Opana, Percocet, and Percodan), Janssen Pharmaceuticals (maker of Duragesic and Ultram), and Teva/ Cephalon (maker of Actiq and Fentora). Legal observers in California argued that industry would challenge Orange County's authority, standing, and jurisdiction over federally regulated drugs, but they noted that there was also a strong precedent set in 2007 when Purdue Pharma, in a federal lawsuit, was forced to pay $635 million to defendants and to admit that it engaged in fraudulent conduct that directly led to the illicit sale and use of OxyContin. Orange County later joined the City of Chicago in the suit. Due to the exceptionally expensive nature of going up against heavily funded industry lawyers, Chicago authorities worked with private law firm Cohen, Milstein, Sellers & Toll to file their suit (Schwartz, 2014, p. 10).

The lawsuits cite as evidence the staggering levels of opioids flowing throughout the United States as well as the behemoth profits the industry enjoyed. They noted that although the United States contains less than 4% of the world's population, by the 2010s Americans consumed 80% of the world's supply of opioids, including 99% of global supplies of hydrocodone (Berger, 2015). In 2010 alone, the lawsuit explained that the sale of opioids generated $8 billion in revenue for the pharmaceutical industry. The suit brought by Chicago also cited that in 2009, opioid abuse and overdoses led to 1,100 emergency room visits in the city, which cost Chicago $9.5 million in pre-scription insurance claims and far more in other health-related expenses. Attorneys in Chicago also obtained internal documents from industry-funded "patient information groups" like the American Pain Foundation. The industry paid that organization $10 million, which marketed the drug as safe and "rarely addictive when used properly for the management of chronic pain." However, that statement contradicted the organization's internal documents that discussed "the lack of confirmatory data about the long-term safety and efficacy of opioids in non-cancer chronic pain" (Schwartz, 2014, p. 9).

In 2015, California Judge Moss dismissed the cases against Purdue, Actavis, and others noting that the situation should be handled by the FDA (Palmer, 2015). Moss contended that in their lawsuit, the plaintiffs were essentially asking the court to ascertain the marketing and safety of the specific prescription drugs, which made the court the de facto regulator rather than the FDA. The same year, US District Judge Jorge Alonso ruled essentially the same in Chicago's lawsuit against the drug-makers, arguing that the plaintiffs' allegations had not been specific enough, with the exception of their case against Purdue Pharma. Alonso gave the plaintiffs 30 days to amend the lawsuit against the pharmaceutical makers and provide more explicit claims regarding deceptive marketing (Pierson, 2021).

NEW STRATEGIES AGAINST INDUSTRY AND SUCCESSFUL SETTLEMENTS

Learning from these failed cases against the industry, cities and states now under-stood that they had to sue on more specified grounds. The narrowed claims allowed governments to more easily possess standing before the courts. Both individual cases and class action lawsuits had much more success in the courts through this avenue. This was evident in the City of San Francisco's case against a major industry player, Walgreens. In 2022, Judge Charles R. Breyer of the US District Court for the Northern District of California ruled that Walgreens was liable for enabling San Francisco's opioid epidemic. The decision was instrumental in that it was the first bench trial to find the Walgreens company liable for the national opioid epidemic. The court found that Walgreens failed to employ proper due diligence in their over-dispensing of opioids and failed to identify, report, cease, and deter suspicious orders as required by law (City Attorney of San Francisco, 2022). Hence this lawsuit was narrower and did not make claims surrounding the drug's safety or the addictiveness. The plaintiffs sued using the public nuisance liability legal framework.

Judge Breyer in his decision discussed the misconduct Walgreens had engaged in for years that contributed to staggering statistics in the city. Between 2006 and 2014, 163,645,704 opioid pills were distributed throughout San Francisco. This amounts to 22 pills per person (including children) per year. Walgreens distributed hundreds of thousands of such pills, including countless times in which there were numerous red-flag warnings. This entailed tens of thousands of prescriptions ordered by physicians with dubious patterns of prescribing. The evidence also documented that pharmacists were not given sufficient time, staffing, or resources by Walgreens corporate to comply with due diligence requirements. Pharmacists instead were compelled to fill as many prescriptions as possible without the resources for proper review. The plaintiffs in this case were able to prove that Walgreens filled and dis-tributed large volumes of prescription opioids that were clearly diverted for illegal use, which ultimately flooded the illicit market with millions of pills. A forthcoming trial will determine the monetary damages awarded to San Francisco by Walgreens corporate (Lin, 2022).

The City of Chicago's case against the drugmakers was eventually transferred to the Northern District of Ohio and evolved into a multidistrict litigation (*City of Chicago v. Purdue Pharma L.P.*, 2021). This was the trajectory of numerous cases that were initiated at the local level. As lawsuits eventually overwhelmed judicial systems throughout the country and legal fees increasingly consumed the revenues of drug makers and other industry players, multistate settlements against the indus-try became increasingly common by 2020. Significant national settlements took place in 2022 against drugmakers Teva and Allergen; pharmacies CVS, Walgreens, Walmart, and Johnson & Johnson; and distributors Cardinal Health, McKesson, and AmerisourceBergen. Purdue Pharma was forced into a separate 47-state national settlement, which will be discussed subsequently.

The total amount of settlements reached nearly $50 billion, with $17.3 billion specifically from Teva, Allergen, CVS, and Walgreens. The state of Illinois share of the $17.3 billion amounted to $518 million over 15 years. California's portion of the settlement—beginning with lawsuits dating back to Orange County's and those prior—amounted to $1.56 billion. In addition to monetary payments the settle-ments also regulated and restricted these companies' business practices. Teva was forced to abide by strict prohibitions against the marketing of opioids and had to ensure that systems were established to prevent drug misuse. Punishments against Allergan were even stronger. The company was barred from selling opioids over the next 10 years (National Opioid Settlement, 2022b).

As part of the settlement Walgreens and CVS were required to enact much stronger systems to monitor their pharmacies and report data on suspicious activity associated with opioid prescriptions. Walgreens's and CVS's monetary settlements amounted to $4.79 billion and $4.9 billion, respectively (National Opioid Settlement, 2022a). Walmart's involvement in the settlement amounted to payments of $3.1 billion in restitution and abatement (Hoffman, 2022). Part of Walmart's portion of the settlement will fund drug treatment and prevention programs. Like CVS and Walgreens, the court ordered Walmart to strictly monitor prescriptions to prevent patients from seeking multiple opioid prescriptions and to thwart the proliferation of pill mills that were ubiquitous in the early days of the epidemic.

Of the roughly $50 billion, $26 billion in national settlements came from Johnson & Johnson, Cardinal Health, McKesson, and AmerisourceBergen. Johnson & Johnson, the behemoth consumer health company, provided many of the key ingredients to produce opioids and manufactured and sold generic opioid medications. As part of the settlement, the company agreed to pay $5 billion and discontinued their manufacturing of opioids. Cardinal Health, McKesson, and AmerisourceBergen are the nation's largest pharmaceutical distributors. AmerisourceBergen will pay $6.1 billion, Cardinal Health will pay $6 billion, and McKesson, $7.4 billion (Mann, 2022). Attorneys general from New York, Vermont, and Washington State alleged that these distributors blatantly devised schemes to evade regulators, gave pharmacies advance notice of audits concerning the quantity of substances being sold and distributed, and notified pharmacies in advance that they were at risk of being reported to the DEA (Hakim et al., 2019).

Furthermore, major lawsuits were brought against McKinsey & Company, the major US consulting firm that assisted Purdue Pharma and other players in new ways of marketing and selling their opioid products. McKinsey will pay nearly $600 million to settle numerous claims against the company. Beyond the financial payments, McKinsey must assemble and make public online tens of thousands of internal memos and documents that describe and specify its client work with Purdue Pharma and other opioid makers. McKinsey also agreed to a stringent plan to retain documents after investigations suggested its corporate partners attempted to destroy documents related to investigations of Purdue Pharma. McKinsey also agreed to halt its advising of companies pertaining to dangerous Schedule II and Schedule III narcotics (State of California Department of Justice, 2021).

Thanks to numerous court cases that resulted in a consolidated national settlement, the public is aware of the nefarious ways in which McKinsey accelerated the epidemic. McKinsey was central in assisting Purdue Pharma's maximizing of profits by targeting the highest-volume physician prescribers of opioids and with marketing schemes that sought to persuade additional physicians to prescribe Oxy-Contin to more patients. McKinsey also assisted Purdue in circumventing pharmacy restrictions that were intended to prevent the type of high-volume prescriptions that inundated communities with opioids and contributed to the thriving black market in these substances. McKinsey also destroyed thousands of documents that detailed how its partners worked with Purdue to advance these marketing and sales tactics (State of California Department of Justice, 2023).

Thousands of lawsuits brought by cities, counties, states, and tribal nations were resolved by these national settlements. It is important to note, however, that in these settlements none of the major players admitted to any wrongdoing. This was also the case with the separate, national $6 billion settlement with Purdue Pharma and the Sackler family. Although the Sacklers never had to admit any wrongdoing, in addition to the $6 billion in financial payments to various parties, the Sacklers were forced to issue a statement of regret for their part in creating a national opioid epidemic. They must also permit institutions to remove their names from buildings, scholarships, and fellowships if they so choose. Purdue Pharma must also hold public hearings in which victims and survivors of opioid addiction can directly communicate with the families. Finally, the settlement compelled Purdue to make additional company documents available to the public. Some of these documents include advocacy materials that it used in congressional lobbying activities, documents used in the promotion, sale, and distributing of Purdue opioids, including those documents showing collaboration with McKinsey & Company and other consultants (New Hampshire Department of Justice, 2022).

THE EUROPEAN COUNTERPART AND WHAT THE UNITED STATES CAN LEARN

Although opioid addiction, overdoses, and deaths grew throughout the world beginning in the 1990s, European countries have experienced far less fallout from prescription opioid abuse and the subsequent street drug epidemic that has plagued the United States. The key deterrent in the European experience has been the far stricter oversight and use of powerful opioids in the European marketplace. Germany provides a good counterfactual example to the US experience. Germany has had one-tenth the rate of opioid overdose deaths as the United States, and opioid addiction rates have remained flat in that country even though Germans have the second highest rate of prescription opioid use in the world after the United States. The types of opioid use, however, have been very different. The German government has long restricted the practice of using synthetic opioids like OxyContin for use in chronic pain management. Instead, powerful opioids are almost always used only during and immediately following surgeries in Germany. In Germany physicians cannot prescribe potent synthetic opioids for long-term pain management unless all other pain medication alternatives have been documented to be insufficient or ineffective for patient pain management. Therefore, in contrast to opioids being dispensed relatively at will in the United States, they are used only as a last resort in Germany. As a result of these policies, only 0.2% of the German population struggles with opioid addiction—less than one-fourth the rate in the United States (Luthra, 2019).

Germany, as well as every other country in Western Europe, also has guaranteed health coverage. Having a system of universal health care coverage has contributed to lower levels of general drug addiction and opioid addiction. Unlike in the United States in which 26 million Americans still lack coverage and another 50 million have inadequate coverage, the German government ensures that all German residents have comprehensive medical coverage. This aids in the prevention of drug addiction in a few ways. First, because insurance is guaranteed and much more affordable than in the United States, patients who have undergone surgeries can receive long-term rehabilitative care for pain through physical therapy services. Because of the lack of medical coverage in the United States, many patients who leave surgery or who have chronic pain are simply prescribed pain pills (Humphreys et al., 2020).

Second, because the German system is universal and far more affordable than its American counterpart, patients are far more likely to plan routine health checkups with their physicians than they are in the United States. German doctor's visits often come with no co-payment (or a nominal co-payment of 2–5 Euros) and therefore there is no financial disincentive for patients who are on pain medication to not regularly check in with their physicians. These routine visits allow German physicians more opportunities to witness potential signs of addiction in their patients. In contrast, physician visits in the nonuniversal, for-profit medical care system in the United States are often quite expensive. Patients routinely have co-payments of $30–$80 per visit and this does not count other costs like expensive insurance deductibles. These costs deter patients who might be struggling with addiction from visiting their healthcare provider and receiving care (Humphreys et al., 2020).

Finally, universal medical systems in other countries tend to have far less fragmentation and more coordination than the American experience. Physicians in Germany are more likely to work together and coordinate care, whereas in the United States the numerous and variant health provider networks artificially set up by the private insurance industry often have physicians not communicating with each other at best, and at worst, working at cross purposes. Coordinated care in places such as Germany, Canada, the United Kingdom, and France has medical providers working together as a team on patient care, including professionals who work in local and regional public health offices.

Although Germany and other European nations have worked diligently to prevent the kind of opioid free-for-all that enveloped the United States over the last 20 years, the industry has descended on the European landscape and threatens to produce a similar wave of addiction and chaos that washed over the American terrain. The Sackler family owns Mundipharma—the European analog of Purdue Pharma—and is actively lobbying European governments to deregulate their policies on synthetic opioid prescriptions and distribution. They are also using the exact same marketing tactics as they did in the United States in relation to sponsoring a select number of physicians who will then market its use to patients, medical bodies, and pharmacists (Humphreys et al., 2020).

A wave of industry public relations and government lobbying is also taking place in India and China. The problem is particularly worrisome in India, as that country manufactures more pharmaceuticals than any other country, and the industry as a whole wields considerable political leverage there. European and Asian policymakers and regulators, however, have the benefit of witnessing what the natural experiment of unfettered prescription opioid distribution and use did to the United States. We now know that once powerful synthetic opioids are unleashed on a society, they are nearly impossible to control and halt. Powerful prescription opioids like OxyContin led to the illicit use of heroin among a significant minority of patients, and now synthetic fentanyl ravages communities. Like OxyContin's origins in corporate America, fentanyl was first developed by another corporation, Insys.

The opioid epidemic in the United States clearly but sadly illustrates the profits-at-any-cost culture of corporate America. The crisis demonstrates that without strong government regulation and oversight, private corporations will not act in the public interest and protect patients, consumers, local communities, and the society as a whole. Corporations cannot be counted on the police themselves. Not only did Purdue and other firms not abide by US law, but they sought partnerships with other players like McKinsey & Company who assisted them in actively circumventing US law. Although states, cities, tribes, and private plaintiffs won billions of dollars in settlements against the corporations involved in the epidemic, in each of the major settlements, the pharmaceutical companies and other industry players never had to admit any wrongdoing. Furthermore, no American corporate executive went to prison over their actions. Fines paid by McKinsey, Purdue, Walgreens, and others simply amounted to the cost of doing business. This shows the limits of American law enforcement, particularly against monied and powerful interests. These outcomes also show the danger of regulatory capture, in which revolving door officials in the FDA and DEA failed to adequately act in the public interest due to their ties to industry. The entire experience provides a strong heed and warning to European and Asian governments who are being pressured to relax regulations and oversight. The American crisis provides a blueprint of what not do, and if European and Asian lawmakers actually purport to represent the public's interest, they must not bow down to corporate power and influence.

REFERENCES

Ausness, R. C. (2020). A progress report on opioid litigation. *Journal of Legal Medicine*, 40(3–4), 429–46.

Berger, E. (2015). Orange County sues opioid drug makers: Suit broadens assault on spiraling opioid abuse. *Annals of Emergency Medicine*, (61)1, PA15–A17.

Caves, J. P. (2019, December 4). *Fentanyl as a chemical weapon.* Center for the Study of Weapons of Mass Destruction. National Defense University. https://wmdcenter.ndu.edu/Publications/Publication-View/Article/2031503/fentanyl-as-a-chemical-weapon/

Centers for Disease Control and Prevention. (2017). *Prescription opioids.* https://www.cdc.gov/opioids/basics/prescribed.html

Centers for Disease Control and Prevention. (2023). *Understanding the opioid overdose epidemic.* https://www.cdc.gov/opioids/basics/epidemic.html

Chakradhar, S., & Ross, C. (2019, December 3). *The history of OxyContin, told through unsealed Purdue documents.* STAT. https://www.statnews.com/2019/12/03/oxycontin-history-told-through-purdue-pharma-documents/

Childers, T. (2019). The opioid crisis: The states' and local governments' response to big pharma's deception and why the supremacy clause may provide a cloak for opioid manufacturers to hide behind. *Barry Law Review, 24*(1), 59–77.

City Attorney of San Francisco. (2022, August 10). *Legal community and San Francisco officials react to win in landmark opioid trial against Walgreens.* https://www.sfcityattorney.org/2022/08/10/legal-community-and-san-francisco-officials-react-to-win-in-landmark-opioid-trial-against-walgreens/#:~:text=The%20Court%20found%20Walgreens%20over,trial%20to%20find%20Walgreens%20liable

City of Chicago v. Purdue Pharma L.P. (2021). Case No. 14 CV 4361 (N.D. Ill. Mar. 31). https://casetext.com/case/city-of-chi-v-purdue-pharma-lp-8

Department of Justice. Drug Enforcement Administration. (2020). *Fentanyl.* https://www.dea.gov/sites/default/files/2020-06/Fentanyl-2020_0.pdf

Feldscher, K. (2022, February 9). *What led to the opioid crisis and how to fix it.* Harvard T. H. Chan School of Public Health. https://www.hsph.harvard.edu/news/features/what-led-to-the-opioid-crisis-and-how-to-fix-it/

Hakim, D., Rashburn, W., & Rabin, R. (2019, April 22). The giants at the heart of the opioid crisis. *The New York Times.* https://www.nytimes.com/2019/04/22/health/opioids-lawsuits-distributors.html

Hall, S. (2015, October 26). Exxon knew about climate change almost 40 years ago. *Scientific American.* https://www.scientificamerican.com/article/exxon-knew-about-climate-change-almost-40-years-ago/

Hamby, C., & Forsythe, M. (2022, June 29). Behind the scenes, McKinsey guided companies at the center of the opioid crisis. *New York Times.* https://www.nytimes.com/2022/06/29/business/mckinsey-opioid-crisis-opana.html

Hoffman, J. (2022, November 15). Walmart agrees to pay $3.1 billion to settle opioid lawsuits. *New York Times.* https://www.nytimes.com/2022/11/15/health/walmart-opioids-settlement.html

Humphreys, K., Caulkins, J. P., & Felbab-Brown, V. (2020, January 13). What the US and Canada can learn from other countries to combat the opioid crisis. Brookings Institute. https://www.brookings.edu/articles/what-the-us-and-canada-can-learn-from-other-countries-to-combat-the-opioid-crisis/

Lin, S. (2022, August 10). Walgreens fueled San Francisco's opioid epidemic with thousands of "suspicious orders," judge rules. *Los Angeles Times.* https://www.latimes.com/california/story/2022-08-10/walgreens-helped-fuel-san-franciscos-opioid-crisis-judge-rules

Luthra, S. (2019, October 19). How Germany averted an opioid crisis. *NBC News.* https://www.nbcnews.com/health/health-news/how-germany-averted-opioid-crisis-n1068286

Mann, B. (2022, February 25). Four U.S. companies will pay $26 billion to settle claims they fueled the opioid crisis. *Morning Edition National Public Radio.* https://www.npr.org/2022/02/25/1082901958/opioid-settlement-johnson-26-billion

Millar, A. (2018, February 27). Fentanyl: Where did it all go wrong? *Pharmaceutical Technology.* https://www.pharmaceutical-technology.com/features/fentanyl-go-wrong/?cf-view&cf-closed

Mills, C. W. (1956). *The power elite.* Oxford University Press.

Monea, N. C. (2019). Cities v. big pharma. *The Urban Lawyer, 50*(1), 87–146.

National Institute on Drug Abuse. (2023, June 30). *Drug overdose death rates*. https://nida.nih
.gov/research-topics/trends-statistics/overdose-death-rates

National Opioid Settlement. (2022a). *Statement on CVS and Walgreens' agreement in prin-
ciple*. https://nationalopioidsettlement.com/wp-content/uploads/2022/11/CVS-Walgreens
-Agreement-In-Principle.pdf

National Opioid Settlement. (2022b). *Statement on Teva/Allergen settlements*. https://nationa
lopioidsettlement.com/wp-content/uploads/2022/11/Teva-Allergan-Statement.pdf

New Hampshire Department of Justice. (2022, March 3). *Attorney General Formella
announces up to $6 billion national settlement with Purdue Pharma and Sacklers; New
Hampshire to receive $46 million if agreement approved*. https://www.doj.nh.gov/news/2022
/20220303-settlement-purdue-pharma-sacklers.htm

Palmer, E. (2015, August 28). *Judge halts lawsuit blaming Purdue, Endo, and other for epidemic
of drug abuse*. Fierce Pharma. https://www.fiercepharma.com/regulatory/judge-halts-lawsuit
-blaming-purdue-endo-and-others-for-epidemic-of-drug-abuse

Pierson, B. (2021, March 31). *Drugmakers must face Chicago opioid claims, judge claims*.
Reuters. https://www.reuters.com/article/idUSL1N2LT3W2/

Schwartz. J. (2014, August 24). Chicago and 2 California counties sue over marketing of
painkillers. *New York Times*. https://www.nytimes.com/2014/08/25/us/chicago-and-2
-california-counties-sue-drug-companies-over-painkiller-marketing.html

Shmerling, R. H. (2022, October 20). *Why life expectancy in the US is falling*. Harvard
Health Publishing. https://www.health.harvard.edu/blog/why-life-expectancy-in-the-us
-is-\falling-202210202835

State of California Department of Justice. (2021, February 4). *Attorney General Becerra
announces $573 nationwide settlement with McKinsey & Company for its role in the opioid
epidemic*. https://oag.ca.gov/news/press-releases/attorney-general-becerra-announces-573
-million-nationwide-settlement-mckinsey

State of California Department of Justice. (2023, June 9). *Attorney General Bonta announces
four multi-billion dollar nationwide opioid settlements*. https://oag.ca.gov/news/press-releases
/attorney-general-bonta-announces-four-multi-billion-dollar-nationwide-opioid

State of Rhode Island Office of the Attorney General. (2022, March 3). *Attorney general
announces settlement of at least $5.5 billion with Purdue Pharma and Sackler family*. https://
riag.ri.gov/press-releases/attorney-general-announces-settlement-least-55-billion-purdue
-pharmaand%20sackler#:~:text=Purdue%20Pharma%20filed%20for%20bankruptcy,
pursuing%20claims%20against%20the%20family

State of Rhode Island Superior Court. (2022). *State of Rhode Island Superior Court v. Purdue
Pharma*. C.A. No. PC-2018-4555. (R.I. Super. Feb. 18). https://cases.justia.com/rhode
-island/superior-court/2022-18-4555.pdf?ts=1645460532

State v. Purdue Pharma L.P. (2019). C.A. PC-2018-4555 (R.I. Super. Aug. 16).

7

An Examination of the Opioid Crisis in the "Live Free or Die" State

David A. Mackey

New Hampshire typically ranks near the top of state ratings in terms of quality of life, best places to raise children, and lowest crime rates in the nation. Recently, New Hampshire was rated as number six in the nation for the best state to raise a family (Fitzgerald, 2022). In particular, the violent crime rate and homicide rate annually rank among the lowest in the country. These favorable statistics mask a significant threat to the health and well-being of its population. New Hampshire has experienced a rapid and profound increase in the number of opioid deaths fueled largely by fentanyl as well as other prescription and illicitly manufactured opioids. The negative impact has been felt across urban, suburban, and rural communities, income strata, and age. New Hampshire has seen opioid-related overdose and overdose-attributed deaths quickly outstrip its harm reduction capacity.

The opioid crisis in New Hampshire has received considerable national attention. President Trump described New Hampshire as a "drug-infested den" (Seelye, 2018, para. 4). Seelye noted New Hampshire's shared border with Massachusetts and easy highway access to New Hampshire's populated southern tier facilitated Massachusetts's role in becoming a primary source of New Hampshire's illicitly manufactured drugs. Likewise, pharmacy prescription records detailed a pattern of high rates and doses of controlled pain medication. With the rapid and significant increase in opioid use, the state did not have an extensive treatment system established to meet the need. It should be noted that New Hampshire has a history as a fiscally conservative state with no sales tax or income tax. Likewise, the state has a tradition of libertarian leanings. These leanings contributed to laws such as no mandatory seat belts or motorcycle helmets for adults, as well as unlicensed open carry for firearms. New Hampshire's state motto, "Live free or die," is one of the better-known state mottos. It is derived from a letter from General John Stark to the troops he commanded at the Battle of Bennington in the American Revolution: "Live free or die. Death is not the worst of evils" (Stark, 1860, p. 313). This background had significant negative impacts on the availability of treatment and harm reduction strategies available at the onset of the surge in opioid use.

The state places considerable limitations on its elected officials. The New Hampshire governor has a two-year term, but much executive branch oversight is provided by an elected executive council. In addition to its state senate, it has 400 members in its lower house. State representatives are paid $200 a year plus mileage when traveling for official House business. Stansel et al. (2023) noted that New Hampshire is the most economically free state in the nation. A key indicator of this measure is government expenditures. New Hampshire ranked as the lowest state in the nation for government spending, taxes, and regulations. Based on these metrics, New Hampshire has the lowest governmental expenditures and the lowest tax burden. The downside of this distinction would be limited state funding, staffing, and treatment infrastructure to respond to the opioid crisis.

THE CRISIS QUANTIFIED

The Centers for Disease Control (CDC, 2022) has noted the rise in the opioid overdose death rate over the last two decades. The rate of opioid overdose deaths in the nation was 2.9 per 100,000 in 1999, and in 2021 the rate increased to 24.7 per 100,000 (CDC, 2022). This represents an astronomical 752% increase, a truly clear and present danger to the nation. In January 2020, roughly 80% of adults in the United States stated that they either strongly or somewhat agree that opioid abuse and addiction is a major problem in their community (Research America, 2022).

New Hampshire, unfortunately, would have a major role in the surge of drug use. Daly et al. (2017) examined the syndromic surveillance system in New Hampshire, which, at that point, included data from 25 of the 26 acute care hospitals in New Hampshire. The researchers identified nearly 21,000 opioid-related emergency room encounters during the five years from 2011 to the end of 2015. The rate of opioid-related overdose deaths in New Hampshire rose to 35.8 per 100,000 in 2018, ranking the sixth highest in the nation (Hedegaard et al., 2020). In 2017, the per capita cost of a fatal opioid overdose was computed. New Hampshire ranked fifth in the nation in the United States with an estimated cost of $3,650 (CDC & Morbidity and Mortality Weekly Report, 2021). It was estimated that in 2017, the total financial cost of nonfatal opioid use in the United States was almost $471 billion when factoring in reduced quality of life, criminal justice expenditures, treatment, and lost productivity (NCBI, 2021).

Cao et al. (2019) examined spatial access to opioid treatment locations in New Hampshire in 2015–2016. The state's increase in fentanyl-related overdoses prompted a National Drug Early Warning System (NDEWS) HotSpot study. Cao et al.'s (2019) work discussed the complexity of computing the geographic distribution of treatment locations available based on the identified people in need of treatment services. The majority of New Hampshire is characterized as rural except for the southcentral and southeast counties. Cao et al. (2019) calculated the distance to treatment programs, buprenorphine treatment practitioners, and Safe Stations (access hubs for treatment) for the roster of individuals entering treatment as well as every decedent resident whose death was attributed to fentanyl. Distance was calculated for each town to each of the nearly 50 treatment centers in the state considering street networks and driving time. Visual graphs produced documented the seven towns with both higher numbers of treatment admissions and decedents. Cao et al. (2019) noted that while the opioid crisis impacted every community in the state, roughly 40% of the communities were not in the higher categories for access to treatment facilities and emergency medical services (EMS). These areas had less convenient access, specifically longer drive times, to treatment and intervention services. Cao et al. (2019) noted that Manchester, the largest city in the state, had access to treatment services and EMS aided largely by Safe Station, but it also had the highest number of fentanyl deaths.

Mattson et al. (2022) noted nearly 92,000 drug overdose deaths occurred nation-wide in 2020 as recorded in the State Unintentional Drug Overdose Reporting System. Among these deaths, 70% of the reported deaths were attributed to illicitly manufactured fentanyl. The rate of overdose deaths was much higher for males (43.3 per 100,000) than females (18.1 per 100,000). Mattson et al. (2022) note that in about 20% of the overdose deaths the decedent was administered naloxone during their overdose event. Over 60% overdosed at home. Potential bystanders were present in less than half of the events. They also noted for decedents of an opioid death, 9% had previously witnessed a fatal overdose in the past. These statistics are key when considering the presence of another person available to administer naloxone at the onset of an overdose, which can occur very quickly with fentanyl.

Suzuki and El-Haddad (2017) noted the rise in the amount of overdose deaths associated with synthetic opioids other than methadone. The one-year increase in overdose deaths for these types of drugs was about 80% in one year from 2013 to 2014. They noted some individuals purposely sought out fentanyl-laced heroin due to the potency of the drug while they acknowledged the risk for overdose was higher due to its presence. Suzuki and El-Haddad noted fentanyl is 50–100 times more potent than morphine and was developed and marketed as an intravenous anesthetic intended for surgical patients due to its powerful and immediate effects and shorter duration of effect. The initial success of intravenous fentanyl would then lead to the development of fentanyl patches prescribed for the treatment of pain. Problems with overdoses and misuse of patches occurred early in their rollout. Suzuki and El-Haddad noted most of their use may be considered inappropriate given the drug's potency. Among overdose deaths, fentanyl deaths can occur rapidly regardless of the method of ingestion. They noted that illicitly manufactured fentanyl was earlier produced as a designer drug to avoid both detection and legal classification. They noted the emergence of illicitly manufactured fentanyl such as acetyl-fentanyl, butyryl-fentanyl, and beta-hydroxy-thio-fentanyl. Street names included China White, China Girl, and Tango and Cash, while Captain Cody is a street name sometimes linked to codeine and other times fentanyl. Suzuki and El-Haddad noted the more recent methods to produce illicitly manufactured fentanyl have been able to lower the technical sophistication of production, making the process easier and less costly and thus incentivizing the illicit market.

In their analysis of public health data in 11 contiguous rural New England counties in three states (Massachusetts, Vermont, and New Hampshire), Stopka et al. (2019) identified several factors they believed contributed to New Hampshire's fatal overdose statistics. Among these negative factors included a tax base model insufficient to provide the scale of preventive services needed, late adoption of a safe syringe program, emphasis on a drug treatment model emphasizing abstinence, and limited access to mental health services and medical care (Stopka et al., 2019). They also noted the slower funding and deployment of safe syringe exchanges once legislative approval was secured, less readily available naloxone coupled with concerns about its legality and associated stigma, and fewer treatment options in more rural areas of New Hampshire; these factors were often accompanied by lack of health insurance coverage and lower income among people who use opioids. It is interesting to note that alcohol revenues from New Hampshire's monopoly on state liquor sales provide a funding source for treatment (Stopka et al., 2019).

ACCESS TO NALOXONE

Naloxone is used to counter the physiological effects of an opioid overdose. It has been used outside of hospital settings to provide immediate prehospital emergency treatment to counter opioid overdose (Gulec et al., 2018). Gulec et al. (2018) examined the controversy surrounding access and ability to administer intranasal naloxone shaped in part by the *National EMS Scope of Practice* guidelines. Based on a study in northern New England, they found no significant differences in the provider ratings of the Glasgow Coma Scale between Advanced Life Support (ALS) and Basic Life Support (BLS) personnel; both groups had a 64% improvement percentage for patients (Gulec et al., 2018). In Gulec et al.'s (2018) study, it was interesting to note providers administered a second dose 20–24% of the time and a third dose in less than 10% of the cases. These results provide support for continued deployment of intranasal naloxone with police and fire personnel, rather than relying solely on advanced life support personnel such as advanced emergency medical technicians (EMTs) and paramedics, due to the additional response time considering the time from making a 911 call to EMS personnel arriving on scene. It should be noted that non-EMS people may likely be the first to encounter a distressed individual experiencing symptoms of opioid overdose. Gulec et al. (2018) noted the number of states that allowed basic life support (BLS) personnel to administer naloxone jumped from 13 to 37 from 2013 to 2014. Their research helped inform the National EMS Scope of Practice Model, which provides guidelines for the scope of responsibilities and limitations for EMS personnel. They noted the policy implications of the study have major implications for states such as New Hampshire with its rural populations as well as urban areas with a reliance on BLS personnel. According to Saunders et al.

(2019), "The NH House Bill 271 was passed in June 2015, expanding naloxone access within the state . . . and revising scope-of-practice protocols to allow basic emergency medical technicians (EMTs) and licensed police officers to administer intranasal naloxone" (Saunders et al., 2019, para. 3).

NATIONAL DRUG EARLY WARNING SYSTEM (NDEWS)

With the highest rate of overdose deaths in the nation in 2016, the New Hampshire fentanyl-related overdose rate was three times the national average (as cited in Moore et al., 2021). To examine factors associated with the high rates of overdose deaths, Meier et al. (2020) interviewed 76 participants in six New Hampshire counties examining their experiences with opioid use and overdose. Meier et al. (2020) noted the existing research on drug-seeking behavior was, not surprisingly, mixed with some users seeking heroin rather than fentanyl, while other individuals purposely sought fentanyl-laced products due to its potency, even while knowing the presence of fentanyl substantially increased their risk for a fatal overdose. In Meier et al.'s (2020) study, opioid users noted the lower cost and greater availability of fentanyl and fentanyl-laced heroin. In New Hampshire specifically, they noted fentanyl contributed to nearly 90% of the fatal overdoses in 2017. Meier et al. (2020) reported that illicitly manufactured fentanyl is approximately 50 to 100 times more potent than morphine and active in the scale of measured in micrograms. Alarmingly, for participants in their study, they reported "Eighty-four percent of interviewees had knowingly used fentanyl in their lifetime, 70% reported overdosing at least once, and 42% had sought a batch of drugs known to have caused an overdose" (Meier et al., 2020, para. 2). They noted nearly 90% of their participants reported using prescription opioids prior to using heroin or illicitly manufactured fentanyl. Nearly 70% identified chronic pain or injuries as a precursor to their opioid misuse. This aspect underscores the importance of controlled substance prescription monitoring and physician and patient education and awareness about the dangers associated with prescription opioids.

One female participant in the study stated:

> We want whatever is strongest and the cheapest. It's sick. I know me using, when I hear of an overdose, I want it because I don't want to buy bad stuff. I want the good stuff that's going to almost kill me. (Meier et al., 2020, para 3.2.4)

They noted some participants used fentanyl test strips to confirm the presence of fentanyl as a positive indicator for use rather than to avoid using the drug mixture. Participants offered their fear of precipitated withdrawal as reasons associated with continued use of opioids as well as fear of the abrupt recovery from overdose. One of their participants stated, "It's like your pain sensors are covered up with a nice, cozy blanket, and some a**hole comes and rips it off you" (Meier et al., 2020, para 3.2.6.). Their participants provided insights about available treatment options. Meier et al. (2020) noted that "barriers to treatment in NH included lengthy waitlists, trouble navigating the treatment system, payment challenges, and the lack of long-term programs" (para. 3.2.8). One pathway to addiction appears to be that patients with chronic pain move to illicitly manufactured fentanyl as prescriptions run out due to lapses in insurance coverage.

These findings were also corroborated by Ciccarone et al. (2017) in their study of opioid users in Massachusetts and New Hampshire. They noted the increased presence of fentanyl in heroin in the region. They conducted interviews in Worcester, Lowell, and Lawrence, Massachusetts, as well as Nashua, New Hampshire. They noted the heroin in New Hampshire was supplied through Massachusetts connections in Lowell and Lawrence, Massachusetts. An interesting aspect of this study was that it included researchers videotaping drug use preparation and injection by study participants while in the field. Long-time heroin users in their study noted the time when fentanyl was first introduced into the region's heroin supply. Their study participants stated they sought out fentanyl for the rush it provided countering the tolerance they built up using heroin as well as its ability to thwart Suboxone. One respondent in their study stated that "dope in general is killing people, but the fentanyl is something different. It's a different animal completely and it really is killing people. One little fuckin', one little mistake and you're fuckin' dead" (Ciccarone et al., 2017, p. 10). Participants detailed their experience and skills to determine whether heroin contained fentanyl, although dealers interviewed in the study provided some contradictory information on users' skills. The reality may be no one knows the actual composition of the product at a given moment due to repeated adulterations.

Bessen et al. (2019) conducted interviews with 76 opioid users and 36 emergency responders in six New Hampshire counties. Their research focused on the impact of New Hampshire's Department of Health and Human Services 2015 Naloxone Distribution Campaign. The campaign established standing orders throughout 188 of the licensed pharmacies operating in the state to allow naloxone to be distributed without a prescription to those at risk, or in a position to assist another at risk, who have received opioid overdose prevention training. Bessen et al. (2019) reported that nearly 14,000 naloxone kits were distributed in less than 2.5 years during the height of the opioid overdose deaths. The impact of the available naloxone is difficult to measure given the peak period of overdose deaths; some numbers may escape official reporting structures on the extent of harm. First responders, interviewed by Bessen et al. (2019), identified the possible downside of naloxone provided the opioid user with the opportunity to escalate the use of opioids and to push the boundaries of dosage relying on naloxone as a safety net. Their first responder participants noted the possibility of a violent reaction from the patient who had been revived by naloxone as they immediately experienced withdrawal symptoms. Opioid users reported numerous misperceptions about the availability and legality of naloxone. Users who experienced naloxone noted the immediate negative withdrawal experience. Their participants noted that "experiences with overdose are more traumatizing for bystanders (often first responders) than the users who overdose, and second, the severity of symptoms associated with precipitated withdrawal often drives users to seek opioids in order to eliminate the symptoms" (Bessen et al., 2019, para. 24). Based on these observations, first responders recognized the need to titrate the dosage of naloxone to gradually revive the patient rather than putting them into immediate symptoms of withdrawal.

Likewise, Saunders et al. (2019) conducted qualitative interviews with first responders in New Hampshire concerning their perceptions of the opioid crisis. Among their key findings were the views of first responders on the tremendous negative impact caused by the potency and inconsistency of fentanyl-laced heroin as the key driver for overdoses in the state. Saunders et al. (2019) conducted interviews with 18 emergency personnel (fire, police, and EMS) and 18 emergency department personnel in New Hampshire to examine their experiences and insights regarding responding to opioid-related overdoses. In their interviews, fire, police, and EMS personnel noted the importance of assessing the scene of an unconscious individual, most likely either not breathing or with shallow breathing, to identify signs and clues as to contributing factors, such as an opioid overdose. Likewise, they noted the presence of drug paraphernalia, especially needles sometimes still in their arms, while also ruling out other possible causes such as trauma. Participants also noted the possible physical threat once the patient regained consciousness. One of their fire department participants noted one major deficiency was the lack of follow-up care for patients revived from opioid overdose. First responders reported responding to potentially four or five overdoses on a shift, resulting in compassion fatigue. Participants also noted the negative effects of overdoses on patients' families, especially children. Their EMS participants noted the critical nature of formal counseling, informal connections, and for some, transitions out of the field into administrative positions. Their participants noted mixed feelings about the distribution of naloxone beyond trained first responders.

OPERATION SAFE STATION

By the midpoint of the decade, the overdose death rate in New Hampshire had reached a critical stage as New Hampshire had the highest opioid mortality death rate in the nation. The impact of the opioid crisis was felt in loss of life, disrupted family situations, exacerbation of co-occurring mental health issues, and EMS calls for service (Saunders et al., 2019) related to opioid overdose. In May 2016, the Manchester Fire Department (MFD) (in Manchester, New Hampshire) launched Operation Safe Station to reduce the stigma and barriers for individuals to connect with drug use treatment services. Others have noted the long wait time for treatment programs due to an array of factors including available bed space and insurance coverage (Meier et al., 2020). Safe Station became a point of entry for services for both the city as well as the state. Operation Safe Station gained national attention during the 2016 presidential election season as candidates toured and touted the mobilized resources during their visits to New Hampshire, and in its first national primary, President Trump would return to highlight Safe Station (Moore et al., 2021).

Moore et al. (2021) conducted an evaluation of the Safe Station program utilizing qualitative interviews with various stakeholders including MFD firefighters and administrative leadership, emergency room staff, ambulance service staff, treatment recovery staff, and program clients. The objective of their research was to identify Safe Station characteristics that were engaging, effective, replicable, and sustainable (Moore et al., 2021). Moore et al. (2021) detailed the negative conditions present in New Hampshire at the time of the inception of the Safe Station program: stigma surrounding treatment, limited overall capacity of availability of treatment services, limited public funding, lack of insurance coverage for some individuals needing treatment, geographic distribution of services within the state, and a perception of a reactive model to the opioid crisis. At the heart of the program, individuals seeking assistance were able to physically enter any of the 10 MFD stations to initiate the intake and referral process for treatment. The MFD became the hub of opioid treatment and intervention services, connecting an array of public health and public safety agencies in the public and private sectors. MFD personnel would assess the individual and determine an appropriate transition, in terms of a handoff to specific services including the emergency room for immediate medical needs, behavioral health services, respite, or counseling (Moore et al., 2021).

Moore et al. (2021) noted the direness of the situation, with New Hampshire ranking first in the nation in the rate of opioid-related overdose deaths for three consecutive years. MFD was already responding to every 911 overdose call in the city (Moore et al., 2021). The Safe Station program encouraged individuals to enter any of the 10 fire stations in the city for immediate access to treatment, and the program was actively publicized in a variety of ways. Fire respondents recognized the critical state of the crisis necessitating a response, which literally focused on being the point of intervention to save lives. Respondents noted MFD was best situated to be the initial point of contact given its status of responding to overdose calls, geographic distribution throughout the city, and 24/7 professional coverage. Several points identified by Moore et al. (2021) centered on the rollout of the Safe Station program. The researchers noted there was little planning, training, or lead time prior to the public rollout of Safe Station. In interviews, firefighters noted the program was devised by the top leadership of the MFD without input from rank-and-file firefighters; some noted they learned about it along with the public (Moore et al., 2021).

Several negative aspects were also identified by Moore et al. (2021). There were perceptions among firefighters that the Safe Station program was being taken advantage of as it drew clients from outside of the city of Manchester. Likewise, they noted program clients entering the Safe Station program more than once. They noted little to no communication in terms of the success of individual clients once they departed MFD. Likewise, they note MFD personnel identified the lack of specific training dealing with the counseling and mental health aspects associated with Safe Station calls. Although the firefighters have advanced medical training for responding to an overdose call as a medical call, they noted the lack of training in counseling skills, especially those skills associated with co-occurring mental health disorders. Compassion fatigue, burnout, and dissatisfaction may become issues due to the sheer volume of calls; one participant noted 3,000 calls (Moore et al., 2021, p. 8). Firefighters also noted no additional funding was provided or other resources supported the program. Station intakes tied up a fire company taking it out of service for other types of calls. As Moore et al. (2021) noted, "by launching Safe Station, the MFD identified their organization as de facto champions of the implementation effort, demonstrating the capacity to lead" (p. 10). The client interviews indicated a very positive view of Safe Station. Of note, Moore et al. (2021) observed that clients identified the accessibility and nonjudgmental response of MFD as a positive feature of the program.

PRESCRIPTION DRUG MONITORING PROGRAM

There are several gateways and pathways in opioid use and misuse, with one tract involving prescription medications. As part of the $21 billion settlement with three pharmaceutical distributors, New Hampshire will eventually receive $115 million paid out over 18 years (New Hampshire Department of Justice, 2022a). In addition to the financial settlement, the companies will implement systems to track shipments and identify and terminate shipments from pharmaceutical distributors to pharmacies with red flag warnings indicating suspicious opioid orders. Following the settlement in the pharmaceutical distributors' case, New Hampshire's attorney general filed suit against several pharmacy chains operating in New Hampshire for overly dispensing opioids. In the New Hampshire Department of Justice (2022b) news release, Governor Chris Sununu stated, "Sadly, some of these national pharmacy chains failed to provide the people of New Hampshire the type of pharmacy care and protection they had a right to expect. Instead, they helped fuel an opioid epidemic in the Granite State" (para. 2). The lawsuit alleges the pharmacy failed to exercise diligence in dispensing controlled drugs, which contributed to the opioid crisis in New Hampshire. Some of the red flags included cash payments, doctor prescriptions from more distant locations, order diversion, and prescriptions to seemingly healthy patients (New Hampshire Department of Justice, 2022b).

Harm reduction programs may present ethical challenges. On one hand, some may view these programs as either aiding or condoning drug use, while on the other hand, programs address the associated negative conditions with sharing dirty needles. Syringe services programs (SSPs) are designed to avoid some of the negative conditions of sharing needles such as hepatitis and HIV (Taylor et al., 2021). Taylor et al. (2021) noted SSPs reduce some of the associated harms associated with intravenous opioid use.

Taylor et al. (2021) examined attitudes toward supervised consumption sites (SCSs) among NH opioid users and key stakeholders. While New Hampshire has added SSPs as the opioid crisis has worsened, the state does not have supervised consumption sites. Taylor et al. (2021) stated, "SCSs are facilities where PWUO can obtain drug use materials (e.g., syringes) and consume already-purchased street drugs (not necessarily limited to opioids) in a non-judgmental environment in the presence of trained staff who monitor them for overdose" (para 2). They conducted focus group interviews with key informants in two counties in New Hampshire and two counties in Ohio. Participants noted SCSs have the potential for life-saving interventions due to the presence of medically trained staff for overdose intervention and clean needle exchange. Among the participants who used opioids, they noted the reluctance to travel to an SCS after purchasing drugs, instead opting for more immediate use of the drugs. One stakeholder participant noted New Hampshire's reluctance and opposition to a needle exchange program, and even once legislatively approved, the difficulty in obtaining state funding. Other participants noted the perception of SCSs as condoning drug use and as a moral failing among users for their addiction. Stakeholders reported that even if SCSs were legalized, it would be difficult to agree on a site due to not-in-my-backyard issues.

Good Samaritan law in NH 318-B:2 mandates that a person in good faith and in a timely manner requests medical assistance for another person who is experiencing a drug overdose, or in good faith and in a timely manner reports that another person has been the victim of a violent crime (New Hampshire RSA, 2022). A person who in good faith and in a timely manner requests medical assistance for another person who is experiencing a drug overdose, or in good faith and in a timely manner reports that another person has been the victim of a violent crime, shall not be arrested, prosecuted, or convicted for possessing, or having under his or her control, a controlled drug in violation of RSA 318:B-2, if the evidence for the charge was gained as a proximate result of the request for medical assistance or the report to law enforcement (New Hampshire RSA, 2022).

GOOD SAMARITAN LAW

Although New Hampshire has a Good Samaritan Law allowing individuals to call 911 to request medical assistance for suspected overdoses, New Hampshire has also made dispensing drugs that lead to death a specific criminal offense. Specifically, Chapter 318-B of the Controlled Drug Act states:

> Any person who manufactures, sells, or dispenses methamphetamine, lysergic acid, diethylamide phencyclidine (PCP) or any other controlled drug classified in schedules I or II, or any controlled drug analog thereof, in violation of RSA 318-B:2, I or I-a, is strictly liable for a death which results from the injection, inhalation or ingestion of that substance, and may be sentenced to imprisonment for life or for such term as the court may order. (New Hampshire RSA, 2017)

The Good Samaritan Law in New Hampshire shields the individual from criminal charges of drug possession.

CONCLUSION

New Hampshire has experienced some positive changes in recent years. In particular, the opioid prescription rate dropped 58% from 83.7 in 2012 per 100 persons to 35.2

in 2020 (CDC, 2021). The rate in 2020 would place New Hampshire in the bottom 10 in a ranking of the 50 states (CDC, 2021). This is a significant improvement given the pathway of addiction from prescription drugs to illicit opioids identified by Meier et al. (2020). During this period of decline, the CDC (2021) also measured prescription dosage in morphine milligram equivalents per day in addition to prescription rates. While the overall rate of opioid prescriptions in New Hampshire was in decline, dosage patterns remained troubling. Specifically, New Hampshire's daily dosage rate for prescriptions of 90 and more morphine milligram equivalents in 2018 would be the fifth highest rate in the nation (CDC, 2019). By 2021, New Hampshire's opioid-specific overdose death rate was 28.4 per 100,000, ranking the state 21st in the nation and the lowest among the six New England states (Kaiser Family Foundation, 2023a). West Virginia, with a rate of 77.2 per 100,000, had the highest rate in the country. Considering all overdose deaths, New Hampshire ranked slightly below the national average in drug overdose death rates in the United States in 2021 (Kaiser Family Foundation, 2023b), with West Virginia having the highest rate (90.9) at nearly three times the national average of 32.4 deaths per 100,000.

REFERENCES

Bessen, S., Metcalf, S. A., Saunders, E. C., Moore, S. K., Meier, A., McLeman, B., Walsh, O., & Marsch, L. A. (2019). Barriers to naloxone use and acceptance among opioid users, first responders, and emergency department providers in New Hampshire, USA. *International Journal of Drug Policy, 74*, 144–51. https://doi-org.libproxy.plymouth.edu/10.1016/j.drugpo.2019.09.008

Cao, Y., Stewart, K., Wish, E., Artigiani, E., & Sorg, M. H. (2019). Determining spatial access to opioid use treatment and emergency services in New Hampshire. *Journal of Substance Abuse Treatment, 101*, 55–66.

CDC. (2019, November 1). *Rate of opioid prescriptions in the U.S. in 2018, by state and daily dosage (per 100 persons)* * [Graph]. In Statista. Retrieved March 27, 2024, from https://www-statista-com.libproxy.plymouth.edu/statistics/754278/opioid-rx-rate-by- daily- dosage-in-the-us-by-state/

CDC. (2021, November 10). *Rate of prescription opioids dispensed in the United States in 2012 and 2020, by state (per 100 persons)* [Graph]. In Statista. Retrieved February 28, 2024, from https://www-statista-com.libproxy.plymouth.edu/statistics/1300781/change-rate-of-opioid-rx-prescriptions-dispensed-in-us-by-state/

CDC. (December 21, 2022). *Death rate due to opioid overdose in the U.S. from 1999 to 2021 (per 100,000 population)* [Graph]. In Statista. Retrieved February 29, 2024, from https://www-statista-com.libproxy.plymouth.edu/statistics/798338/rate-of-opioid-overdose-deaths-in-us/

CDC & Morbidity and Mortality Weekly Report. (2021, April 16). *Per capita cost of fatal opioid overdose in the United States in 2017, by state* * (in U.S. dollars) [Graph]. In Statista. Retrieved February 29, 2024, from https://www-statista-com.libproxy.plymouth.edu/statistics/1231489/fatal-opioid-overdose-per-capita-cost-us-by-state/

Ciccarone, D., Ondocsin, J., & Mars, S. (2017). Heroin uncertainties: Exploring users' perceptions of fentanyl-adulterated and -substituted heroin. *International Journal on Drug Policy, 46*, 146–55.

Daly, E. R., Dufault, K., Swenson, D. J., Lakevicius, P., Metcalf, E., & Chan, B. P. (2017). Use of emergency department data to monitor and respond to an increase in opioid overdoses in New Hampshire, 2011–2015. *Public Health Reports, 132*, 73s–79s.

Fitzgerald, M. (2022). The best states to raise a family. *U.S. News and World Report*. https://www.usnews.com/news/best-states/articles/best-state-to-raise-a-family

Gulec, N., Lahey, J., Suozzi, J. C., Sholl, M., MacLean, C. D., & Wolfson, D. L. (2018). Basic and advanced EMS providers are equally effective in naloxone administration for opioid overdose in Northern New England. *Prehospital Emergency Care, 22*, 163–69.

Hedegaard H., Miniño, A. M., & Warner, M. (2020). *Drug overdose deaths in the United States, 1999–2018. NCHS Data Brief, no 356*. National Center for Health Statistics.

Kaiser Family Foundation. (2023a, August 9). *Opioid overdose death rate in the United States in 2021, by state (per 100,000 population)* [Graph]. In Statista. Retrieved February 28, 2024, from https://www-statista-com.libproxy.plymouth.edu/statistics/676209/death-rate-from-opioid-overdose-us-states/

Kaiser Family Foundation. (2023b, August 9). *Drug overdose death rate in the United States in 2021, by state (per 100,000 population)* [Graph]. In Statista. Retrieved February 29, 2024, from https://www-statista-com.libproxy.plymouth.edu/statistics/686415/top-ten-leading-states-concerning-death-rate-of-drug-overdose-in-the-us/

Mattson, C. L., Kumar, S., Tanz, L. J., Patel, P., Luo, Q., & Davis, N. L. (2022). *Drug overdose deaths in 28 states and the District of Columbia: 2020 data from the State Unintentional Drug Overdose Reporting System (SUDORS). SUDORS Data Brief, No 1*. Centers for Disease Control and Prevention, U.S. Department of Health and Human Services.

Meier, A., Moore, S. K., Saunders, E. C., McLeman, B., Metcalf, S. A., Auty, S., Walsh, O., & Marsch, L. A. (2020). Understanding the increase in opioid overdoses in New Hampshire: A rapid epidemiologic assessment. *Drug and Alcohol Dependence, 209*. https://doi.org/10.1016/j.drugalcdep.2020.107893

Moore, S. K., Saunders, E. C., McLeman, B., Metcalf, S. A., Walsh, O., Bell, K., Meier, A., & Marsch, L. A. (2021, September). Implementation of a New Hampshire community-initiated response to the opioid crisis: A mixed-methods process evaluation of Safe Station. *International Journal of Drug Policy, 95103259*.

NCBI. (2021, January 1). *Estimated nonfatal costs of opioid use disorder in the United States in 2017, by type of cost (in million U.S. dollars)* [Graph]. In Statista. Retrieved February 29, 2024, from https://www-statista-com.libproxy.plymouth.edu/statistics/935176/nonfatal-opioid-use-disorder-costs-us-by-type/

New Hampshire Department of Justice. (2022a). *Drug distributors commit to $21 billion opioid agreement; New Hampshire to receive $115 million to fight the opioid crisis*. https://www.doj.nh.gov/news/2022/20220225-opioid-agreement.htm

New Hampshire Department of Justice. (2022b). *New Hampshire sues pharmacies for overly dispensing opioids*. https://www.doj.nh.gov/news/2022/20220726-pharmacies-suit.htm

New Hampshire RSA. (2017). *Chapter 318-B Controlled Drug Act Section 318-B:26*. https://www.gencourt.state.nh.us/rsa/html/xxx/318-b/318-b-26.htm

New Hampshire RSA. (2022). *Chapter 318-B:2 Controlled Drug Act Section 318-B:28-b*. https://law.justia.com/codes/new-hampshire/2022/title-xxx/title-318-b/section-318-b-28-b/

Research America. (2022, March 24). *Percentage of U.S. adults who agree that opioid abuse and addiction is a major problem from 2020 to 2022* [Graph]. In Statista. Retrieved February 29, 2024, from https://www-statista-com.libproxy.plymouth.edu/statistics/1302088/public-perception-on-opioid-abuse-and-addiction-us/

Saunders, E., Metcalf, S. A., Walsh, O., Moore, S. K., Meier, A., McLeman, B., Auty, S., Bessen, S., & Marsch, L. A. (2019). "You can see those concentric rings going out": Emergency personnel's experiences treating overdose and perspectives on policy-level responses to the opioid crisis in New Hampshire. *Drug and Alcohol Dependence, 204*, 107555. https://doi.org/10.1016/j.drugalcdep.2019.107555

Seelye, K. Q. (2018, January 21). "Perfect Storm" fuels New Hampshire opioid crisis. *New York Times.* https://www.proquest.com/newspapers/perfect-storm-fuels-new-hampshire-opioid-crisis/docview/1989328991/se-2

Stansel, D., Torra, J., McMahon, F., & Carrión-Tavárez, A. (2023). *Economic freedom of North America 2023.* Fraser Institute. DOI: https://doi.org/10.53095/88975015

Stark, C. (1860). *Memoir and official correspondence of Gen John Stark.* Steam Press of McFarland and Jenks.

Stopka, T. J., Jacque, E., Kelso, P., Guhn-Knight, H., Nolte, K., Hoskinson Jr., R., Jones, A., Harding, J., Drew, A., VanDonsel, A., & Friedmann, P. D. (2019). The opioid epidemic in rural northern New England: An approach to epidemiologic, policy, and legal surveillance. *Preventive Medicine, 128.* https://doi.org/10.1016/j.ypmed.2019.05.028

Suzuki, J., & El-Haddad, S. (2017). A review: Fentanyl and non-pharmaceutical fentanyls. *Drug and Alcohol Dependence, 171*, 107–16. https://doi-org.libproxy.plymouth.edu/10.1016/j.drugalcdep.2016.11.033

Taylor, J., Ober, A. J., Kilmer, B., Caulkins, J. P., & Iguchi, M. Y. (2021). Community perspectives on supervised consumption sites: Insights from four U.S. counties deeply affected by opioids. *Journal of Substance Abuse Treatment, 131.* https://doi.org/10.1016/j.jsat.2021.108397

8

Opioids in Medical Practice

Deborah L. Morris

Before opioids there were opiates, and before opiates, opium. These drugs derived from or based on the products of the opium poppy have offered medicine, recreation, and risk for thousands of years, possibly since prehistoric times. Artistic and written references to the opium poppy are seen from several ancient civilizations including the Sumerian, Babylonian, Egyptian, and Greek, from material as old as a Sumerian clay tablet that dates to 2100 BCE. Greek and Roman writings document the use of the poppy for pain, sedation, and diarrhea, effective uses that continue to this day (Norn et al., 2005).

Early Western medicine as it developed in Europe had few truly effective remedies, often relying on spurious theories, using herbs based on shape or color, techniques like bleeding or cupping, and only slowly beginning to rely on empiric evidence in the 19th and 20th centuries. However, throughout history when most of what a medical provider, whether physician, barber surgeon, or midwife could offer was comfort, human touch, and some knowledge of physical diagnosis, the products of the poppy were used to induce sleep, relieve cough, treat diarrhea, provide sedation, and relieve pain.

Papaver somniferum, the opium poppy, contains several chemical compounds that have pharmaceutical properties. The alkaloid chemicals codeine, morphine, and thebaine are considered opiates, natural derivatives of this medicinal plant (Pathan, 2012). These compounds have their effects by interacting with proteins, called receptors, on cell membranes of human neurons. While there are three known types of opiate receptors, the ones most associated with many of the medicinal effects of opioids are called μ (mu) opioid receptors or sometimes MOR or MOP (Dhaliwal & Gupta, 2023). These same receptors respond to chemicals made in the central nervous system (CNS) called enkephalins and endorphins, sometimes called endogenous opioids, produced within the body (Cullen, 2023). Drugs that are based on the opium compounds, whether natural, modified, or synthetic, are exogenous opioids, meaning that they are produced outside the body.

Laudanum, opium resin dissolved in alcohol and sometimes called tincture of opium, was widely used in the 18th and 19th centuries, both prescribed by physicians and pharmacists and unprescribed. Opium was an ingredient in many widely available patent medicines, recommended as panaceas for a wide range of real and imagined ailments (Crocq, 2007).

As the science of chemistry developed, German chemist Friedrich Serturner was able to isolate, refine, and purify the component of opium he named morphine in 1806. Fifty years later, with the development of the hypodermic needle, this effective and potent drug became widely available to relieve pain, but also to misuse. Morphine was important in treating wounded soldiers in the Civil War, but many of these patients developed addiction and continued using the drug, starting a wave of morphine addiction in the late 19th century. While opium use could be addictive, and there are ancient accounts of the use of opium for recreation, purified morphine was both much more potent and much more addictive (Norn et al., 2005).

In the late 19th century, the morphine molecule was chemically modified into heroin. It was produced and marketed by the German company Bayer beginning in 1898. Heroin was noted to be stronger than morphine and was initially thought to be less addictive. In fact, the higher potency of heroin makes it more addictive than morphine. Although the drug was promoted as a treatment for morphine addiction in the early 1900s, heroin addiction began to rise sharply. This created enough of a societal problem that its use was restricted, first requiring a doctor's prescription in 1914, and then outlawed, even for medical use, in 1924 (United Nations Office on Drugs and Crime, 1953).

The drug known as oxycodone was first created in 1916, synthesized from thebaine, an opium-derived compound, and it became available in the United States as an oral pain medication in 1939. A combination of oxycodone and acetaminophen (Tylenol) called Percocet was approved in the United States in 1976 and became a commonly prescribed pain medication, often used for acute injuries and as an oral pain reliever after surgery (Moradi et al., 2012).

Pharmaceutical research in the mid-20th century also led to the production of several drugs that worked like morphine but were entirely synthesized in the laboratory, not derived from the opium poppy. The first was meperidine in 1939, followed by methadone in 1946 and fentanyl in 1959. These drugs found widespread use for analgesia, the treatment of pain, and surgical anesthesia. Many other synthetic and semi-synthetic opioid drugs were developed and marketed in the last half of the 20th century (Shafi et al., 2022). In addition, drug companies developed new formulations of existing drugs and promoted their use. Some of these included time-release mechanisms to prolong the action of previously known drugs, and combinations of drugs meant to decrease the abuse potential. One of these formulations was long-acting oxycodone, OxyContin, now known to be a major contributor to the opioid overuse crisis.

The Food and Drug Administration (FDA), a federal agency "responsible for protecting the public health by assuring the safety, efficacy, and security of human and veterinary drugs," is responsible for assuring that drugs are safe and effective and approves all drugs that are prescribed for humans (US Food and Drug Administration, n.d.). The Drug Enforcement Administration (DEA) is a separate agency that controls opioids and other drugs with abuse potential, enforcing "the controlled substance laws and regulations of the United States." Drugs with abuse potential are placed into one of five "schedules" and are often referred to as scheduled drugs. Schedule I drugs have a high abuse risk and are considered to have no legitimate safe medical use. Heroin is a Schedule I drug. Many of the opioid drugs commonly used today fall into Schedule II, including all oxycodone drugs, meperidine, methadone, fentanyl, morphine, and others. These drugs are known to have high abuse potential and risk of dependence. Some codeine-containing drugs fall under Schedule III, which is considered to have less abuse potential. Schedule IV and V drugs have even lower abuse potential. Some of the opioids in Schedule V include drugs used for cough and diarrhea (US Drug Enforcement Administration, n.d.).

All drugs are associated with potential side effects, referred to as adverse drug events (ADEs). Opioids have some common ADEs, and some are less common but potentially serious. We will discuss the most common ADEs of opioids and their negative consequences, but there are many less common ADEs, both minor and serious.

Nearly all opiates can cause constipation because they slow the motility of smooth muscle in the walls of the gastrointestinal organs, particularly the small and large intestines. They also impact the secretion of water into the intestines. Anyone who is prescribed opiates should be warned of this ADE and encouraged to consume additional water and fiber. People on chronic opioid therapy often need to use laxatives to maintain bowel function (Benyamin et al., 2008).

Other common gastrointestinal ADEs associated with opioids are nausea and vomiting. The causes of these symptoms are complex and include action on both peripheral enteric nervous system receptors, and CNS receptors in a part of the brain called the chemoreceptor trigger zone. For people using opioids to relieve pain related to advanced cancer, this can become a serious problem, requiring routes of drug administration other than oral, additional drugs and strategies to treat nausea and vomiting, and nutritional support (Smith & Laufer, 2014).

Most opioids cause sedation. Even the opioid drugs designed to work peripherally and to not cross the blood-brain barrier may have CNS effects in high doses. Almost all opioid drugs, even over-the-counter (OTC) agents like dextromethorphan and loperamide (Imodium) can cause drowsiness and dizziness, central effects. Opioid analgesics are labeled by the pharmacist as causing drowsiness and they should not be taken when driving or operating heavy equipment. Many people experience some degree of itching when they use opioid drugs and the mechanisms vary, though true allergy is rare, occurring in less than 2% of people. This interesting ADE often does not respond to antihistamines and may be severe enough to limit the use of opioids in some patients (Bigliardi & Bigliardi, 2014).

A common characteristic of opioids is that they produce an effect called tolerance. After even a few doses of an opioid, the body requires more drugs to achieve the same effect, whether that effect is medically desired analgesia, or the euphoria or "high" sought by illicit drug users (Collett, 1998). This characteristic can be troublesome when these drugs are used for other than acute, short-term pain. Over time, for the drug to continue to provide pain relief, the dose may need to be increased. The development of tolerance with repeated doses of opioids can create problems for people on long-term opioid therapy for serious pain (Benyamin et al., 2008).

Tolerance also contributes to the addictive potential of these drugs. Taking repeated and increasingly high doses of the opiate may lead to physical and psychological dependence, even when the drug is prescribed for very real pain and not used inappropriately. Opioid dependence means that the body requires the drug to avoid withdrawal symptoms. It is different from addiction. When the need for the drug interferes with normal life, resulting in compulsive drug-seeking behavior and use, even despite adverse consequences, addiction has occurred. Opioid dependence and addiction are adverse drug effects of opioids (Collett, 1998).

A life-threatening ADE of opioids is the depression of the normal drive to breathe. This is called respiratory depression and occurs more often with higher-potency drugs. Breathing is an automatic process regulated by areas in the brain stem that respond to changes in carbon dioxide levels. When we breathe less, carbon dioxide is not eliminated through the lungs, and levels rise in the blood and cerebrospinal fluid. There are μ opioid receptors in the same parts of the brain stem that, when activated by the presence of opioids, inhibit the drive to breathe and block the normal response to increased carbon dioxide. Respiratory depression is the cause of death in most opioid overdoses. Some other drugs, such as benzodiazepine tranquilizers like diazepam (Valium) and alprazolam (Xanax), worsen this serious ADE and make overdose death more likely (Benyamin et al., 2008).

Despite the potential for ADEs, opiates and opioids are used in medical practice for an assortment of conditions and symptoms. FDA-approved opioids range from weak preparations to drugs of incredibly high potency relative to morphine, often used as the standard for assessing opioid potency.

In Table 8.1, some of the common opioids are compared. If morphine is used as the standard, with a potency of 1, then heroin is twice as potent, and fentanyl is a hundred times stronger. The use of more potent opioids is more likely to lead to tolerance, dependence, and addiction, and especially to cause respiratory depression with a higher risk of overdose and death.

One of the common uses of codeine, a natural low-potency opiate, has been in the treatment of cough. It is thought to decrease cough by interacting with opioid receptors in the cough center of the brain stem. Although codeine-containing cough syrups were available in many states without a prescription until the last few years, they now require a prescription and are scheduled from III–V depending upon the amount of codeine per dose.

Dextromethorphan, a drug developed for cough that is a synthetic opioid, acting on those same central receptors in the cough center, has been available for more than

Table 8.1 Opioid Comparison Table

Drug	Class	Route(s)	Relative Potency	Controlled Substance Act Schedule
Morphine	Natural opiate derived from the opium poppy	Oral, injected	1	II
Codeine	Natural opiate derived from the opium poppy	Oral	0.1	III
Heroin	Semisynthetic opiate derived from morphine	No currently accepted medical uses. Snorted, smoked, or injected for illicit use	2	I
Oxycodone	Semisynthetic opioid derived from thebaine	Oral medically, snorted and injected for illicit use	1.5–2	II
Fentanyl	Synthetic opioid	Topical (through skin), oral, through mucous membrane, injected	100	II

50 years. This common ingredient in OTC cough medicines, like Robitussin DM, was long thought to have low potential for abuse or misuse. However, used in high doses it can cause euphoria and potentially even hallucinations. Its misuse, especially by adolescents, has led to more control over its sale, with proof of age required for its purchase in many states.

Even though opioid cough suppressants remain available, both OTC and prescribed, the scientific evidence for their effectiveness is weak and their use is increasingly discouraged, especially in children. Cough is a protective reflex that prevents us from accidentally inhaling foreign substances (like food) and helps to clear excessive mucous and other respiratory secretions. While cough suppressants remain widely used, many productive coughs are better left unsuppressed.

Opioids are well-known to have effects on gastrointestinal (GI) motility. As discussed earlier, one of the common ADEs of their use is constipation. They have long been used in the treatment of diarrhea. These GI effects occur because there is a network of neural cells throughout the GI system known as the enteric nervous system (ENS), sometimes referred to as the gut-brain. This extensive mesh-like structure of interconnected nerve cells can function independently of the CNS but also has connections with it. Many of the same kinds of receptors found in the neurons of the brain and of the peripheral nervous system (PNS) are found in the ENS. Not surprisingly, opioid receptors are distributed throughout the ENS and have profound effects on its function (Galligan & Sternini, 2017).

Opioids inhibit the motor activity of the intestines, slowing the movement of digestive products and resulting in increased time for water to be absorbed while also inhibiting the secretion of water in the colon. This makes them effective in treating diarrhea, and results in the common adverse drug event of constipation.

Paregoric is a solution of opium in water and alcohol with anise oil, camphor, and benzoic acid, and has been available since the 17th century. Until the mid-20th century it was available at pharmacies without a prescription and used not only for diarrhea but for pain, including infant colic and teething. Because paregoric is an opium preparation, it was commonly misused and eventually became a scheduled drug requiring a prescription.

In 1960 a synthetic opioid called diphenoxylate, combined with another drug that slows gastrointestinal activity, was released and marketed for the treatment of diarrhea under the trade name Lomotil. One of the reasons for the additional ingredient in Lomotil, atropine, is to prevent its misuse. Atropine has unpleasant side effects when taken in higher doses. By itself, diphenoxylate is a Schedule II drug, thought to have high abuse potential. While it has potent effects on the neurons of the ENS, it also has similar effects on the CNS as other opioids, like sedation, euphoria, and the potential for dependence and addiction. As is true of many opioids, it is not safe to use in young children because of the possibility of respiratory depression.

A newer antidiarrheal drug called loperamide, Imodium, is also an opioid. It is sold OTC because it has relatively little CNS effect and low abuse potential. While it is widely used, it still must be approached with caution. It should not be used in infants and very young children. Also, in the same way that suppressing cough is not always in a patient's best interest, suppressing diarrhea can cause problems. Some infectious causes of diarrhea, when suppressed by opioids, lead to further intestinal damage. Also, there have been increasing cases of the misuse of this drug taken in high doses, in some cases leading to heart arrhythmias (Galligan & Sternini, 2017).

Opioids play a key role in surgical anesthesia. General anesthesia during surgery has three elements. A drug called a hypnotic is given to sedate the patient, causing unconsciousness so there will be no memory of the surgery. For serious operations, another drug called a paralytic is given to prevent the anesthetized patient from moving. But for all operations, even when the patient is unconscious and paralyzed, it is important to provide pain relief to prevent both physiologic and psychological harm from the effects of pain, even though the patient is sedated. Drugs used to provide pain relief are called analgesics.

While morphine and other drugs are still used, fentanyl and its close relatives are the most common analgesics in general anesthesia because of their potency, rapid onset of action, and ease of dosing. The anesthesiologist or anesthetist monitors the patient's oxygen levels to assure safety, and provides breathing support if needed, but also monitors some of the physiological responses to pain, like pulse and blood pressure, to assure that the anesthetized patient is not experiencing pain.

Another way that opiates are used in anesthesia is administered along with the numbing agents that are used in epidural, spinal, and similar regional anesthesia techniques. Small doses of morphine or fentanyl improve and prolong the pain control provided by these modes of surgical anesthesia with fewer systemic effects (Ferry et al., 2023).

An increasingly important use of opioids is in the treatment of opioid use disorders (OUDs). While this may seem counterintuitive, research has repeatedly demonstrated the effectiveness of what has been called medication-assisted treatment (MAT) for OUDs, previously called opioid addiction.

Drugs that interact with opioid receptors may have different effects. The drugs that cause the same effects as opiates and endorphins are called opioid agonists. Some drugs interact with opioid receptors in a way that blocks the receptors, preventing the effect of opioids, and these are called opioid antagonists. Other opioid drugs have both effects on distinct types of opioid receptors; these are called agonist-antagonists and have mixed effects.

Drugs from all three groups have been used in the treatment of OUDs and can be effective when given in a supervised and controlled way. One well-known example of an opioid antagonist is naloxone (Narcan) which is used as an emergency drug to treat opioid overdose. It is available as an injection and a nasal spray. By binding with opiate receptors in the CNS's respiratory centers, this drug reverses the respiratory depression that leads to opioid overdose deaths.

Another opioid antagonist is naltrexone, a drug usually given orally though it can also be given as an injection for patients likely to relapse or be noncompliant with the oral form. Naltrexone prevents opiates and opioids from creating the euphoria and sedation that contribute to addiction. It also is reported to block cravings. The person being treated with naltrexone must have completed detoxification from opioids or they will be rapidly thrown into withdrawal, with all the unpleasant symptoms that come with it. If they are taking naltrexone and relapse, using an opioid, they will not experience the high they seek. Interestingly, naltrexone is also used to treat alcohol use disorder. It both reduces alcohol craving and blocks some of the effects of alcohol that are mediated by μ opioid receptors.

Methadone, a synthetic opioid introduced and used for pain treatment, was the earliest form of medication-assisted treatment for opioid addiction. In the 1960s it was recognized that methadone could be used to treat heroin addicts because of its long time of action and status as an opioid agonist. By relieving cravings, suppressing withdrawal symptoms, and inhibiting the euphoric effects of heroin use, it allowed many addicts to live productive lives. In addition, as the AIDS epidemic emerged, methadone was recognized as preventing the infections associated with intravenous heroin use. Despite evidence of effectiveness and harm reduction, its use was politicized and very highly regulated. This has long limited access to methadone maintenance therapy (Joseph et al., 2000).

Methadone is often used to treat people with serious OUDs such as addiction to injected heroin and similar drugs. In most cases treatment requires medically supervised withdrawal from the drug followed by supervised daily administration of oral methadone to control craving. For many years methadone as a treatment for opioid addiction could only be prescribed at specialized methadone centers and had to be given as a liquid dose witnessed by staff to prevent diversion. As the opioid crisis developed and the use of MAT for OUDs entered the mainstream, some of the restrictions on methadone prescribing have loosened. Unfortunately, bias against this inexpensive and effective treatment for OUD persists.

Buprenorphine, a newer synthetic opioid (Suboxone and others), is an agonist-antagonist (also called a partial agonist). It is used to treat pain but has found its widest use in medication-assisted treatment of OUD. The regulations regarding the treatment of OUD with buprenorphine have relaxed as evidence for the effectiveness of MAT and its acceptance in medical practice has increased. The DEA now requires all practitioners who prescribe controlled drugs to receive continuing medical education both on the risks of opioid prescribing, and on the treatment of OUD.

Buprenorphine given at the correct dose treats OUD in the same way methadone does, by blocking cravings and preventing withdrawal symptoms. At the doses prescribed for OUD, it does not cause the euphoria of opioid misuse and allows patients to lead normal lives. In addition, because of the opioid antagonist effects of this drug, it also in some ways resembles naltrexone, preventing the concurrent use of illicit opioids from causing a "high" (Deyo-Svendsen et al., 2020).

The most common and arguably most important medical use for opioids has been and continues to be the treatment of pain. Everyone experiences pain in their life due to injury, illness, and aging effects. While there are many ways to manage pain, opioids remain useful in many situations, despite the risks.

Opioids relieve pain by binding to opioid receptors in both the central (brain and spinal cord) and peripheral (everything else) nervous systems. There are three known types of opiate receptors, and all can be involved in pain relief, but the most important is thought to be the MOP or μ receptor. In the CNS, opioids have been observed to activate pathways that inhibit the transmission of pain signals from the periphery (Dhaliwal & Gupta, 2023).

There are opioid receptors on sensory nerve ends in the PNS as well as on immune cells and, while the opioid effect on inflammation is not yet understood, their anti-inflammatory action likely also contributes to pain relief. A great deal of current research is focused on finding opioids that interact with peripheral receptors, providing analgesia without the side effects of sedation, respiratory depression, and addiction potential (Sehgal et al., 2011).

Pain comes from many causes and in many varieties. The approach to opioid use varies with the source, severity, timing, and other characteristics of pain. In recent years, the CDC has updated its recommendations regarding the treatment of pain and recommends for most causes of acute pain, including injuries, dental pain, and kidney stones, that nonsteroidal anti-inflammatory drugs (NSAIDs) like ibuprofen be used whenever possible to avoid the risk of dependence and addiction (Dowell et al., 2022).

While the use of opioids has decreased since the recognition of the opioid epidemic in the 2010s, there is still a role for the short-term use of oral mid-potency opioids such as oxycodone-acetaminophen combinations in the treatment of pain from acute injuries such as fractures. Acute pain is usually defined as less than 30 days in duration, but in the primary care and emergency room settings, most acute injuries are treated with a very short course of opioids, a few days to a week-long prescription, along with other treatments for pain, such as NSAIDs or OTC analgesics like acetaminophen.

Similarly, orthopedic surgeons, who treat fractures both operatively and nonoperatively, may provide a prescription for opioids for use in the first few days after the treatment or surgery and discourage opioid use for the expected pain during the rest of the time required to heal. Dentists and oral surgeons also often prescribe short courses of opioids for acute painful conditions but again recommend NSAIDs. Other methods to decrease pain such as ice, heat, topical agents, rest, exercise, physical therapies, and immobilization (splinting and casting) should be the primary modes of pain control according to current recommendations. Episodes of acute pain that are likely to recur, conditions such as migraine headache, kidney stone, and low back pain are usually not treated with opioids to avoid the potential for dependence.

Opioids are still used in the inpatient setting for severe pain associated with injury (related to things like trauma and burns), diseases that cause episodes of severe acute pain like sickle cell disease, and surgery, but far fewer patients are discharged from the hospital on opioids than in the past.

Acute surgical pain is often treated with intravenous opioids, often morphine, given using a system called patient-controlled analgesia. Morphine given intravenously works quickly but has a short duration of action. A programmable pump allows a patient in pain to self-administer morphine in small doses and intervals programmed into the pump as they need it. The programming should allow for adequate pain relief but limit the risk of overuse. This requires a patient physically and cognitively able to manage the mechanism and is not always appropriate, but can be highly effective in managing the severe acute pain that often occurs in the period after serious operations (Deyo-Svendsen et al., 2020).

Many kinds of cancer cause pain, sometimes from direct tumor effect, pressure on organs or nerves, and sometimes more indirectly because of treatments like surgery, radiation, chemotherapy, and immunotherapy. The assessment of pain in cancer patients is important and its treatment is a crucial part of care. Not all types of cancer pain respond to opioids, but it is widely recognized that opioids play a key role in treating cancer-related pain, along with all other treatment modalities that have been shown effective in pain relief (Caraceni & Shkodra, 2019).

Opioids for cancer pain can be given through many routes including oral, transdermal (through the skin), and injected. In most cases these patients are given more potent opioids and a combination of drugs formulated to be long-acting, with additional doses of short-acting opioids for what is called breakthrough pain (Scarborough & Smith, 2018).

Whenever a patient is given opioids for chronic pain, including cancer pain, it is important to anticipate and manage expected side effects like constipation. In addition, drug dose and effectiveness must be monitored, and tolerance and physical dependence must be expected and managed. Changing the drug used and/or the route of administration, taking breaks from opioids, using other techniques such as nerve blocks, and adding non-opioid drugs that contribute to pain relief may all help manage opioid tolerance, but in cancer patients increasing the dose is often helpful. It is important for those who treat cancer patients to remember that tolerance and physical dependence are different from addiction (Scarborough & Smith, 2018).

The treatment of chronic pain, pain lasting more than 90 days, with opioids has become much more controversial. During the 1990s, the medical community encouraged assessing pain in all patients and treating pain aggressively. Before that, ongoing opioid therapy had been reserved for patients near the end of life, especially cancer patients.

The use of opioids has fluctuated over time. During times when the public and the medical profession are more concerned about the potential for opioid abuse, prescribing has been more careful and more restricted. The widespread availability of opiates in the late 19th and early 20th centuries led to overuse and addiction. As a result, government restrictions and the attitudes of medical providers led to much less opioid use for anything but the most severe pain.

By the 1970s, there was concern about the undertreatment of severe pain, especially postoperative and cancer pain. In the 1990s medical writers and some organizations began to promote the use of opiates for non-cancer-related chronic pain, and the American Pain Society promoted the addition of pain to the assessment of all patients as the "fifth vital sign." At the same time, pharmaceutical companies introduced long-acting pain medications such as OxyContin, marketed as being less prone to abuse, and heavily promoted for use in patients with chronic pain.

OxyContin and other long-acting opioids became widely prescribed, along with more traditional short-acting opioids, for chronic noncancer pain. While some of this prescribing was done in specialized pain management clinics, many primary care providers (family medicine and general internal medicine) also prescribed potent long-acting opioids to patients with chronic pain.

The increase in availability of potent prescription opiates led to tolerance, dependence, misuse, and overuse, and prescription opiate overdoses began to increase. With the increase in prescribing also came an increase in diversion, both from patients who sold their increasingly valuable pills and from unethical prescribers and pharmacies.

When patients physically dependent on opioids lost access to prescribed drugs because of events like doctor changes or loss of insurance coverage, some began purchasing their supply from illegal sources, and increased demand led to higher prices on the street. The increased cost of oxycodone per milligram led many of these individuals, now clearly misusing the drugs, to switch to heroin to maintain their habit and avoid withdrawal since it was less expensive. And thus the opioid crisis of the early 21st century was born (Jones et al., 2018).

Heroin doses are much less predictable than pharmaceutical-grade opioids since pure heroin is rare and supplies are "cut" with inert substances and, sometimes, other drugs that cause drowsiness, like benzodiazepines. Because of this, opioid overdoses have become more common. This problem has become much worse as very inexpensive and highly potent illicit fentanyl has contaminated the street supply of heroin.

The history of opioids in medical use is littered with unintended consequences, and the blame for the current crisis has been widely distributed. As in previous eras, the use of opioids in medical care has diminished sharply due to increased awareness, tighter regulation, and prescriber fear of legal consequences for inappropriate prescribing.

This leads us back to the use of opioids in the treatment of chronic, noncancer-related chronic pain. Long-term pain can occur from many causes, autoimmune diseases that affect the joints, the chronic joint damage of degenerative joint disease, imperfectly healed injuries, nerve compression or damage, and many diseases and conditions including some that are poorly understood, like fibromyalgia. Such pain can be debilitating and disabling; it needs to be recognized and treated.

Current recommendations advise using all effective potential non-opioid modalities to relieve pain when possible, and this is sensible (Dowell et al., 2022). However, opioids, while not effective or indicated for many kinds of chronic pain, are still an important option that should be considered for the treatment of chronic noncancer-related pain.

In cases where opioids are indicated, care must be taken to prevent overuse and misuse. In many cases, this care is best managed by providers who specialize in pain management and can provide all appropriate care including procedures like nerve blocks. In all cases, the patient must be educated to understand the risks, and it is standard practice to have a signed agreement between the patient and prescriber. This can include provisions such as periodic drug screening to assure that the patient is not using drugs outside of the agreement, either from other prescribers or illicitly obtained. Drug screens also can show that a patient is using the prescribed drug and not diverting it to someone else or selling it (Dowell et al., 2022).

Many primary care providers and those who treat some of the injuries and illnesses likely to cause chronic pain, like orthopedists and rheumatologists, have become extremely reluctant to prescribe opioids. Before the 1990s, there was real concern about the lack of treatment for such patients. That concern was not wrong. Pain causes suffering, and those who care for those in pain have an obligation to do what they can to treat it and to ease the burden of these disabling and debilitating conditions when possible.

Inappropriate and excessive prescribing of opioids has had truly terrible consequences, but the swing of the pendulum to the opposite extreme of ignoring pain has its own set of unintended and awful consequences. Opioids are effective at relieving pain and may be useful for other symptoms. They are one option among many, but it is important to recognize their value and utility and to ensure that all options for effective pain relief are available to those who suffer.

CONCLUSION

To summarize, opioids are one of the earliest effective drugs known to medicine. Over time, as our understanding of chemistry, pharmacology, and molecular biology has increased, opioids of increasingly higher potency have been introduced. The potential for misuse, and for the development of tolerance, dependence, and addiction, has risen with the strength of available opioids.

With the advent and wide use of these higher-potency synthetic products, the risk of many adverse drug events, along with the risk of fatal overdose, has increased exponentially. However, in this time of crisis, with thousands dying of overdose, it is important to remember that there are important, even crucial, legitimate medical uses for opioid drugs.

Physicians and other prescribers must address serious pain using all potential treatments, including opioids, to assure humane treatment of this troubling and universal symptom, while using caution to assure the safety of their patients and limiting misuse and diversion. They also need to responsibly treat individuals with OUD, using evidence-based therapies including MAT.

REFERENCES

Benyamin, R., Trescot, A. M., Datta, S., Buenaventura, R., Adlaka, R., Sehgal, N., Glaser, S. E., & Vallejo, R. (2008). Opioid complications and side effects. *Pain Physician, 11*(2 Suppl), S105–S120.

Bigliardi, P. L., & Bigliardi-Qi, M. (2014). Peripheral opioids. In E. Carstens & T. Akiyama (Eds.), *Itch: Mechanisms and treatment.* CRC Press/Taylor & Francis. Available from: https://www.ncbi.nlm.nih.gov/books/NBK200922/

Caraceni, A., & Shkodra, M. (2019). Cancer pain assessment and classification. *Cancers, 11*(4), 510. https://doi.org/10.3390/cancers11040510

Collett, B. J. (1998). Opioid tolerance: The clinical perspective. *British Journal of Anaesthesia, 81*(1), 58–68. https://doi.org/10.1093/bja/81.1.58

Crocq M. A. (2007). Historical and cultural aspects of man's relationship with addictive drugs. *Dialogues in Clinical Neuroscience, 9*(4), 355–61. https://doi.org/10.31887/DCNS .2007.9.4/macrocq

Cullen, J. M., & Cascella, M. (2023, March 20). *Physiology, enkephalin.* StatPearls. https:// www.ncbi.nlm.nih.gov/books/NBK557764/

Deyo-Svendsen, M., Cabrera Svendsen, M., Walker, J., Hodges, A., Oldfather, R., & Mansukhani, M. P. (2020). Medication-assisted treatment for opioid use disorder in a rural family medicine practice. *Journal of Primary Care & Community Health, 11*, 2150132720931720. https://doi.org/10.1177/2150132720931720

Dhaliwal, A., & Gupta, M. (2023, July 24). *Physiology, opioid receptor.* StatPearls. https:// www.ncbi.nlm.nih.gov/books/NBK546642/

Dowell, D., Ragan, K. R., Jones, C. M., Baldwin, G. T., & Chou, R. (2022). CDC clinical practice guideline for prescribing opioids for pain—United States, 2022. *MMWR*

Recommendations and Reports, *71*(No. RR-3), 1–95. http://dx.doi.org/10.15585/mmwr .rr7103a1

Ferry, N., Hancock, L. E., & Dhanjal, S. (2023, December 14). *Opioid anesthesia*. StatPearls. https://www.ncbi.nlm.nih.gov/books/NBK532956/

Galligan, J. J., & Sternini, C. (2017). Insights into the Role of opioid receptors in the GI tract: Experimental evidence and therapeutic relevance. *Handbook of Experimental Pharmacology*, *239*, 363–78. https://doi.org/10.1007/164_2016_116

Jones, M. R., Viswanath, O., Peck, J., Kaye, A. D., Gill, J. S., & Simopoulos, T. T. (2018). A Brief history of the opioid epidemic and strategies for pain medicine. *Pain and Therapy*, *7*(1), 13–21. https://doi.org/10.1007/s40122-018-0097-6

Joseph, H., Stancliff, S., & Langrod, J. (2000). Methadone maintenance treatment (MMT): A review of historical and clinical issues. *The Mount Sinai Journal of Medicine, New York*, *67*(5–6), 347–64. https://doi.org/10.1016/j.ejphar.2013.09.074

Moradi, M., Esmaeili, S., Shoar, S., & Safari, S. (2012). Use of oxycodone in pain management. *Anesthesiology and Pain Medicine*, *1*(4), 262–64. https://doi.org/10.5812/aapm.4529

Norn, S., Kruse, P. R., & Kruse, E. (2005). [History of opium poppy and morphine] [Abstract from PubMed]. *Dansk medicinhistorisk arbog*, *33*, 171–84. https://pubmed.ncbi .nlm.nih.gov/36675147/

Pathan, H., & Williams, J. (2012). Basic opioid pharmacology: An update. *British Journal of Pain*, *6*(1), 11–16. https://doi.org/10.1177/2049463712438493

Scarborough, B. M., & Smith, C. B. (2018). Optimal pain management for patients with cancer in the modern era. *CA: A Cancer Journal for Clinicians*, *68*(3), 182–96. https://doi .org/10.3322/caac.21453

Sehgal, N., Smith, H. S., & Manchikanti, L. (2011). Peripherally acting opioids and clinical implications for pain control. *Pain Physician*, *14*(3), 249–58.

Shafi, A., Berry, A. J., Sumnall, H., Wood, D. M., & Tracy, D. K. (2022). Synthetic opioids: A review and clinical update. *Therapeutic Advances in Psychopharmacology*, *12*, 20451253221139616. https://doi.org/10.1177/20451253221139616

Smith, H. S., & Laufer, A. (2014). Opioid induced nausea and vomiting. *European Journal of Pharmacology*, *722*, 67–78. https://doi.org/10.1016/j.ejphar.2013.09.074

United Nations Office on Drugs and Crime. (1953). Retrieved from https://www.unodc.org /unodc/en/data-and-analysis/bulletin/bulletin_1953-0101_2_page004.html

US Drug Enforcement Administration. (n.d.). Mission. Retrieved from https://www.dea.gov /about/mission

US Food and Drug Administration. (n.d.). About FDA. Retrieved from https://www.fda.gov /about-fda

9

Is It Acceptable to Prescribe Opioids to a Recovering Addict Suffering from Chronic Pain?

A Virtue Ethics Approach

Michael Potts

This chapter focuses on the ethical acceptability of prescribing opioids to opioid addicts who are in chronic pain, focusing mainly on cancer pain. This issue is fraught with difficulties and moral dilemmas for which the traditional rule-based approach to ethics will be inadequate. An ethical system that focuses more on the discernment of morally relevant individual features of a situation is virtue ethics. Virtues such as compassion and prudence can help a physician weigh the alternatives in a situation in which it is usually impossible to find one correct course of action. The chapter begins with a survey of the relevant moral issues involving pain, in particular cancer pain, and its treatment with opioids. A case study will be presented followed by an analysis. This, in turn, will be followed by a list of variations from the case study to reveal how complicated the moral issues can become when discussing opioids and pain. The next section will discuss virtue ethics along with two key virtues, compassion and prudence, that play a role in decision-making concerning pain treatment. The final section will apply a virtue ethical approach to some of the scenarios discussed previously.

ISSUES REGARDING PAIN MANAGEMENT AND OPIOIDS

A significant percentage of cancer patients suffer pain, though surveys vary widely from 14% to 100% (Smith & Saiki, 2015). In total, the percentage of late-stage cancer patients experiencing pain is around 64%, and of those in any stage, 53% feel

Michael Potts

pain. Even of those who have ended the sometimes painful curative treatments, 33% have pain (Smith & Saiki, 2015). It is clear that, as Smith and Saiki (2015) point out, "Safe, effective, and evidence-based management of cancer pain is a cornerstone of comprehensive cancer care" (p. 1428).

Thapa et al. (2011) state that excellent pain care using available resources "should result in excellent pain control in nearly 95% of patients with cancer pain" (p. 162). The authors do not provide the physiological data backing this optimistic claim, but even if we controlled the pain of over 95% of cancer patients, that still leaves around 5% without adequate pain control. Given the number of people suffering from cancer worldwide, even 5% would be a large number of people. The difficulty of managing cancer pain is shown by the fact that during the last four weeks of their lives, more than 50% of cancer patients required "three or more routes" of administration of pain-control agents (Glare, 1997, p. 445). Given the extent of pain, many cancer patients find it difficult to follow their usual routine, and they report that their quality of life is severely reduced by their pain (Smith & Saiki, 2015). Given that medicine tends to focus on curative care with the important exception of specialists in palliative care and given the notion among some doctors that death is a failure, there can be a reluctance to focus on strictly palliative care to control symptoms including pain. In tests of their treatments for chronic pain, oncologists do much worse than specialists in pain care in alleviating their patients' pain (Smith & Saiki, 2015).

Pasternak (2014) correctly says that the management of cancer pain "is an art." It is an art because therapy for pain must fit particular individuals, and each individual is different in pain levels, pain tolerance, and which drugs effectively relieve pain (Pasternak, 2014, p. 1655). This individualized care can become problematic if an opioid addict suffers from severe cancer pain. Unfortunately, opioids remain the best drug to control cancer pain (Bruera et al., 1992; Mandala et al., 2006). Addiction to opioids, especially the synthetic opioid fentanyl, is a serious social and healthcare problem. In 2022, the death toll from synthetic opioids was 73,838. The total death toll in 2022 from all opioids was 81,806 (National Institute on Drug Abuse, 2024). However, recent research has shown that the risk of opioid addiction is low for cancer patients who take their medications as prescribed (American Cancer Society, 2024; Pasternak, 2014; Portenoy, 1996; Walsh, 1984).

Another concern in prescribing opioids for cancer pain is the side effects of opioids, among which are sleepiness, constipation, nausea, vomiting, dizziness, itching, nightmares, confusion and hallucinations, slow or shallow breathing, or trouble urinating (American Cancer Society, 2024). Organic hallucinosis is one of the most serious side effects, but it usually occurs only with high doses of opioids and can often be stopped by using a different opioid (Bruera et al., 1992). Some of these symptoms may resolve over time, and most of them are not as serious as severe chronic pain.

An opioid addict who seeks opioids for pain can be faking, but I wish to focus on an opioid addict diagnosed with terminal cancer and who is in constant, severe pain. There are multiple individual factors that can be involved in ethical decision-making about prescribing opioids to an addict, and the issues differ from patient to patient. Legalism concerning policy can cause more harm than good to a patient (Nicholson & Hellman, 2020). However, there are borderline cases in which it is difficult to know what to do, and a rules-based approach to ethics is inadequate to deal with those patients. Rules must be carefully defined with clear parameters, but here we are dealing with matters not subject to exact solutions. Thus, a virtue-oriented approach can supplement a rules-oriented approach to ethical decision-making regarding the treatment of opioid addicts with cancer pain.

CASE STUDY PLUS VARIATIONS

A 54-year-old male who has been on buprenorphine to treat opioid addiction for five years has terminal pancreatic cancer with a prognosis of one to three months' survival. He had become addicted to opium he derived from poppies and was pleased that a drug other than methadone was available to treat his addiction. However, he now suffers from severe cancer pain that is so agonizing he constantly moans and sometimes screams. All attempts to use non-opioid drugs have not relieved his pain, and even a nerve block had limited efficacy. His physician wishes to try opioid treatment, but he is afraid of the moral implications of giving opioids to an addict and fears potential law enforcement or medical board responses. The patient is in so much pain he screams for opioids. What should the physician do?

This may not seem like a clear-cut ethical case, but actually it is. Pain is not the only issue for the patient who suffers it constantly and severely. The patient should be given an opioid; if none of the available opioids work, then more extreme measures such as psychological counseling, nerve blocks, or, in the most extreme cases when nothing else works, "central neurodestructive procedures" that actually cut nerve connections, though probably not until the patient is within a few months of death (three months before expected death is a reasonable option) (Nersesyan & Slavin, 2007, p. 384).

One objection could be that this patient has been successfully treated for opioid addiction to this point, and the doctor is violating nonmaleficence by harming the patient and bringing back addiction. However, one must weigh the absence of excruciating pain versus the risk of addiction; in addition, in a patient soon to die, it is irrational to be concerned about addiction since the patient is better off addicted and not in pain in this situation (Fine, 2007).

Violating state or federal laws is another concern many doctors have. Federal restrictions on Schedule II and III drugs (opioids are Schedule II) given for operative and postoperative pain are not operative for the terminally ill (North Carolina Medical Board, 2019). In addition, "Federal law allows partial filling of Schedule III and IV prescriptions for up to six months, and, for terminally ill patients, partial filling of Schedule II prescriptions for up to 60 days." This is done not only to prevent an unnecessarily high dose but also to lower expenses for the patient and the patient's

Table 9.1   Considerations for Decision-Making Regarding Prescribing Opioids to Opioid Addicts with Intractable Pain

Pain Level and Duration	Patient's Attitude Toward Pain	Patient's Prognosis	Addiction History	Legal Concerns
Severe (levels 7–10)	Pain must be suffered to please God	Less than 3 months' survival	Constantly addicted to opioids	Overly strict state laws or local regulations
Moderate (levels 4–6)	Pain interferes with quality of life	4–6 months' survival	Periods of active addictions/ periods of inaction	Overzealous law enforcement
Mild (levels 3–5)	Enjoys pain	7–12 months' survival	Recovering addict under treatment—short time under treatment	Legal concerns of hospital administration
Breakthrough pain—new pain, severe that arises after successful treatment for other pain	Pain is worse than death	1–3 years' survival	Recovering addict under lengthy treatment and maintenance	Legal concerns of other hospital staff
Acute pain	Religious objections to pain relief	More than 3 years' survival		
Chronic pain				
Intermittent pain				

family (North Carolina Medical Board, 2019). State laws should follow federal guidelines, which take care not to harm the patient while allowing for adequate aid.

What if the patient is malingering? Although this is possible, especially with an addict, "to treat the patient with the respect that is owed . . . the doctor must trust her patient to accept her testimony about her pain" (Nicholson & Hellman, 2020, p. 302). This is an even stronger imperative in the terminally ill; if the doctor makes an incorrect judgment about malingering, the consequences for the patient could be catastrophic.

What about deviations from this case study? How would they affect the ethics of prescribing opioids? Consider the modifications in Table 9.1 of the case study (the only constant is that only opioids can relieve the patient's pain).

Any combination of these factors may be present for consideration in decision-making. Utilitarian calculation would have to occur at such a general level that it would be difficult to do since it tends to overlook subtle nuances in an individual patient. A virtue approach to ethics can be a more solid approach to ethical decision-making in these difficult cases.

VIRTUE ETHICS

Virtue ethics, in this case, focuses on the character of the healthcare provider. A "virtue" is defined by Aristotle (1999) as "a state that decides, consisting in a mean, the mean relative to us, which is defined by reference to reason, that is to say, to the reason by reference to which the prudent person would define it. It is a mean between two vices, one of excess and one of deficiency" (Eth. Nic. II.7.15). The idea is that the right thing to do is a middle way between extremes. For example, if someone drinks too much, is promiscuous, and cannot control urges, that person is in excess of pleasures that are not for the good since he lacks the virtue of temperance. On the other hand, someone who is serious all the time and thinks that having fun is sinful is lacking in pleasure and also lacks the virtue of temperance. Temperance is a middle way between those two extremes, that is, enjoying pleasure but being moderate about it. The way people learn the mean is to focus on a role model ("the prudent person") or role models to emulate. Ask the question, "How would my role model behave virtuously in this situation." For physicians and other medical practitioners, there can be professional and moral role models, yet even at the professional level, medicine is a moral enterprise. Medicine involves a relationship between a vulnerable patient and a physician who has the knowledge and power to try and help the patient. The power disparity automatically generates ethical responsibilities to use medical power responsibly, to care about the patient, to "do no harm" to the patient, and hopefully to benefit the patient (Wiggins & Schwartz, 2005; Zaner, 1988). Thus, there cannot be any strict separation between clinical and moral judgment.

Now, a mean between extremes does not imply coming up with an exact answer. Aristotle rightly says that particular cases of ethical action "fall under no craft or profession, [but] the agents themselves must consider in each case what the opportune action is, as doctors and navigators do" (Eth. Nic. II.2.4). Just as a physician must consider the patient's particularities and all the facts of the case in making an inexact though hopefully accurate diagnosis and treatment plan, so people making ethical decisions cannot reach an exact conclusion concerning a case but will hopefully choose in a way that is a reasonable moral course of action. The problem is that so many parameters are involved in deciding what to do in a given case. After mentioning states such as being angry or having pity, Aristotle says that "having these motives at the right times, about the right things, toward the right people, for the right end, and in the right way is the intermediate and best condition, and this is proper to virtue" (Eth. Nic. II.6.11). It takes particular virtues to achieve a result close to the proper balance; reaching the exact mean may be practically impossible, but one can at least be close to the target. That is the best one can hope for in an uncertain and complex moral world. Practical reason (*phronesis*) is the virtue that gives a person the skill to make a good decision in a particular situation.

Virtues of character help a person approach the mean more accurately in particular situations. For Aristotle, ethics is not primarily about general rules, but about decision-making in particular and often complex situations—precisely the kind that arise in considering opioids for addicts in severe pain. The key virtues for moral decision-making in medicine, according to Pellegrino and Thomasma (1993) are fidelity to trust, compassion, *phronesis* (prudence or practical reason), justice, fortitude, temperance, integrity, and self-effacement. Fidelity to trust arises from the very nature of medical practice, with the vulnerable patient who is ill coming to the healthcare provider for help. This implies a certain amount of trust on the part of the patient in the healthcare provider to give the best care she can. A violation of trust (as occurs, for example, in sexual abuse by physicians) is something that destroys the patient-provider relationship which is founded on trust. A physician who does not care about a patient's pain and lets the patient suffer is violating trust, as is a physician who unnecessarily denies adequate pain care.

Compassion is also at the heart of good medical care. A sociopath or psychopath would probably not make a good physician, lacking the desire or capacity to empathize with a patient in her illness. Yet, compassion is more than emotion; it is a habituated trait, or virtue, that has implications for patient care. A compassionate physician will have compassion for a patient in pain and desire to relieve that pain. A physician lacking compassion would not be as motivated to help a patient in pain as someone with that virtue. Compassion, like all the virtues, must be balanced with other virtues in determining the good course of action.

Phronesis, or practical wisdom, is probably the most important virtue since it is involved in clinical judgment as well as ethical judgment. Prudence is the ability to do the right thing in a particular situation. It arises from practice, from clinical experience, and from experience dealing with ethical issues in day-to-day practice. *Phronesis* can weigh compassion against other virtues such as justice or integrity in a given situation. This is not done through some formal procedure but automatically stems from the physician's experience in the past as well as wisdom honed from other physicians' experiences. The physician may have a role model and ask, "What would my role model do?" in a moral dilemma. Prudence is an all-encompassing virtue that applies to clinical judgment in diagnosis, decisions about treatment, decisions about pain management, and decisions regarding end-of-life care. None of these areas is morally neutral but is filled with moral pitfalls and dilemmas. The nuances of these pitfalls and dilemmas are going to differ from patient to patient. The individual patient and her reactions to her disease or injury, medication, surgery (if needed) and end-of-life situations should be taken into account given the exigencies of a situation.

Practical reason (prudence) will not yield an exact answer—sometimes there is no "exact answer" to a moral dilemma—or to most situations of morality with the exception of actions that are always wrong, such as murder. Almost always we will miss something, but that is more true if only intellectual analysis and calculation are used to resolve a moral dilemma. A quantitative approach to moral decision-making in medicine is a category mistake. Moral judgment is not a matter of mathematics, but a matter of practical art. If moral judgment is an art, the artist must be skilled in having the virtues to judge a particular case. The judgment will not be perfect, but it should be at least one good option among others. In situations such as debates over pain care, it is easy to err on one extreme or another; for example, a physician may totally sedate his patients who are terminally ill and in severe pain. This is applying his own rule to a given situation without taking individual nuances into account. A patient may want to say "goodbye" to family members or inform the family what he wants concerning the funeral and whether to be buried or cremated. A totalizing approach does not work to do justice to all patients in severe pain at the end of life. On the other extreme, a doctor may give minimal pain medications and be reticent to use opioids to treat any patient in pain. Such reticence led to inadequate pain management at one Chinese hospital (Ye et al., 2001).

"Justice" traditionally meant "desert," giving people what is due to them in a fair way. The virtue of justice, as opposed to the rule, represents a state of character that leads a person to make just decisions. Unfortunately, the virtue of justice has not always shown its result in pain care. Treatment disparities between races have been discovered, with African Americans receiving fewer opioids for pain than Americans of other races and often receiving lower doses even if they were prescribed opioids (Knoebel et al., 2021). While there may be bureaucratic rules in place to try and prevent these abuses, it would be better to have physicians with the virtue of justice who would treat people as individuals rather than in terms of their race or racial stereotypes.

In pain management, the just treatment for a patient in the old sense of desert is to relieve the patient's pain. Human beings' pain often takes away their sense of meaning in life and can lead to depression, despair, and sometimes suicide. Every human being in pain deserves the offer of pain relief if drugs and other treatments are available. In nations where key drugs are not available due to the nations being poor, programs can be devised to arrange transporting these drugs to needy nations at an affordable rate. At the individual level, physicians should realize it is just and good for them to treat their patients' pain to the best of their ability. Intentional failure to do so reveals not only a lack of compassion and violation of trust, but is also unjust to the patient.

Fortitude is the ability to patiently deal with difficult or adverse situations without losing one's emotional bearing. It also involves the patience to allow a drug to work before going for a change. Impatience at a cancer patient receiving opioids because the physician thinks that the patient is an addict is a vice. Fortitude involves caring for a patient even when all hope for a cure is lost. If a physician is frightened by dying, she may not treat the dying patient palliatively because she cannot emotionally deal with death and dying. It may become necessary, if such a physician cannot change, that another doctor be moved to the case, perhaps a different oncologist, perhaps a palliative care expert. There is no room for a lack of fortitude in pain care; this leads to patient neglect, doctors abandoning patients, when the doctors have a duty to care.

Temperance is the ability to restrain the sensory inputs that please a person. It is sometimes called "self-control" or "impulse control." Temperance is an important virtue; doctors, for instance, must have self-control over any sexual thoughts lest they harm a patient, destroying trust. Self-control in prescribing opioids could involve avoiding being overzealous about promoting and using opioids—not all people in severe pain need them. They should be a last resort, not a first resort. Considering the case for moderation in opioid prescribing is important (Harden, 2007). Overzealous pessimism about opioids, due to the opioid epidemic, is understandable but wrong if it harms patients—Puritanism is just as much of a lack of temperance as libertinism.

Integrity is consistency in being true to one's principles and not giving them up in the face of opposition. If a physician believes it is necessary to give opioids to an opioid addict because it is the only treatment that mitigates the patient's severe pain, she should be true to her convictions. Sometimes administrative decisions or insurance company coverage decisions go against treatments that are effective, and opioids in pain control are an easy target due to the opioid crisis. Hospital administrators may put pressure on physicians to hold back some on opioid prescriptions. A senior physician may have reservations about prescribing opioids in general and would completely oppose prescribing opium to a drug addict. A physician with integrity would do his best to change the senior physician's or hospital administrator's mind.

Integrity implies honesty, but honesty by itself is not sufficient to define integrity. Honesty is the virtue that enables one to consistently tell the truth. Integrity is broader—its opposite is hypocrisy, a failure to live according to one's convictions. Those convictions should be in line with the other virtues. Thus, if a physician claims to be compassionate but out of self-interest or fear of reprisal refuses to prescribe opioids when other pharmaceuticals do not relieve pain, that physician lacks integrity (as well as compassion).

Self-effacement does not mean self-hatred but humility. The old paternalistic attitude of "physician knows best" is for the most part dead in bioethics, except in cases of regulation needed to protect the public such as drug safety regulations and making sure those who practice medicine have the proper credentials to do so. If a physician becomes arrogant to the point of not listening to a patient or comes to believe that all patients are ignorant and he knows best what they need, then that physician will not treat the patient in the best way. The physician's own assumptions, including false assumptions, may get in the way. He may be convinced that the patient is really malingering without sufficient evidence or believe that the patient should have more pain tolerance than she shows. He may also disagree with the patient's values concerning pain control and impose his own values onto the patient. A willingness to be humble and listen to the patient, to try to understand the pain from the patient's point of view as best he can, will lead to better treatment for that patient, both medically and from a moral point of view.

VIRTUE ETHICS AND THE ISSUE OF OPIOID TREATMENT FOR OPIOID ADDICTS IN SEVERE PAIN

The case study presented earlier is clear-cut both in the four principles approach of "standard" bioethics from Beauchamp and Childress (2019) and from the standpoint of a virtue approach to ethics. The physician should treat the terminally ill opioid addict cancer patient's pain when there is only a short time for the patient to live by any pharmaceutical or other method that works. Compassion and practical wisdom both dictate in this particular case that caring for an opioid addict is consistent with treating her pain with as much pharmaceutical or other treatments as are warranted to relieve such pain. It would not be compassionate to say, "This patient's addiction will become active again; thus, I cannot prescribe opioids" when such failure to prescribe becomes a failure to reduce the patient's pain. Instead, such an approach would be legalistic to the point of cruelty.

Altering the scenario, what if the opioid addict has a three-year prognosis of mortality and claims to be in severe pain? If there is no contravening evidence that is beyond a reasonable doubt, the compassionate course of treatment may be to prescribe opioids if the patient claims they are the only drug that works. But *phronesis*, practical wisdom, could suggest caution. If the patient is observed making normal movements claimed to be too painful in an earlier interview, especially if this is consistently done, this has to be considered—if opioids have a tapering off effect, prescribing them if there is empirical evidence for malingering would only harm the patient. Suppose this same patient is within a few months of dying and the pain really does become severe. In that case, the compassionate thing to do would be to hold off on opioids until it is clear that the patient is no longer malingering. Thus, if the patient does not make his usual movements and is physically limited as well as in clear psychological distress, and other drugs do not work, the good thing to do seems to be prescribing opioids to see if they work. If going through a series of opioids does not work, then other measures can be considered, but if a particular opioid does relieve the patient's severe pain to the point that he is either in no distress or in a low level of distress, a continued prescription for the opioid that works is the compassionate thing to do. There is no violation of integrity in this case because the situation of the patient at time A when he is malingering is different from the situation at time B when he really is in severe pain.

I am not convinced that the best thing to do is to withhold opioids in noncancer cases. In both cases, the patient may become physically dependent on an opioid, but that is not the same as addiction; it does suggest caution if the physician thinks it best to withdraw a particular opioid since that process must occur slowly. Regulative policies allowing liberal use of opioids, even for addicts, have been loosened for cancer patients and the terminally ill, but for severe pain in other illnesses, including fibromyalgia, regulations may discourage a physician from giving opioids. However, the virtue of temperance as well as prudence suggests caution in such cases. One wants to be just to a patient and not discriminate against a patient by suggesting, "Sorry, your severe pain can't be treated with opioids, even though they are the only drugs that work, since your pain is not caused by cancer." That sounds ludicrous, but it is the result of a globalizing ban affecting nonterminal patients with severe noncancer pain. The extent of pain and how much it interferes with quality of life is the real issue, not the terminal nature of the patient's illness or the type of illness from which the patient suffers. However, temperance also suggests that there should be careful precautions that such patients take only the correct dosage of the opioids prescribed to them and not more. The patient should not go to the street to seek other opioids. If the patient is actually in severe pain and a particular dose of opioids does not work on the original pain or on breakthrough pain, then the patient has a responsibility to communicate that fact with his or her physicians. The patient's virtues or lack thereof come into play, too.

Cases of addicts in severe pain are nuanced, as are all other serious medical issues, but are more nuanced given the complexity of the moral issues. Having the virtues may help a physician approach the correct action to help the patient more than only using principles. There may be no 100% best moral action to be taken, and any decision has benefits and drawbacks. But a virtuous physician learns from both clinical experience and the character she has developed over time via habituation to the point that she is reliable in making decisions that at least help the patient more than harm, and better deal with the problem in medicine of undertreating pain.

REFERENCES

American Cancer Society. (2024). *Opioids for cancer pain*. Retrieved September 19, 2024, from https://www.cancer.org/cancer/managing-cancer/side-effects/pain/cancer-pain/opioid-pain-medicines-for-cancer-pain.html

Aristotle. (1999). *Nicomachean ethics* (2nd ed.). Translated by Terence Irwin. Hackett Publishing Company.

Beauchamp, T. L., & Childress, J. F. (2019). *Principles of biomedical ethics* (8th ed.). Oxford University Press.

Bruera, E., Schoeller, T., & Montejo, G. (1992). Organic hallucinosis in patients receiving high doses of opioids from cancer pain. *Pain, 48*, 397–99.

Fine, R. L. (2007). Ethical and practical issues with opioids in life-limiting illness. *Proceedings of the Baylor University Medical Center, 20,* 5–12.

Glare, P. (1997). Problems with opioids in cancer pain: Parenteral opioids. *Support Care Cancer, 5,* 445–50.

Harden, R. N. (2007, March). Chronic pain and opioids: A call for moderation. *Archives of Physical Medicine and Rehabilitation, 89*(3), supplement 1, 572–76.

Knoebel, R. W., Starck, J. V., & Miller, P. (2021). Treatment disparities among the black population and their influence on the equitable management of chronic pain. *Health Equity, 5*(1), 596–605.

Mandala, M., Moro, C., Labianca, R., Cremonesi, M., & Barni, S. (2006). Optimizing use of opioids in the management of cancer pain. *Therapeutics and Clinical Risk Management, 2*(4), 447–53.

National Institute on Drug Abuse. (2024). *Drug overdose deaths: Facts and figures.* Retrieved September 18, 2024, from https://nida.nih.gov/research-topics/trends-statistics/overdose-death-rates

Nersesyan, H., & Slavin, K. V. (2007). Current approach to cancer pain management: Availability and implications of different treatment options. *Therapeutics and Clinical Risk Management, 3*(3), 381–400, DOI: 10.2147/tcrm.s12160412

Nicholson, K. M., & Hellman, D. (2020). Opioid prescribing and the ethical duty to do no harm. *American Journal of Law and Medicine, 46*(2–3), 297–310.

North Carolina Medical Board. (2019). *Joint statement on medication management of pain in end-of-life care.* Retrieved July 13, 2023, from https://www.ncmedboard.org/resources-information/professional-resources/laws-rules-position-statements/position-statements/joint_statement_on_pain_management_and_end-of-life_care

Pasternak, G. W. (2014, June 1). Opioid pharmacology and relief of pain. *Journal of Clinical Oncology, 16,* 1655–61.

Pellegrino, E. D., & Thomasma, D. C. (1993). *The virtues in medical practice.* Oxford University Press.

Portenoy, R. K. (1996). Opioid therapy for chronic nonmalignant pain: A review of the critical issues. *Journal of Pain and Symptom Management, 11*(4), 203–17.

Smith, T. J., & Saiki, C. B. (2015). Cancer pain management. *Mayo Clinic Proceedings, 90,* 10, 1428–39.

Thapa, D., Rastogi, V., & Ahuja, V. (2011, April–June). Cancer pain management—current status. *Journal of Anaesthesiology and Clinical Pharmacology, 27,* 162–68.

Walsh, T. D. (1984). Oral morphine in chronic cancer pain. *Pain, 18,* 1–11.

Wiggins, O. P., & Schwartz, M. A. (2005). Richard Zaner's phenomenology of the clinical encounter. *Theoretical Medicine and Bioethics, 26*(1), 73–87. doi: 10.1007/s11017-004-4805-3.

Ye, S., Wang, X. S., Cheng, Y., Yang, J., & Cleeland, C. S. (2001). Special aspects of cancer pain management in a Chinese general hospital. *European Journal of Pain* 5 (Suppl. A), 15–20.

Zaner, R. M. (1988). *Ethics and the clinical encounter.* Prentice-Hall.

10

Psychology and Opioids

Mark Kline, Laura Mars, and Madison Brunson

This chapter explores harm-reduction strategies, pathways to addiction, mental health concerns, and underlying socioeconomic factors that make certain communities more vulnerable to addiction. This chapter also addresses the role of corporate greed and ineffective regulation and how the overprescription of opioids by various healthcare providers, including dentists, nurse practitioners, and physician assistants, has contributed to the opioid epidemic. Additionally, this chapter examines alternative perspectives on addiction, such as those proposed by Gabor Maté and the Rat Park experiment, which emphasize the importance of environmental and psychological factors in the development of addictive behaviors.

HARM-REDUCTION AND REGULATORY METHODS

Harm reduction is a set of practical strategies and ideas aimed at reducing the negative consequences associated with drug use. It acknowledges that drug use is a complex issue that requires a multifaceted approach to address the various health and social problems associated with it. Developed and popularized by psychologist Dr. Alan Marlatt in the 1980s, harm reduction emerged as a response to traditional "zero-tolerance" or abstinence-based approaches, which often alienated individuals struggling with substance use disorders. Marlatt's harm-reduction framework emphasizes meeting people where they are in their drug use journey and providing them with nonjudgmental support to reduce potential harm. This pragmatic approach focuses on minimizing the risks associated with drug use, rather than solely aiming for abstinence. As Marlatt argued, harm-reduction strategies can empower individuals, promote dignity and respect, and ultimately lead to healthier outcomes for people who use drugs and their communities (Marlatt et al., 2012).

CASE STUDY: JOHN'S STRUGGLE WITH OPIOID
ABUSE AND THE ROLE OF HARM REDUCTION

John, a 35-year-old man from a small town in the United States, began using prescription opioids after a work-related injury. Initially, he was prescribed oxycodone to manage his severe back pain. However, over time, John became dependent on the medication. As his tolerance increased, he began using higher doses to achieve the same pain-relieving effects. When John's doctor refused to prescribe more opioids due to concerns about addiction, John turned to the streets to buy pills. Eventually, he started using heroin as it was cheaper and more easily accessible. His opioid use began to negatively impact his job, relationships, and overall quality of life.

John decided to seek help and entered a local substance abuse treatment program. The program introduced John to harm-reduction strategies, including medication-assisted treatment (MAT) with methadone or buprenorphine. This treatment approach allowed John to stabilize his life and reduce the risks associated with opioid use. In addition to MAT, John's treatment plan also involved participation in a needle exchange program to minimize the risk of HIV and hepatitis C transmission. He was provided with naloxone, an opioid overdose reversal drug, in case of emergency. The program connected John with counseling services and support groups that helped him address underlying issues contributing to his addiction.

John's story illustrates the importance of harm-reduction approaches in treating opioid abuse. By focusing on reducing the negative consequences associated with drug use rather than solely aiming for abstinence, harm-reduction strategies enabled John to regain control of his life and minimize health risks associated with opioid use.

In recent years, numerous countries have adopted harm-reduction approaches to tackle drug addiction and related issues. This section will discuss the impact of these harm-reduction approaches in four countries: Portugal, the United Kingdom, the United States, and Canada.

Drawing from Marlatt's principles, these countries have implemented various harm-reduction strategies such as needle exchange programs, supervised injection sites, substitution therapy with methadone or buprenorphine, and the distribution of naloxone to reverse opioid overdoses. By adopting these evidence-based interventions, significant progress has been made in reducing drug-related harms such as HIV transmission rates, overdose deaths, and criminal activity associated with drug use. While challenges remain in fully implementing and scaling up harm-reduction strategies across different cultural and political contexts, the legacy of Alan Marlatt's work has provided an essential foundation for addressing substance use disorders from a compassionate and evidence-based perspective.

Each of these countries has implemented different harm-reduction strategies based on their unique contexts, needs, and resources. By examining these diverse approaches, we can gain valuable insights into what works best in different settings and identify opportunities for further improvement in global drug policy.

Ultimately, understanding the successes and challenges faced by each country can help inform the development of evidence-based policies that effectively address drug addiction and its associated harms.

HARM-REDUCTION APPROACHES IN PORTUGAL

In 2001, Portugal made a groundbreaking decision to decriminalize drug use and implement a comprehensive harm-reduction strategy. This bold move was a response to the country's escalating drug problem, which had led to high rates of HIV infection and drug-related deaths. The Portuguese government recognized that punitive measures were not effectively addressing the issue and shifted its focus toward public health and social support.

The Portuguese harm-reduction strategy included several key components. First, needle exchange programs were established to reduce the spread of HIV and other blood-borne infections among people who inject drugs. These programs provided clean needles and syringes, as well as information on safer injection practices. Second, substitution therapy with methadone or buprenorphine was made widely available to help individuals with opioid use disorder manage their addiction and reduce the risk of overdose. Third, access to treatment and social support services was expanded, including drug counseling, housing assistance, and employment support.

As a result of these comprehensive harm-reduction measures, Portugal experienced a significant decrease in drug-related deaths, HIV infection rates, and overall addiction rates. According to a study by Stevens and Hughes (2010), the number of drug-related deaths in Portugal fell from 131 in 2001 to 20 in 2008, while the number of new HIV diagnoses among people who inject drugs dropped from 1,016 in 2001 to 56 in 2012. Furthermore, the overall prevalence of drug use in the country declined, particularly among young people.

The success of Portugal's harm-reduction approach can be attributed to several factors. First, the decriminalization of drug use removed the stigma associated with seeking help for addiction while encouraging more individuals to access treatment and support services. Second, the focus on public health and social support allowed for a more holistic approach to addressing the complex needs of people with substance use disorders. Finally, the implementation of evidence-based interventions, such as needle exchange programs and substitution therapy, directly targeted the most pressing health risks associated with drug use.

Portugal's experience demonstrates the potential benefits of adopting a comprehensive harm-reduction strategy, particularly in countries facing similar drug-related challenges. By prioritizing public health and social support over punitive measures, Portugal has been able to significantly reduce the negative consequences associated with drug use and improve the overall well-being of its citizens.

HARM-REDUCTION APPROACHES
IN THE UNITED KINGDOM

The United Kingdom has implemented various harm-reduction strategies, such as needle exchange programs, safe consumption sites (drug consumption rooms), and naloxone distribution programs. These initiatives have contributed to a reduction in drug-related deaths, HIV rates, and addiction rates (Rhodes et al., 2019). However, the United Kingdom still faces challenges in fully implementing harm-reduction strategies due to political and funding constraints.

HARM-REDUCTION APPROACHES
IN THE UNITED STATES

The United States has adopted harm-reduction strategies such as syringe exchange programs, MAT with methadone or buprenorphine, and naloxone distribution programs. These initiatives have shown positive impacts on drug-related deaths, HIV rates, and addiction rates (Des Jarlais et al., 2005). However, barriers to implementing harm-reduction strategies persist in some areas due to political opposition and lack of funding.

HARM-REDUCTION APPROACHES IN CANADA

Canada has implemented harm-reduction strategies such as supervised injection sites (e.g., Insite), needle exchange programs, and suboxone and methadone treatment programs. These initiatives have led to a reduction in drug-related deaths, HIV rates, and addiction rates (Wood et al., 2006). However, challenges remain in expanding these programs to reach more individuals in need.

COMPARISON OF HARM-REDUCTION SUCCESSES
AND CHALLENGES ACROSS COUNTRIES

Each country's harm-reduction approach has similarities and differences, influenced by a variety of cultural, political, and legal factors. These factors play a significant role in shaping the way each nation addresses drug use and addiction within its borders. Lessons can be learned from each country's experiences, such as the importance of political support and adequate funding for harm-reduction initiatives. These initiatives can include needle exchange programs, supervised injection sites, and access to addiction treatment services.

By examining these diverse approaches, we can identify best practices and opportunities for improvement in global drug policy. For example, some countries may have more successful strategies for reducing overdose deaths, while others may excel in providing resources for those struggling with addiction. Comparing and contrasting various harm-reduction models can help policymakers and public health experts determine which methods are most effective in addressing the complex issue of drug use.

In addition to learning from each other's successes and challenges, international collaboration can be invaluable in the ongoing effort to improve harm-reduction policies worldwide. Sharing research findings, exchanging ideas, and collaborating on new initiatives can lead to more informed and effective policy decisions. By working together, countries can develop a more comprehensive and evidence-based approach to addressing drug use and its associated harms, ultimately benefiting individuals, families, and communities around the world.

PHYSIOLOGICAL PATHWAYS TO OPIOID ADDICTION

Opioid addiction involves a variety of physiological pathways and mechanisms that contribute to the development and maintenance of addictive behaviors. Gaining a deeper understanding of these processes can help inform more effective prevention and treatment strategies for opioid addiction (Nestler, 2004).

1. **Opioid Receptors:** Opioids primarily act on mu opioid receptors, which leads to decreased neurotransmitter release and produces effects such as analgesia, euphoria, and respiratory depression. Research, including Matthes et al.'s (1996) study, has highlighted the crucial role of mu opioid receptors in mediating the effects of opioids.

2. **Reward Pathway and Dopamine Release:** The mesolimbic dopamine system, which originates in the ventral tegmental area (VTA) and projects to the nucleus accumbens (NAc), is central to opioid addiction. Opioids increase dopamine release in the NAc, contributing to their rewarding and reinforcing properties. Work by researchers like Koob and Le Moal (2008) has emphasized the importance of understanding how dysregulation of the brain's reward system contributes to addiction.

3. **Tolerance, Dependence, and Withdrawal:** Chronic opioid use can lead to tolerance (requiring higher doses for the same effect), dependence (appearance of withdrawal symptoms upon discontinuation or reduction), and withdrawal symptoms such as anxiety, agitation, and increased pain sensitivity. The locus coeruleus (LC) plays a critical role in opioid withdrawal due to its involvement in the stress response.

4. **Neuroplasticity in Opioid Addiction:** Opioid addiction is associated with long-term changes in neuronal function and structure, referred to as neuroplasticity. DeltaFosB, a transcription factor that accumulates in the NAc following chronic drug exposure, has been implicated in addiction-related neuroplasticity. Research by Nestler (2004) supports deltaFosB's role in mediating addiction and its potential as a target for addiction treatments.

OPIOID RECEPTORS AND THEIR ROLE IN ADDICTION

Opioids exert their effects by binding to specific receptors on the surface of neurons called opioid receptors. There are three main types of opioid receptors: mu (μ), delta (δ), and kappa (κ). The activation of these receptors, particularly the mu opioid receptor, leads to a decrease in neurotransmitter release, resulting in various physiological effects such as analgesia, euphoria, and respiratory depression. The binding of opioids to mu opioid receptors triggers a cascade of intracellular events that lead to the inhibition of adenylate cyclase, which ultimately decreases the production of cyclic AMP (cAMP). This decrease in cAMP levels results in the hyperpolarization of neurons and a subsequent reduction in neurotransmitter release. One prominent study by Matthes et al. (1996) generated mice lacking the mu opioid receptor gene. These mice did not respond to morphine treatment, supporting the critical role of mu opioid receptors in mediating the effects of opioids.

THE REWARD PATHWAY AND DOPAMINE RELEASE

The mesolimbic dopamine system plays a central role in opioid addiction. This neural pathway originates in the VTA and projects to the NAc, a brain region involved in reinforcement and reward-related behavior. Opioids increase dopamine release in the NAc, contributing to their rewarding and reinforcing properties. Koob and Le Moal's (2008) work on the neurobiology of addiction highlights the importance of understanding the reward pathway. Their research suggests that addiction involves dysregulation of the brain's reward system, leading to compulsive drug-seeking behavior and a decreased sensitivity to natural rewards.

TOLERANCE, DEPENDENCE, AND WITHDRAWAL

Long-term opioid use can lead to tolerance, dependence, and withdrawal. Tolerance occurs when the body adapts to the presence of opioids, requiring higher doses to achieve the same effect. Cellular adaptations such as receptor desensitization and downregulation contribute to the development of tolerance.

Physical dependence is characterized by the appearance of withdrawal symptoms when opioid use is discontinued or reduced. Withdrawal symptoms include anxiety, agitation, increased pain sensitivity, and flu-like symptoms. The LC, a region in the brainstem involved in the stress response, plays a crucial role in opioid withdrawal. Inhibition of LC neurons by opioids results in a compensatory increase in neuronal excitability. When opioids are removed, this increased excitability contributes to withdrawal symptoms.

NEUROPLASTICITY IN OPIOID ADDICTION

Opioid addiction is associated with long-term changes in neuronal function and structure, referred to as neuroplasticity. One key player in addiction-related neuroplasticity is deltaFosB, a transcription factor that accumulates in the NAc following chronic drug exposure. Research by Nestler (2004) has shown that deltaFosB over-expression in the NAc increases an animal's sensitivity to the rewarding effects of drugs, while its suppression reduces drug self-administration. This evidence supports deltaFosB's role in mediating addiction-related neuroplasticity and its potential as a target for addiction treatment.

In conclusion, understanding the physiological pathways to opioid addiction, including the complex interactions between opioid receptors, the reward pathway, tolerance, dependence and withdrawal, and neuroplastic changes in the brain, is essential for developing effective prevention and treatment strategies for opioid addiction.

STRESS AND COPING

The relationship between stress and substance use is well-established. People often turn to drugs like opioids as a way to cope with stress and alleviate negative emotions. Khantzian's (1985) self-medication hypothesis posits that individuals use substances to manage psychological distress and regulate emotional states. This theory suggests that understanding an individual's reasons for drug use can help tailor treatment approaches to address the underlying issues driving addiction.

NEGATIVE AFFECT, ANXIETY, AND DEPRESSION

Negative affect, which includes emotions such as sadness, anxiety, and irritability, has been linked to drug-seeking behavior. Individuals struggling with opioid addiction often have comorbid mood disorders such as anxiety and depression. Baker's (2017) negative reinforcement model of addiction posits that individuals use substances to escape or avoid negative affective states. This model emphasizes the role of negative reinforcement in maintaining addiction.

SOCIAL FACTORS AND PEER INFLUENCE

Social learning theory suggests that individuals learn behaviors by observing others in their social environment. This theory has been applied to understand the initiation and continuation of substance use, including opioid addiction. Peer influence plays a significant role in drug-taking behavior, particularly during adolescence when susceptibility to peer influence is high. Hawkins and colleagues' (2021) social development model integrates various social learning concepts to explain how protective and risk factors in an individual's social environment contribute to substance use.

PERSONALITY TRAITS AND IMPULSIVITY

Certain personality traits have been associated with an increased risk of developing substance use disorders, including opioid addiction. Cloninger's (2018) tridimensional personality theory identifies three dimensions of personality (novelty seeking, harm avoidance, and reward dependence) that are relevant to addiction vulnerability. Impulsivity, a facet of novelty seeking, has been consistently linked to substance use disorders. High impulsivity can lead to poor decision-making and increased risk-taking behavior, which may contribute to the development of addiction (Cloninger, 2018; Howard et al., 1997).

THE ROLE OF CORPORATE GREED
AND INEFFECTIVE REGULATION

The opioid epidemic has been fueled not only by overprescribing but also by corporate greed and ineffective regulation. Purdue Pharma, the manufacturer of Oxy-Contin, played a significant role in exacerbating the crisis. Despite pleading guilty to criminal charges of misbranding OxyContin and minimizing addiction risks, Purdue Pharma continued to aggressively market the drug, defrauding the United States, paying kickbacks to companies that would steer patients to OxyContin, and ultimately contributing to the escalation of the opioid epidemic.

Purdue Pharma's actions were driven by profit motives, as evidenced by the company's continued marketing efforts and the involvement of the Sackler family, who owned Purdue Pharma. The company faced numerous lawsuits alleging that it contributed to the opioid crisis through deceptive OxyContin marketing practices. In 2019, Purdue Pharma filed for bankruptcy as it faced over 2,000 lawsuits, and in 2020, the company pleaded guilty to three felony offenses, including conspiracy to defraud the United States, and violating the federal Anti-Kickback Statute.

THE ROLE OF MEDICAL OVER-PRESCRIPTION
IN THE OPIOID EPIDEMIC

While the Purdue Pharma case highlights the unethical marketing practices that contributed to the opioid epidemic, it is important to recognize that medical over-prescription of opioids, more generally, has been a significant factor in the crisis. Inadequate training, misinformation, and a lack of alternative pain management options have led to a culture of overprescribing opioids by healthcare professionals.

Beginning in the late 1990s, aggressive marketing tactics by pharmaceutical companies, including Purdue Pharma, resulted in a widespread belief that opioids were safe and nonaddictive. This belief was further reinforced by guidelines from prominent medical organizations supporting the prescription of opioids for chronic pain management. However, as opioid prescriptions increased, so did addiction rates and overdose deaths. As the dangers of opioids became more apparent, regulatory bodies and healthcare providers began to reevaluate prescribing practices. More recent guidelines emphasize a cautious approach to opioid prescription and encourage healthcare providers to explore alternative pain management strategies.

THE ROLE OF DENTISTS IN OPIOID PRESCRIBING

Dentists are a significant source of opioid prescriptions, particularly for adolescents and young adults. Studies have shown that opioids prescribed by dentists accounted for over 10% of adolescents and nearly one-third of young adults receiving their first opioid prescription in 2015 (Schroeder et al., 2019). Furthermore, among those who received opioids from dentists, 6.9% went on to receive another opioid prescription within a year, and 5.8% had subsequent healthcare encounters associated with opioid abuse (Schroeder et al., 2019).

According to a study conducted by Suda et al. (2019), for many adolescents, dentists account for their first exposure to opioids. Evidence has shown that exposure to opioids at such young ages was later associated with higher rates of opioid use between three months and a year in comparison to participants in a control group. Additional studies have shown that compared to other professionals, dentists also tend to prescribe opioids in greater quantities and at higher doses than what is necessary to help with dental pain (Thornhill et al., 2019).

A 2016 study conducted by Maughan et al. (2016) compared opioid prescribing between dentists in the United States and England. Data showed that the US dentists' opioid prescription rate was 37 times greater than dentists in England, adjusted based on population. The number of opioid prescriptions written in 2016 in the United States was 11.4 million while only 28,082 were written in England (U.S. Department of Health and Human Services, 2019). This shows huge disparities between opioid prescriptions between the United States and England where the dental procedures are the same and the overall oral health of citizens are similar.

The most frequently prescribed opioids by US dentists include hydrocodone, codeine, and oxycodone. In comparison, hydrocodone is equivalent in strength to morphine while oxycodone is 1.5 times more powerful than morphine. These drugs are most associated with drug dependency and overdose death. Compared to dentists in England, the only opioid prescribed is dihydrocodeine, which in comparison to morphine is only one-fifth of the potency.

Large amounts of opioid prescriptions from dentists often go unused. This amount comes from dentists prescribing opioids "as needed" and prescribing higher quantities than needed, in which patients end up filling those prescriptions but leaving them unused. Sahebi-Fakhrabad et al. (2023) examined the consumption patterns of patients and found that after three weeks post-dental surgery, 54% of pills remained unused. These unused pills pose a risk to other people such as family and friends obtaining and using them. Surveys suggest that dentists are perhaps a significant source of misuse and have contributed to nonmedical opioid use (Ashrafioun et al., 2014; U.S. Department of Health and Human Services, 2019).

Studies of pain management associated with invasive dental procedures such as third molar extractions have been studied more extensively. The American Dental Association Council on Dental Practice requested an overview of reviews of analgesic medications used in dental pain management. A 2019 study conducted by Schroeder et al. found that the best pain management options for postoperative dental pain were nonsteroidal anti-inflammatory drugs (NSAIDs) either alone or in conjunction with acetaminophen. This same study also showed that NSAIDs resulted in equal or superior results compared to opioid medications for pain relief (Schroeder et al., 2019).

Despite evidence suggesting that a combination of NSAIDs and acetaminophen may provide more effective pain relief, surveys indicate that many dentists continue to prescribe opioids following surgical tooth extraction (Schroeder et al., 2019). Dentists also represent a high volume of total opioid prescribing, with a study in South Carolina finding that they were responsible for most immediate-release opioids dispensed in the state (Schroeder et al., 2019).

To address this issue, organizations such as the Centers for Disease Control and Prevention (CDC) and the American Dental Association (ADA) have issued opioid prescribing guidelines recommending non-opioids as the first-line treatment and limits on opioid prescription durations. Additionally, state oral health programs have worked on provider education, guidelines, promotion of prescription drug monitoring programs, and interdisciplinary collaboration (Suda et al., 2019).

THE ROLE OF NURSE PRACTITIONERS AND PHYSICIAN ASSISTANTS IN OPIOID PRESCRIBING

Nurse practitioners (NPs) and physician assistants (PAs) also play a significant role in opioid prescribing, with some studies suggesting that they prescribe opioids at higher rates than medical doctors. These higher rates of opioid prescriptions by NPs and PAs have raised concerns about the potential impact of their prescribing habits on the opioid crisis.

A 2020 cross-sectional analysis found that while most NPs and PAs prescribed opioids similarly to medical doctors, they had more outliers who prescribed high-frequency or high-dose opioids (Ellenbogen & Segal, 2020). This is particularly concerning as high-dose prescriptions can lead to an increased risk of opioid misuse and overdose.

Another study comparing generalist physicians, NPs, and PAs filling Medicare Part D opioid claims found that NPs had the highest total volume of claims, followed by PAs and then physicians (Ellenbogen & Segal, 2020). These results suggest that NPs and PAs may be contributing to a larger proportion of opioid prescriptions than previously thought.

Interestingly, scope of practice laws granting NPs and PAs independent prescribing authority without physician oversight were linked to higher-risk opioid prescribing patterns. Clinicians in states with independent authority were over 20 times more likely than those in restrictive states to overprescribe opioids, which raises concerns about the potential consequences of these laws on patient safety (Spetz et al., 2019). However, less restrictive NP scope of practice laws were associated with a slightly higher percentage of NPs obtaining waivers to prescribe buprenorphine for opioid addiction treatment (Spetz et al., 2019). This indicates that in some cases, expanded scope of practice laws may have a positive impact on addressing the opioid crisis by increasing access to evidence-based treatments. In conclusion, while NPs and PAs play a crucial role in healthcare delivery, their involvement in opioid prescribing patterns warrants further examination and potential policy interventions to ensure patient safety and mitigate the ongoing opioid crisis.

Addressing medical over-prescription of opioids requires comprehensive changes within the healthcare system. This includes providing healthcare professionals with better education on pain management and addiction, establishing monitoring programs to track opioid prescriptions, and improving access to alternative pain management options such as physical therapy or non-opioid medications. By understanding the broader context of medical over-prescription, we can better address the root causes of the opioid epidemic and work toward developing more effective strategies to prevent future addiction crises.

SOCIOECONOMIC FACTORS AND THE OPIOID CRISIS

The opioid epidemic has disproportionately affected communities with worse economic prospects, as poverty and financial instability are highly correlated with opioid use and addiction. People with lower incomes are more likely to misuse opioids and have opioid use disorder than the general population. Financial instability fosters stress, increasing the likelihood of addictive behaviors, and lower-income individuals are more likely to suffer from chronic pain, mental illness, or trauma, which can increase their vulnerability to opioid misuse.

Furthermore, the opioid epidemic has reduced labor force participation in the United States, particularly among men. Increases in opioid prescriptions might account for 20% of the decline in men's labor force participation since 1999, as opioid misuse can compromise labor supply through absenteeism, workplace accidents, disability, incarceration, or death (CDC, 2021).

The intensity of the opioid crisis also varies significantly across states and regions, with some parts of the country, such as Appalachia, New England, and the Midwest, bearing the brunt of the recent increases in overdose deaths. These areas tend to have higher rates of poverty, unemployment, and economic distress than other regions.

ALTERNATIVE PERSPECTIVES ON ADDICTION: GABOR MATÉ AND THE RAT PARK EXPERIMENT

While traditional approaches to addiction treatment often focus on abstinence and punishment, alternative perspectives emphasize the importance of addressing underlying emotional and psychological factors, as well as environmental influences. Gabor Maté, a renowned physician and author, proposes a compassionate and holistic approach to addiction treatment. Maté (2008) defines addiction as any behavior that an individual cannot stop engaging in, despite negative consequences, and argues that addictive behaviors are coping mechanisms developed in response to early life stress, trauma, or abuse. Maté (2008) advocates for trauma-informed therapies that address the root causes of addiction, as well as harm-reduction strategies that prioritize minimizing the negative consequences associated with drug use without necessarily requiring abstinence.

The Rat Park experiment, conducted by Canadian psychologist Bruce K. Alexander in the late 1970s and early 1980s, challenged the prevailing notions of addiction and its causes. The experiment demonstrated that environmental factors, such as social isolation and stress, play a significant role in the development of addiction (Gage & Sumnall, 2019). When rats were placed in an enriched environment (Rat Park) with opportunities for social interaction and exploration, they showed little interest in consuming a morphine solution, even when it was readily available (Gage & Sumnall, 2019). These results suggest that addressing environmental and social factors should be an essential component of addiction treatment.

Both Gabor Maté's ideas and the Rat Park experiment highlight the importance of considering the psychological and environmental factors that contribute to addiction, rather than solely focusing on the addictive properties of substances. By addressing these underlying factors, and incorporating approaches such as harm reduction, trauma-informed therapy, and environmental enrichment, addiction treatment can become more comprehensive and effective.

CONCLUSION

The opioid epidemic is a complex issue driven by various physiological, psychological, social, and regulatory factors. At the physiological level, understanding the role of opioid receptors, the brain's reward pathway, and mechanisms like tolerance and neuroplasticity is crucial for developing effective treatments. Psychological factors such as stress, negative affect, peer influence, and personality traits also contribute to vulnerability to opioid addiction.

The over-prescription of opioids by healthcare providers, including dentists, NPs, and PAs, has exacerbated the crisis. Corporate greed, ineffective regulation, and aggressive marketing by pharmaceutical companies like Purdue Pharma have fueled the overprescription of opioids. Socioeconomic factors, such as poverty, financial instability, and lack of economic opportunities, have made certain communities more susceptible to opioid addiction.

Alternative perspectives, such as those proposed by Gabor Maté and the Rat Park experiment, emphasize the importance of addressing environmental and psychological factors in addiction treatment, rather than solely focusing on the addictive properties of substances. Harm-reduction approaches, including needle exchange programs, safe consumption sites, and access to MAT, have shown promise in minimizing the negative consequences associated with drug use.

A comparative analysis of harm-reduction strategies across countries like Portugal, the United Kingdom, the United States, and Canada highlights the successes and challenges faced in implementing these approaches. Factors such as political support, adequate funding, and cultural attitudes toward drug use play a significant role in shaping each nation's response to the opioid crisis.

Moving forward, a comprehensive and multifaceted approach is necessary to address the opioid epidemic effectively. This should involve regulating opioid prescribing practices, expanding access to evidence-based addiction treatment, addressing socioeconomic disparities, and adopting harm-reduction strategies. International collaboration, sharing of research findings, and learning from diverse policy approaches can inform more effective and compassionate strategies to combat the opioid crisis and promote overall well-being.

REFERENCES

Ashrafioun, L., Edwards, P.C., Bohnert, A.S., & Ilgen, M.A. (2014). Nonmedical use of pain medications in dental patients. *The American Journal of Drug and Alcohol Abuse, 40*, 312–16.

Baker, D. W. (2017, March). History of the Joint Commission's pain standards: Lessons for today's prescription opioid epidemic. *JAMA, 317*(11), 1117–18. doi: 10.1001/jama.2017.0935

CDC. (2021). *Understanding the epidemic.* https://www.cdc.gov/drugoverdose/epidemic

Cloninger, S. C. (2018). *Theories of personality: Understanding persons* (7th ed.). Pearson.

Des Jarlais, D. C., Perlis, T., Arasteh, K., Torian, L. V., Hagan, H., Beatrice, S., Smith, L., Wethers, J., Milliken, J., Mildvan, D., Yancovitz, S., & Friedman, S. R. (2005, October). Reductions in hepatitis C virus and HIV infections among injecting drug users in New York City, 1990–2001. *AIDS, 19*(Suppl 3), S20–25. doi: 10.1097/01.aids.0000192066.86410.8c

Ellenbogen, M. I., & Segal, J. B. (2020, January 1). Differences in opioid prescribing among generalist physicians, nurse practitioners, and physician assistants. *Pain Medicine, 21*(1), 76–83. doi: 10.1093/pm/pnz005

Gage, S. H., & Sumnall, H. R. (2019). Rat Park: How a rat paradise changed the narrative of addiction. *Addiction (Abingdon, England), 114*(5), 917–22. https://doi.org/10.1111/add.14481

Hawkins, E. J., Malte, C. A., Gordon, A. J., et al. (2021). Accessibility to medication for opioid use disorder after interventions to improve prescribing among nonaddiction clinics in the US Veterans Health Care System. *JAMA Network Open, 4*(12), e2137238. doi:10.1001/jamanetworkopen.2021.37238

Howard, M. O., Kivlahan, D., & Walker, R. D. (1997, January). Cloninger's tridimensional theory of personality and psychopathology: Applications to substance use disorders. *Journal of Studies on Alcohol and Drugs, 58*(1), 48–66. doi: 10.15288/jsa.1997.58.48

Khantzian, E. J. (1985, November). The self-medication hypothesis of addictive disorders: Focus on heroin and cocaine dependence. *American Journal of Psychiatry, 142*(11), 1259–64. doi: 10.1176/ajp.142.11.1259

Koob, G. F., & Le Moal, M. (2008). Addiction and the brain antireward system. *Annual Review of Psychology, 59*, 29–53. doi: 10.1146/annurev.psych.59.103006.093548

Marlatt, G. A., Larimer, M. E., & Witkiewitz, K. (Eds.). (2012). *Harm reduction: Pragmatic strategies for managing high-risk behaviors* (2nd ed.). Guilford Press.

Maté, G. (2008). *In the realm of hungry ghosts*. North Atlantic Books.

Matthes, H. W. D., Maldonado, R., Simonin, F., Valverde, O., Slowe, S., Kitchen, I., Befort, K., Dierich, A., Le Meur, M., Dollé, P., Tzavara, E., Hanoune, J., Roques, B. P., & Kieffer, B. L. (1996). Loss of morphine-induced analgesia, reward effect and withdrawal symptoms in mice lacking the mu-opioid-receptor gene. *Nature, 383*, 819–23.

Maughan, B. C., Hersh, E. V., Shofer, F. S., Wanner, K. J., Archer, E., Carrasco, L. R., & Rhodes, K. V. (2016). Unused opioid analgesics and drug disposal following outpatient dental surgery: A randomized controlled trial. *Drug and Alcohol Dependence, 168*, 328–34.

Nestler, E. J. (2004, April). Historical review: Molecular and cellular mechanisms of opiate and cocaine addiction. *Trends in Pharmacological Sciences, 25*(4), 210–18. doi: 10.1016/j.tips.2004.02.005

Rhodes, E., Wilson, M., Robinson, A., Hayden, J. A., & Asbridge, M. (2019, November 1). The effectiveness of prescription drug monitoring programs at reducing opioid-related harms and consequences: A systematic review. *BMC Health Services Research, 19*(1), 784. doi: 10.1186/s12913-019-4642-8

Sahebi-Fakhrabad, A., Sadeghi, A. H., Kemahlioglu-Ziya, E., Handfield, R., Tohidi, H., & Vasheghani-Farahani, I. (2023, April 14). The impact of opioid prescribing limits on drug usage in South Carolina: A novel geospatial and time series data analysis. *Healthcare (Basel), 11*(8), 1132. doi: 10.3390/healthcare11081132

Schroeder, A. R., Dehghan, M., Newman, T. B., Bentley, J. P., & Park, K. T. (2019). Association of opioid prescriptions from dental clinicians for US adolescents and young adults with subsequent opioid use and abuse. *JAMA Internal Medicine, 179*(2), 145–52. doi:10.1001/jamainternmed.2018.5419

Spetz, J., Toretsky, C., Chapman, S., Phoenix, B., & Tierney, M. (2019, April 9). Nurse practitioner and physician assistant waivers to prescribe buprenorphine and state scope of practice restrictions. *JAMA, 321*(14), 1407–408. doi: 10.1001/jama.2019.0834

Stevens, A., & Hughes, C. E. (2010). What can we learn from the Portuguese decriminalization of illicit drugs? *British Journal of Criminology, 50*(6), 999–1022. https://kar.kent.ac.uk/29910/

Suda, K. J., Durkin, M. J., Calip, G. S., Gellad, W. F., Kim, H., Lockhart, P. B., . . . Thornhill, M. H. (2019). Comparison of opioid prescribing by dentists in the United States and England. *JAMA Network Open, 2*(5), e194303–e194303.

Thornhill, M. H., Suda, K. J., Durkin, M. J., & Lockhart, P. B. (2019). Is it time US dentistry ended its opioid dependence? *Journal of the American Dental Association, 150*(10), 883–89.

U.S. Department of Health and Human Services. (2019, May). *Pain management best practices inter-agency task force report: Updates, gaps, inconsistencies, and recommendations*. Retrieved September 19, 2024, from https://www.hhs.gov/ash/advisory-committees/pain/reports/index.html

Wood, E., Tyndall, M. W., Zhang, R., Stoltz, J. A., Lai, C., Montaner, J. S., & Kerr, T. (2006). Attendance at supervised injecting facilities and use of detoxification services. *New England Journal of Medicine, 354*(23), 2512–14. https://doi.org/10.1056/NEJMc052939

11

The War on Patients

Patients' Rights to Receive
Opioid Pain Medications

Eric S. See and Sarah A. See

The opioid epidemic is one of many battles waged as part of the larger war on drugs. The war officially began in 1971 when President Nixon declared drug abuse to be "public enemy number one." It continued into the 1980s with the "Just Say No" campaign of First Lady Nancy Reagan and forever entered the popular culture with the 1987 Partnership for a Drug-Free America ad: "This is your brain on drugs." While various drugs such as cocaine and heroin traded time in the spotlight from the 1970s through the mid-1990s, a different type of drug came to dominate the national conscience in the late 1990s. This drug was not produced in some faraway land and smuggled into the United States by cartels to be sold by street-level dealers. The new drug taking over the streets was manufactured right here at home by reputable pharmaceutical companies and sold through prescriptions after visits to a doctor or clinic. That drug was prescription opioids, which continues to be a significant problem today.

In the late 1990s and early 2000s, opioids in the form of prescription drugs such as OxyContin and other similar formulations flooded communities across the nation, resulting in economic devastation and the deaths of tens of thousands of individuals. This chapter will examine how such powerful medications became so widely available as well as the death and destruction they caused. Even though drastic action was needed 20 years ago to deal with this crisis, this chapter will also focus on the extreme overreaction to opioid medications from both the legal and medical communities and the devastating impact this overreaction has had on legitimate patients. Patients recovering from surgery are often denied opioid medications during recovery, and chronic pain patients have been forced off or denied access to opioid medications altogether. Due to a lack of understanding of the historical and factual events leading to the opioid crisis, the medical establishment has abandoned patients in pain, and the justice system has branded them as criminals or addicts. Finally, the chapter will examine how the opioid epidemic has shifted from prescription pills to the abuse of fentanyl, which is often foreign-made. Policy recommendations will be offered not only to protect patients in pain but also to allow them to be treated humanely and compassionately for their medical needs, while at the same time protecting the general public and those at risk for opioid abuse.

BRIEF HISTORY OF THE PROBLEM

How did we get here? How did we get to a point in this country where approximately 800,000 people have died from opioids since 1999 while patients in pain still suffer today? The beginning of the opioid crisis in this country is difficult to determine. While the approval of OxyContin in 1995 can be viewed as the beginning of the modern crisis, opioid abuse has a long history in the United States, dating back well over 100 years. Medical care during the Civil War was primitive at best, and treatment of the wounded often consisted of amputation. Soldiers were treated with morphine for the intense pain, and morphine addiction among soldiers was not uncommon (Little, 2021). This was perhaps the first recorded wave of opiate addiction in this country.

Morphine addiction brings up an important distinction that is often misunderstood: the difference between opiates and opioids. Morphine is an opiate. Opiates represent chemical compounds that occur naturally in the poppy plant. These compounds are extracted and refined and include opium, morphine, codeine, and heroin. Opioids, on the other hand, are synthetic. They do not come from a plant and are manufactured in a lab. There are hundreds of different manufactured opioids. Common varieties include hydrocodone (Vicodin), oxycodone (OxyContin and Percocet), and fentanyl. While it is important to understand the distinction, it needs to be pointed out that the chemical composition of opiates such as morphine and heroin, and opioids such as oxycodone is nearly identical. They all affect the brain in very similar ways (State of Oregon, n.d.)

Perhaps the greatest distinction between opiates and opioids is public perception. Although the chemical composition of heroin and oxycodone is nearly identical, one comes from a street-level drug dealer and the other comes from a medical doctor. There has always been a general belief that anything that comes from a doctor is good, and anything that comes with a stamp of approval from the Food and Drug Administration (FDA) must be safe and effective. While parents would never dream of giving their children heroin from a street dealer after surgery, pills from a doctor, following an auto accident or a sports injury, have seldom been questioned. Pills coming from a doctor with the approval of the FDA must be safe, right?

Though OxyContin was introduced in 1995, the idea for the pain medication began much earlier. In 1952, Arthur Sackler bought a small pharmaceutical company called Purdue Fredrick, which was renamed Purdue Pharma. Kept in the family and passed down to his children, Purdue Pharma continued growing, and through additional acquisitions, acquired Knapp Laboratories. In the 1970s, Knapp Laboratories produced a drug called MS Contin. Used in England, MS Contin was essentially a morphine pill, but the pill had a special coating the company called Contin. This coating allowed for the active ingredients of the medication to be time-released in the body. This time-release procedure allowed patients to receive cancer pain management and end-of-life pain management at home in the form of a pill as opposed to a morphine drip in a hospital. This advancement allowed patients to be treated for pain and to die at home as opposed to in a hospital setting (Keefe, 2021). In 1985, MS Contin received FDA approval for use in the United States.

With MS Contin, Purdue Pharma had a solid grip on the cancer pain and end-of-life care treatment market. While the pill was revolutionary in that it allowed patients to die with dignity at home, the hospice-care market was financially limited. What Purdue wanted was a bomb-shell drug that would secure the financial future of the company. It wanted a new pain pill that could be used regularly by millions of people for much more common ailments such as back pain, neck pain, and arthritis. Instead of reinventing the wheel, Purdue Pharma looked at medications already in existence that had FDA approval (Keefe, 2021). Oxycodone was first developed in Germany in 1916 and became available in the United States in 1936. Purdue Pharma took oxycodone, which was a well-known, effective, but highly addictive drug for treating pain, and added their time-release Contin coating to create Oxy-Contin. MS Contin had been used successfully for years with a very low incidence of abuse, and the company claimed that the time-release coating prevented the pill from being abused and made the user resistant to addiction. The active ingredients were released into the body slowly over 12 hours as opposed to all at once. This was designed to prevent the drug from creating an immediate and intense high and thus unlikely to cause addiction.

OxyContin was approved by the FDA in 1995. The approval process was completed in about a year, much quicker than the normal approval process. Representatives with Purdue worked hand in hand with the FDA, revising the label for OxyContin 30 times, subtly changing the wording before getting approval. With an FDA-approved label in hand, aggressive marketing by Purdue Pharma convinced doctors that not only was OxyContin safe, but that it was their ethical obligation as doctors to treat pain.

Three main factors made doctors feel comfortable in prescribing OxyContin to their patients, and all three factors were predicated on misinformation. First, as earlier, the label for OxyContin led doctors to believe that the medication was not addictive. The label read in part: "Delayed absorption, as provided by OxyContin tablets, is believed to reduce the abuse liability of a drug" (US Department of Justice, 2006). Doctors were told that the Contin coating, added to the medication, prevented the body from absorbing the medication all at once. As a result, the patient would not experience a high. There was no scientific evidence to support this statement. It must be noted that upon leaving the FDA, the official who approved the OxyContin label, Dr. Curtis Wright, took a high-paying job for Purdue Pharma (US Department of Justice, 2006).

Second, as part of the FDA approval process, in television commercials, and in educational information provided to doctors, Purdue referenced studies showing that "much less" than 1% of pain patients treated by doctors become addicted to pain medication. The problem is there were no such studies. The claim was based solely on a letter to the editor published in the *New England Journal of Medicine* in 1980 that discussed outcomes of patients treated for pain in a hospital setting and was only four sentences long. This letter did not support the claims made by Purdue (Porter & Jick, 1980).

Finally, pain, which had once been merely a symptom, became known as the fifth vital sign, joining heartbeat, breathing rate, temperature, and blood pressure as key factors that doctors had to assess and treat. Patients were asked to quantify their level of pain, and in some instances, patients who self-reported a high enough pain score were automatically prescribed opioids. This change was pushed by various "patients' rights" groups. While this may sound like a positive development, it was not. In fact, many of these patients' rights groups were funded by, and received false information from, Purdue Pharma (Clark & Rogers, 2019).

By 1996, OxyContin was readily available to patients, and it was an immediate success. It was popular with patients and a financial windfall for Purdue. The treatment of pain and the prescribing of pain medication in and of itself was not necessarily a bad thing. However, the way it was done, using false and misleading medical information, in conjunction with phony patients' rights organizations, set the stage for the opioid epidemic that was about to ravage the country and the continued mistreatment of pain patients today.

THE PERFECT STORM: DOSAGE, AVAILABILITY, AND THE LACK OF REGULATIONS

Even understanding the flawed and disingenuous ways in which OxyContin came to the marketplace does not explain the resulting impact the drug would have on society. To understand the impact, three factors must be explored: dosage, availability, and the lack of regulations.

Dosage

The standard dosage today for oxycodone is 5 milligrams every 6 to 8 hours. When OxyContin was first introduced, it was available in 10, 20, and 40 milligram doses. Soon after, Purdue Pharma introduced 60- and 80-milligram pills, and in 2000, it released a 160-milligram pill (Opioid Crisis, 2023). Why the dosage escalation? There are two primary reasons. First, there was a higher profit margin to be made with the higher dosage pills. Pricing was based on the milligram count of the pill. Second, there was a fundamental problem with the 12-hour time-release OxyContin formula: the medication did not always work as advertised. For many people pain relief did not last 12 hours, and they were in extreme pain before it was time for their next dose.

One simple solution to this 12-hour problem would have been to change the dosage schedule and take the medication more often. To Purdue, however, this would be an admission that OxyContin did not work as advertised. That was unacceptable. Purdue's explanation was that the patient was not on a high enough dose. Instead of shortening the interval, Purdue encouraged doctors to increase the dose, which of course, was the more profitable solution for Purdue. Increasing the dosage was also the solution for those patients who had developed a tolerance for the medication and needed more and more of it to obtain sufficient pain relief. Purdue encouraged its sales representatives to aggressively sell the highest dosage of OxyContin that was available.

Availability

How popular was OxyContin? "In 1996, in its first year on the market, OxyContin accounted for $45 million in sales for Purdue. By 2000, OxyContin generated $1.1 billion in sales. In 2010, profits from OxyContin rose to $3.1 billion" (OxyContin and the Opioid Epidemic, n.d.). This increase in sales demonstrates the frequency with which it was being prescribed for patients across the country. Revenue for OxyContin, since its introduction, has exceeded roughly 35 billion dollars (Gross, 2021). Keep in mind, these figures only represent sales of OxyContin and do not account for the dozens of competitor medications that were also available.

Lack of Regulations

The Sackler family and Purdue Pharma are often made out to be the key villains in the opioid epidemic. Time and time again, they put profits in front of human lives, and they were well aware of the devastation their product caused. The negative reputation the family and company earned is accurate and well deserved. They were, however, not alone in their promotion and pushing opioids in the pursuit of profit. While sales of OxyContin grew at exponential rates, a new kind of business emerged, most notably in Florida, that would push the opioid crisis to a whole new level. By the early 2000s, pain clinics took the once covert, back-alley business of drug dealing to strip malls across the state. These clinics would operate in full view of an unsuspecting and ill-prepared community, including law enforcement agencies at both the state and federal levels.

AMERICAN PAIN

While this chapter will discuss the pain clinics that operated in Florida generally, and American Pain specifically, it must be noted that similar operations existed across the country. Pain clinics were not limited to Florida. Unscrupulous businesspeople, doctors, clinics, and pharmacies participated, and billions of pills were shipped nationwide.

Beginning in 2008, the George brothers began operating a series of pain clinics in Florida that would eventually become known as American Pain. Although they were not doctors, they hired doctors with various specialties to practice as pain special- ists. All that was required was the ability to prescribe opioid medications. Doctors were paid on a per-patient basis, and the clinics they operated would see hundreds of patients a day (American Pain, 2023). The goal of the clinics was not treating patients, but rather the sale of pain medication.

New patients to the clinic would typically receive 180 oxycodone pills that were 30 milligrams each. This was a one-month supply. Returning customers would receive a prescription for 240 pills that were also 30 milligrams (American Pain, 2023). This amount greatly exceeds the 60 to 120, 5-milligram pills often prescribed today as a one-month supply for chronic pain patients. Put another way, patients would be prescribed 8 pills containing 240 milligrams of oxycodone per day, as opposed to 4 pills containing 20 milligrams per day. In addition, prescriptions were filled for cash on-site. Patients paid $3 per pill and could resell them for approximately $20 per pill on the street. Because there was no central database tracking these prescriptions, patients could go from clinic to clinic, receiving and filling opioid prescriptions. This led to the creation of a new type of tourism in which out-of-state patients routinely traveled to Florida to obtain pain medications. In fact, at one point, approximately 80% of American Pain clients were out-of-state residents. It was not uncommon for vans or buses full of "patients" from other states to visit multiple clinics in a day, resulting in hundreds to thousands of pills per patient. The clinics operated by the George brothers were clinics in name only. They were pill mills designed for the pro- viders to see as many patients as possible and write as many prescriptions as possible, with only cursory, if any, medical examinations (American Pain, 2023).

While the George brothers were perhaps the most well-known of the Florida pill mill operators, they were hardly alone. The exact number of these clinics operating in Florida may be unknown, but the first year they were required by law to register in 2009–2010, there were 921 (National Institute of Justice, 2018). Just how bad was the problem?

> By the clinics' peak in 2010, 90 of the nation's top 100 opioid prescribers were Florida doctors, according to federal officials, and 85 percent of the nation's oxycodone was prescribed in the state. That year alone, about 500 million pills were sold in Florida. The number of people who died in Florida with oxycodone or another prescription opioid in their system hit 4,282 in 2010, a four-fold increase from 2000, with 2,710 of the deaths deemed overdoses, according to a state medical examiners' report. (Spencer, 2019)

By 2010–2011, opioid prescriptions topped 251 million nationwide (Fink et al., 2020). It was also during this period that the country finally began to scale back on the approval and use of prescription opioid medications. While it was a slow process, doctors became more vigilant and reluctant to prescribe these medications, states began to regulate pain clinics, and the federal government began to become more actively involved in regulating pain medications. These changes were neces- sary and long overdue. Lives were lost and destroyed by the reckless and greedy actions of pharmaceutical companies, pharmacies, pain clinics, doctors, business-men, and those looking to make a profit peddling pills. However, in our efforts to roll back the abuses of the past, did we go too far? Has the pendulum swung too far in the other direction? Are patients now suffering because access has been too severely limited to the pain medications that caused all these problems in the first place?

What began as a necessary course correction reining in the reckless and danger-ous proliferation of opioid medications has become a near-shadow ban of an entire class of medications that provide necessary relief to patients. As a result, millions of patients in pain are untreated or undertreated. While patients in pain can be divided into several subgroups, two primary groups of pain will be discussed here.

UNDERSTANDING PAIN

Pain is one of the most common reasons given as to why patients seek care in the emergency room each year (Weiss & Jiang, 2021). By its very nature, pain can be subjective and difficult to define and quantify. Still, two general types of pain can be identified and discussed: acute and chronic. Acute pain generally is short-term last-ing from a few moments to a few days but can extend to several weeks and generally has an identifiable cause such as an accident, surgical or dental procedure, childbirth, broken bone, or cuts and sprains. Regardless of the severity, the key here is that the pain is normally temporary.

Chronic pain, on the other hand, generally lasts for three months or more. Some examples of chronic pain include back pain, nerve pain, arthritis, sciatica, fibromyal-gia, headaches, osteoporosis, and cancer. In some cases, the exact cause of the chronic pain may never be determined. Some patients will suffer from chronic pain for years if not decades, as no permanent cure exists for many types of chronic pain. While no cure may exist, chronic pain can be treated or at least partially relieved. Approxi-mately 30% of Americans suffer from some form of chronic pain, and that number jumps to over 40% when looking at older Americans (Johannes et al., 2010). There is no reason to expect these numbers to decrease as the population ages.

The country's reaction to opioids and patients in any kind of pain can best be compared to a bus driving down the highway recklessly at a high rate of speed. The massive overprescribing of the medication is the bus swerving wildly off the left side of the road into the ditch. The ditch on the left side of the road is filled with greedy corporations and doctors, pill mills, addiction, overdose, broken families, and death. This was America circa 2014.

Instead of making simple adjustments to the wheel and centering the vehicle, the driver dramatically overcorrected yanking the wheel to the right. The resulting over-correction sent the bus into the other ditch. This ditch is filled with untreated cancer patients, chronic pain patients, surgical patients, and others with untreated pain so severe that sometimes suicide is their only recourse to end the pain they experience. It also includes those patients who have been on long-term opioid therapy and suddenly find themselves cut off from their medications with no medical oversight. This is America circa 2024.

Who are the occupants of this runaway vehicle? The bus is driven by the FDA. Passengers include the Centers for Disease Control and Prevention (CDC), the Drug Enforcement Administration (DEA), pharmaceutical distributors, and the attorneys general of 46 states. While the bus is indeed crowded, sadly the seats reserved for doctors and patient advocates have been left empty. None of this had to happen. There is no dispute that the actions or inactions of the FDA were critical in creating the opioid crisis. The FDA failed numerous times not only in the initial approval process but also in the ongoing oversight role in the proper uses and dosages of OxyContin. This was the massive swerving of the wheel to the left. The yanking of the wheel to the right has been led by the actions of the CDC.

By 2012, opioid prescriptions totaled 259 million. Between 1999 and 2014, over 165,000 Americans lost their lives to the opioid crisis (Dowell et al., 2016). Despite these staggering numbers, according to their 2016 report, 20% of noncancer patients reporting pain in a doctor's office were still being prescribed an opioid. Recall that MS Contin was initially used for cancer and end-of-life pain. Clearly action needed to be taken. Doctors desperately needed guidance.

In 2016, the CDC released 12 guidelines for prescribing opioids for chronic pain (Dowell et al., 2016). While the CDC has consistently claimed that the guidelines were intended to only be recommendations, many doctors have treated them as law, fearing that prescribing opioids would result in investigations and prosecutions (Knopf, 2018). Regardless of intent, the impact of these guidelines has meant that millions of legitimate pain patients across the country have been denied access to pain medications, or their access to pain medications has been sharply limited or ended, often with no medical supervision. The CDC further acknowledged that physicians across specialties were stressed, confused, and seeking guidance. It can be agreed, however, that guidance provided to doctors in the prescribing of medications to their patients should be guided and informed by science. The CDC claimed to do this.

> This CDC guideline offers clarity on recommendations based on the most recent scientific evidence, informed by expert opinion and stakeholder and public input. Scientific research has identified high-risk prescribing practices that have contributed to the overdose epidemic (e.g., high-dose prescribing, overlapping opioid and benzo-diazepine prescriptions, and extended-release/long-acting [ER/LA] opioids for acute pain) (*24,33,34*). Using guidelines to address problematic prescribing has the potential to optimize care and improve patient safety based on evidence-based practice (*28*), as well as reverse the cycle of opioid pain medication misuse that contributes to the opioid overdose epidemic. (Dowell et al., 2016)

While the intentions of the CDC may well have been to advise doctors based on the most recent and best scientific evidence, they failed spectacularly at that task. How can such a bold statement be made? The CDC report states it. Before ever stating its 12 recommendations, however, the CDC went through a three-step process, and each step must be explained. First, they created a hierarchy of four types of evidence that reflected the confidence the CDC would have in their own recommendations. Second, the CDC asked five clinical questions pertaining to opioids. Finally, they then made three general assessments about the prescribing of opioids. All of this was done to ensure that the resulting 12 recommendations would be scientifically sound and accurate.

Step One, the scoring of different types of evidence:

The following four types of scores were created by the CDC:

Type 1. Randomized clinical trial, or overwhelming evidence from observational studies. Very Confident in the result.

Type 2. Randomized clinical trials with important limitations or exceptionally strong observational studies. Likely Confident, but actual results may be substantially different.

Type 3. Observational or randomized clinical trials with notable limitations. Confidence is limited, and actual results may be substantially different.

Type 4. Clinical experience, observations, observational studies with important limitations, or randomized clinical trials with several major limitations. Very Little Confidence, and the actual result is likely to be substantially different. (Dowell et al., 2016)

The CDC created a scale of 1 to 4 that ranges from studies and observations with overwhelming evidence and a very high degree of confidence in the result represented by a 1, and studies and observations with major limitations and likely to be wrong as represented by a 4. The CDC then goes on to ask five clinical questions pertaining to opioids.

Step Two, the creation of five clinical questions:

The CDC devised five clinical questions that deal with the following:

- The effectiveness of long-term opioid therapy versus placebo, no opioid therapy, or nonopioid therapy for long-term (≥1 year) outcomes related to pain, function, and quality of life, and how effectiveness varies according to the type/cause of pain, patient demographics, and patient comorbidities (Key Question [KQ] 1).
- The risks of opioids versus placebo or no opioids on abuse, addiction, overdose, and other harms, and how harms vary according to the type/cause of pain, patient demographics, patient comorbidities, and dose (KQ2).
- The comparative effectiveness of opioid dosing strategies (different methods for initiating and titrating opioids; immediate-release versus ER/LA opioids; different ER/LA opioids; immediate-release plus ER/LA opioids versus ER/LA

opioids alone; scheduled, continuous versus as-needed dosing; dose escalation versus dose maintenance; opioid rotation versus maintenance; different strategies for treating acute exacerbations of chronic pain; decreasing opioid doses or tapering off versus continuation; and different tapering protocols and strategies) (KQ3).

- The accuracy of instruments for predicting risk for opioid overdose, addiction, abuse, or misuse; the effectiveness of risk mitigation strategies (use of risk prediction instruments); effectiveness of risk mitigation strategies including opioid management plans, patient education, urine drug testing, prescription drug monitoring program (PDMP) data, monitoring instruments, monitoring intervals, pill counts, and abuse-deterrent formulations for reducing risk for opioid overdose, addiction, abuse, or misuse; and the comparative effectiveness of treatment strategies for managing patients with addiction (KQ4).
- The effects of prescribing opioid therapy versus not prescribing opioid therapy for acute pain on long-term use (KQ5). (Dowell et al., 2016)

At this point, the CDC can now answer the five questions they asked, based upon the 4-point scale they created. How many of these questions were answered with the CDC's highest level of confidence as indicated with a type 1 label? *None.* Question one had zero evidence to examine and could not be scored like the other questions. Questions two, four, and five were labeled with a 3. Question three received a 4. The CDC examined zero studies looking at the long-term use of opioids (question one) and acknowledges that the answers it provides to every other question *may be* or *is likely to be* substantially different from the answers they provide. The CDC has little to no scientific evidence to back up *any* of the answers it provides to the very questions they felt were important to ask. It is this house of cards, utterly lacking in scientific evidence and foundation, predicated on unsupported assessments and clinical questions lacking scientific credibility, that the CDC then goes on to make three general assessments about the prescribing of opioids.

Step Three, three general assessments:

- No evidence shows a long-term benefit of opioids in pain and function versus no opioids for chronic pain with outcomes examined at least one year later (with most placebo-controlled randomized trials ≤6 weeks in duration).
- Extensive evidence shows the possible harms of opioids (including opioid use disorder, overdose, and motor vehicle injury).
- Extensive evidence suggests some benefits of nonpharmacologic and nonopioid pharmacologic treatments compared with long-term opioid therapy, with less harm. (Dowell et al., 2016)

Looking at the first assessment, the CDC acknowledged in their report that most of the studies they reviewed only lasted six weeks. The most important statement that they made is that opioids were not effective for long-term use. This statement was critical because doctors needed valid findings and recommendations to guide them in their practice and aid them in making safe and effective prescribing decisions. The CDC had absolutely no evidence to back that first assessment up. Assessments two and three were never in question. There have always been potential harms associated with opioids, and other medications that are non-opioid have important and beneficial uses as well. Doctors need to be able to weigh the benefits and risks of opioids, as well as other non-opioid options. Taken as a whole, all three of the assessments that form the backbone of the 12 recommendations made by the CDC had little to no scientific or practical value, nor provided any new information.

After failing to adequately address their own clinical research questions and after making faulty and questionable general assessments, the CDC finally made its 12 recommendations for doctors to consider when prescribing opioids. The 12 recommendations fall under the three categories: (1) determining when to initiate or continue opioids for chronic pain, (2) selecting opioids, dosage, duration, follow-up, and discontinuation, (3) assessing risk and addressing harms of opioid use.

These recommendations were also scored using the same 4-point scale discussed earlier. Disturbingly, not a single recommendation received a type 1 score. This means that not one of the 12 recommendations across the three categories was written based on overwhelming evidence nor with a strong degree of confidence. Only recommendation 12, which says doctors should offer or arrange treatment for those who have an opioid use disorder, received a type 2 score, which means strong to moderate confidence. All other recommendations dealing with issues such as opioid effectiveness, goals for chronic pain patients, types of opioids to use, dosage, time frames for evaluating risk and harm, patient history of drug abuse, urine testing, and prescribing in conjunction with benzodiazepines receive type 3 or 4 scores, with type 4 being the most common (Dowell et al., 2016). To sum up, the most common score given by the CDC for a CDC recommendation was a type 4 score indicating that the result had very little confidence, and that the actual result was likely to vary significantly from what the CDC said would occur (Dowell et al., 2016). Simply put, none of the medical advice the CDC urged doctors to follow came with a high degree of confidence.

After stating that they would offer results backed by the best available science, best practices, and best experts, how does the CDC defend against the charge that their recommendations are not backed by science and cannot be supported? They don't. From the report:

> Although there was widespread agreement on some of the recommendations, there was disagreement on others. Experts did not vote on the recommendations or seek to come to a consensus. Decisions about recommendations to be included in the guideline, and their rationale, were made by CDC. After revising the guideline, CDC sent written copies of it to each of the experts for review and asked for any additional comments; CDC reviewed these written comments and considered them when making further revisions to the draft guideline. The experts have not reviewed the final version of the guideline. (Dowell et al., 2016)

Since then, the situation has only gotten worse for patients in pain. The veering path the bus was traveling on has never been corrected. Bad science has been followed up with bad policies and more bad science. In 2022, the National Opioid Settlement was reached between three of the major opioid distributors and the attorneys general of 46 states. The purpose of this settlement was to fix the abuses of the past while providing financial restitution to the victims of the crisis. While the states and the attorneys have been paid, it is difficult to see a positive impact on individuals. According to the terms of the settlement, "85% of funds [were to] be allocated to programs that will help address the ongoing opioid crisis through treatment, education, and prevention efforts" (National Prescription Opiate Litigation Plaintiffs' Executive Committee, 2022). As is typical in these types of settlements, individual victims and families saw little to no financial settlement.

One of the results of the settlement has been the development of strict limitations on the number of pills shipped to individual pharmacies. These limits have led to many pharmacies running out of pills before the end of the month. How many pills is any particular pharmacy entitled to dispense each month? No one knows. It's a secret. Individual pharmacies are not allowed to know the limits set by the distributors. They are not allowed to ask for additional pills. Pharmacists are afraid of breaking new rules they do not fully understand and being cut off from medication supplies completely. As a result, they are more reluctant than ever to fill legitimate prescriptions (Jewett & Gabler, 2023). This is just part of a series of bad policy decisions that have led to medication shortages and frustrated patients across the country being denied access to necessary medications.

Additionally, in 2022, the CDC released yet another set of guidelines relating to the prescribing of opioids for pain. The report acknowledges the reduction of opioid prescriptions following the 2016 report, along with an increase in the use of non-opioid medications. The 2022 report also acknowledges the negative impacts of the 2016 report, such as a decline in the use of opioids for cancer patients, rapid tapering or discontinuation of medications, insurance denial, as well as patient dismissal and abandonment. The CDC goes on to say that

> These actions are not consistent with the 2016 CDC Opioid Prescribing Guideline and have contributed to patient harm, including untreated and undertreated pain, serious withdrawal symptoms, worsening pain outcomes, psychological distress, overdose, and suicidal ideation and behavior (*66–71*). (Dowell et al., 2022)

These denials of responsibility fall on deaf ears for many patients who have begged for access to medications for years, only to be turned away time and time again. The fact that many patients have turned to suicide as their only pain solution is a testament to the complete breakdown of the government's response to the crisis. It is also clear that major pharmacies changed their practices to match what they determined to be requirements from the CDC (CVS Caremark Opioid Quantity Limits Pharmacy Reference Guide, 2018). The CDC knew for years that their guidelines were being interpreted and acted on in ways that they claim are inconsistent with their original intention. Despite these claims, the agency took no action in the face of policies like the one implemented by CVS in 2018. It took six full years for the CDC to release new guidelines in 2022.

Perhaps the CDC learned from the failures of the 2016 report. Perhaps the 2022 report would make science the key building block of their new recommendations. Sadly, that did not occur. The CDC specifically says that a part of the scope and audience for the 2022 report is clinicians treating chronic pain lasting three months or more. How many studies did the 2022 CDC report examine that looked at intermediate and long-term use of opioids (a year or more)? Again, the answer is *zero*. All the flaws that existed in the 2016 report were replicated in the 2022 report. This marks the second report in a six-year timespan that the CDC made recommendations against the long-term use of opioids, without looking at a single study that examined the long-term use of opioids. It is clear that doctors and patients looking for answers as to the long-term effectiveness of opioids are not going to find results by looking to the CDC for guidance.

However, the CDC is not the only government agency harming patients with arbitrary rules and policies. The DEA is along for the ride as well. It was previously noted that many patients struggle to fill prescriptions at local pharmacies. While the National Opioid Settlement is partly to blame, so is the DEA. Since 2015, the DEA has lowered the manufacturing quotas for most opioids by nearly 66% (Anson, 2023). Despite these massive cuts, the pleas from thousands of patients, and the concerns of doctors, the DEA is set to further reduce these quotas even more in 2024.

These cuts in medication production are cruel. The accompanying policies are even crueler. A pharmacy may not have enough pills to be able to fill an entire prescription. Let's say a patient has a prescription for a one-month supply of 90 pain pills. When they go to fill or refill this prescription, they are told that the pharmacy only has 20 pills, and they are unsure if they can get more. If the patient elects to take the 20 pills available, the remaining portion of the prescription is voided, and they are unable to get the remaining 70 pills even if they later become available. If they don't take the 20 pills, they may very well get nothing.

In most cases, the pharmacy is unable to tell the patient when or if they will get more pills. This is due to the terms of the settlement that keep the total number of pills a pharmacy may distribute a secret as well as the national shortage of pain medications due to the lowered manufacturing quotas. Adding to the struggle, patients with a refillable prescription must call or visit the pharmacy each month and request their pain medications. The pharmacy is unable to refill valid pain prescriptions each month like they do for millions of other patients and non-narcotic prescriptions. Safeguards to minimize pill diversion are already in place. A photo ID is always required to pick up an opioid prescription. Forbidding a pharmacist to refill a reoccurring prescription for pain medication is simply one more hurdle put in the path of patients seeking treatment and relief.

With all these cuts in the production and access to prescription opioid medications, the death rate from opioids has plummeted, correct? No. Despite cutting the legitimate access to opioid medications year after year, deaths attributed to opioids have only risen. As described by the CDC, opioid deaths can be understood in three waves. Wave one deaths were the result of prescription pills, and it lasted from about 1993 to 2010. Once the regulation of prescription medications began around 2010, so did wave two of the crisis. Wave two saw a rapid increase in deaths due to heroin and lasted from 2010 to 2013. Wave three began in 2013 and continues to the present day. Wave three deaths are attributed primarily to illegal synthetic fentanyl (CDC, 2024). Wave two problems with heroin still accounted for 9,000 deaths in 2021. While approximately 17,000 people died from an overdose involving prescription opioids in 2021, approximately 71,000 died from an overdose involving synthetic fentanyl (CDC, 2024). Because we are unable to achieve sufficient progress with heroin and fentanyl deaths, patients in pain remain a prime target for regulations, restrictions, and criminalization. Chronic pain patients provide a convenient target for legislatures and government agencies who are more interested in making headlines than making a difference in opioid-related matters.

CONCLUSION AND RECOMMENDATIONS

It is clear that the unregulated prescribing and dispensing of opioid pain medications was a major mistake that cost tens of thousands of Americans their lives. It was a tragedy of epic proportions. Sadly, we have not learned from our mistakes and gained control of the opioid epidemic. Instead of understanding and relying on science, passing meaningful laws, and developing appropriate policy, we have instead chosen to promote junk science, promote policies that further victimize those already in pain, and create laws that are shrouded in secrecy and impossible to understand. We need a commonsense approach to our nation's opioid policies. The following are recommendations as to how we can create policies that are both compassionate and save lives:

- Recognize that it is no longer 2010. The biggest opioid concern is no longer prescription pills but rather synthetic fentanyl.
- Conduct actual long-term studies of those using opioids for chronic pain for a year or longer. Given the number of adults in chronic pain, this can be accomplished.
- Conduct long-term survey research of both chronic pain patients, and those who prescribe them the medications.
- Leave decisions on the number of pills to be manufactured to experts in the medical field and not career bureaucrats in the FDA and DEA.
- Remove arbitrary limits on the number of pills shipped to pharmacies.
- Allow patients to fill a partial prescription and then the remainder of the prescription if supplies become available as well as allow for the refill of prescriptions monthly for long-term chronic pain patients.
- Better educate physicians and patients on the signs and treatment of chronic pain.
- Continue to invest in opioid education and treatment programs.

- Remove the stigma often found in the medical community surrounding patients who need opioid medications.

Patients in pain have a right to be treated with opioid medications. This includes patients with chronic pain. No patient should be forced to contemplate suicide due to untreated pain. There is no reason that the bureaucrats driving the bus navigating our national policy must continue to crash over and over again. We can course correct as a nation and treat those in pain, while protecting the public from pill mills and the excess of the past. We can demand that our government agencies use science and common sense when crafting future policies, which are the two components they have repeatedly avoided when making policies thus far. We can focus on the current problem of synthetic fentanyl and still treat those in chronic pain. To fail to learn from the mistakes of the past would mean that all of the lives lost in the late 1990s and early 2000s were lost in vain. That is an outcome that is unacceptable and would cause a type of pain so unimaginable that no pain medication yet known to man could treat.

REFERENCES

American Pain. (2023, February 5). CNN.

Anson, P. (2023). *DEA finalizes more cuts in RX opioid supply in 2024.* https://www.painnewsnetwork.org/stories/2023/12/29/dea-orders-more-cuts-in-rx-opioid-supply-in-2024

Center for Disease Control. (2024). *Understanding the opioid overdose epidemic.* https://www.cdc.gov/overdose-prevention/about/understanding-the-opioid-overdose-epidemic.html?CDC_AAref_Val=https://www.cdc.gov/opioids/basics/epidemic.html

Clark, K., & Rogers, H. (2019, May 22). *Corrupting influence Purdue and the WHO.* https://katherineclark.house.gov/2019/5/clark-rogers-release-report-exposing-purdue-pharma-s-corrupting-influence-at-the-world-health-organization

CVS Caremark Opioid Quantity Limits Pharmacy Reference Guide. (2018). Retrieved April 5, 2024, https://www.caremark.com/portal/asset/Opioid_Reference_Guide.pdf

Dowell, D., Haegerich, T. M., & Chou, R. (2016). CDC guideline for prescribing opioids for chronic pain—United States, 2016. *Morbidity and Mortality Weekly Report, 65*(RR-1), 1–49. doi: http://dx.doi.org/10.15585/mmwr.rr6501e1

Dowell, D., Ragan, K. R., Jones, C. M., Baldwin, G. T., & Chou, R. (2022). CDC clinical practice guideline for prescribing opioids for pain—United States, 2022. Retrieved April 28, 2024. *Morbidity and Mortality Weekly Report, 71*(RR-3), 1–95. doi: http://dx.doi.org/10.15585/mmwr.rr7103a1

Fink, B. C., Uyttebrouck, O., & Larson, R. S. (2020, June). An effective intervention: Limiting opioid prescribing as a means of reducing opioid analgesic misuse, and overdose deaths. *Journal of Law, Medicine & Ethics, 48*(2), 249–58. doi: 10.1177/1073110520935336

Gross, T. (2021). *Journalist investigates "crime story" of the Sackler family and the opioid crisis.* https://www.npr.org/2021/04/14/986736258/journalist-investigates-crime-story-of-the-sackler-family-and-the-opioid-crisis

Jewett, C., & Gabler, E. (2023). Opioid settlement hinders patients access to a wide array of drugs. *New York Times.* https://www.nytimes.com/2023/03/13/us/drug-limits-adhd-depression.html

Johannes, C. B., Le, T. K., Zhou, X., Johnston, J. A., & Dworkin, R. H. (2010, November). The prevalence of chronic pain in United States adults: Results of an internet-based survey. *Journal of Pain, 11*(11), 1230–39. doi: 10.1016/j.jpain.2010.07.002

Keefe, P. R. (2021). *Empire of pain: The secret history of the Sackler dynasty.* Doubleday.

Knopf, T. (2018, October 15). *Hundreds of N.C. doctors say they've stopped prescribing opioids.* NC Health News. Retrieved March 6, 2024, https://www.northcarolinahealthnews.org/2018/10/15/nc-doctors-stop-prescribe-opioids/#:~:text=During%20the%20reporting%20of%20this,result%20of%20the%20opioid%20crisis

Little, B. (2021). *How Civil War medicine led to America's first opioid crisis.* History. Retrieved March 6, 2024, https://www.history.com/news/civil-war-medicine-opioid-addiction

National Institute of Justice. (2018). *Florida legislation helps reduce the number of "pill mills."* Retrieved March 6, 2024, https://nij.ojp.gov/topics/articles/florida-legislation-helps-reduce-number-pill-mills#:~:text=The%20E2%80%9Cpill%20mill%20law%2C%E2%80%9D,the%20number%20of%20pill%20mills

National Prescription Opiate Litigation Plaintiffs' Executive Committee. (2022). Press Release February 25, 2022. *Thousands of U.S. communities to receive opioid recovery funds from $26 billion global settlements as soon as May 2022.* nationalopioidsettlement.com

Opioid Crisis. (2023, April 30). *Ten steps to disaster.* Smithsonian Channel.

OxyContin and the Opioid Epidemic. (n.d.). *OxyContin and the opioid epidemic—ethics unwrapped.* Retrieved April 4, 2024, https://ethicsunwrapped.utexas.edu/video/oxycontin-the-opioid-epidemic

Porter, J., & Jick, H. (1980, January 10). *Addiction rare in patients treated with narcotics.* Letter to the Editor. *New England Journal of Medicine.* https://www.nejm.org/doi/10.1056/NEJM198001103020221

Spencer, T. (2019). *Florida "pill mills" were the "gas on the fire" of opioid crisis.* AP News.

State of Oregon. (n.d.). *Opiates or opioids—what's the difference?* Alcohol and Drug Policy Commission, State of Oregon.

U.S. Department of Justice. (2006). https://www.mass.gov/doc/ogrosky-memo/download

Weiss, A., & Jiang, H. (2021). *Most frequent reasons for emergency department visits.* 2018 Statistical Brief #286, December. https://hcup-us.ahrq.gov/reports/statbriefs/sb286-ED-Frequent-Conditions-2018.pdf

12

Opioids and Athletes

Hugh Harling

Drug use for enhancing performance in athletic competitions is as old as competitions. While overall drug use is still lower in athletes, the use of specific drugs to alleviate pain and stress is higher. According to one study by Zandonai et al. (2021) analgesic use by athletes is common. Student-athletes are four times more likely than age-matched individuals to use opioids to relieve pain. Another well-known drug class, opioids, has become an issue for athletes. Opioids are primarily prescribed for pain management, and the International Association of the Study of Pain updated its definition of pain to "An aversive sensory and emotional experience typically caused by, or resembling that caused by, actual or potential tissue injury" (Vandertuin, 2021, p. 5). With this definition, it expands that pain is not solely a biological event but a multifactorial event, with biologic, psychological, sociological, and situation-dependent variables (Vandertuin, 2021, p. 5). The National Collegiate Athletics Association (NCAA) put forth its first discussion of pain and sport in 2017 when its first physician authored a paper "Pain in elite athletes-neurophysiological, biomechanical and psychosocial considerations: A narrative review" (Hainline et al., 2017). Combined with a mindset that often values winning over an individual's health, athletes often make choices that can set them up for a hard road of addiction and risky choices. This chapter will explore the sport ethic mentality; the athletic culture will be brought into focus in response to a hypothetical dilemma. The dilemma leads us to research and studies that best describe the use of performance-enhancing substances and opioids in athletes and how organizations have blurred the lines between ethical drug use versus doping through antidoping policies. Additionally, the chapter will explore how injury, stress, and pressure to perform can lead athletes to use opioids and other drugs. Finally, the chapter will explore the unique issues of how one manages the physical pain associated with certain athletic events and post-athletic career issues with drugs many athletes experience.

Hughes and Coakley (1991) composed a set of values and norms to explain athlete behavior that they termed "sport ethic." The values and norms are considered a part of deviant behavior modeling rather than negative connotations of deviant behavior. The sport ethic casts a positive deviance focused on overcompliance and "too committed to the goals and norms of sport" (Hughes & Coakley, 1991, p. 308). As financial gains and fame have risen, the desire of individuals to participate in sports to excel has become rewarded with greater fame and glory. Sports, like education, are seen as a way to fulfill the American dream and lift, through meritocracy, individuals to the top of society through their hard work (Hughes & Coakley, 1991).

Individuals excelling as athletes are noticed and rewarded in society with special status and often privileges. As Vandertuin (2021) noted, "Athletes have frequently engaged in pain-relieving medication (PRM) to continue to play/practice which is often an accepted practice by those directly involved with athletes. In this culture of sport, athletes are often praised for their strength in being able to play after injury; however, athletes will often rely on medications to quash their pain to allow them to continue to play" (p. 4). Hughes and Coakley (1991) identified four common beliefs in what one must commit to identify as an athlete and have a "sport ethic." The first belief is if one is to identify as an athlete, this requires that "being an athlete involves making sacrifices for the game" (p. 309). This implies that the individual must "prove they care about their sport, participants must have 'the proper attitude,' make a commitment, meet the demands of fellow athletes, and sacrifice to stay involved" (p. 309). Additionally, the "athlete" will "consistently do what is necessary to meet the demands of a team or the demands of competition" (p. 309). The second belief is that the individual must strive for distinction. Hughes and Coakley (1991) described the impact of striving for distinction by stating, "Winning symbolizes improvement and establishes distinction; losing is tolerated only to the extent that it is part of the experience of learning how to win" (p. 309). The third belief is that to be called an athlete "involves the acceptance of risks and playing through pain" (p. 309). Despite pain being a multifaceted response by the body and brain to overload of its systems, Hughes and Coakley (1991), describe that "an athlete does not give in to pressure, pain, or fear. . . . The idea is that athletes never back down from challenges in the form of either physical risk or pressure, and that standing up to challenges involves moral courage" (p. 309). The fourth and final belief is that "being an athlete involves refusing to accept limits in pursuit of possibilities" (Hughes & Coakley, 1991, p. 310). The commitment to being an athlete where anything is possible, or any team can beat another team on any given day, allows the individual to continue their sport ethic even when the goals are no longer possible. The journey is used to gain status and reward by athletes. Athletes are being told to make sacrifices, pay the price, and play with the pain, by their parents, coaches, commentators, and the media. This is all done in pursuit of what is perceived to be dedication to the game, to exalt the virtues of what it takes to become real athletes, and to achieve all that can come with it (Hughes & Coakley, 1991).

Pedersen et al. (2022) describe the current pain management practices among youth athletes as primarily using nonsteroidal anti-inflammatory drugs (NSAIDs) which are notably the most frequently used in sport medicine. Pedersen et al. (2022)

found that "individual studies indicate that youth athletes regularly use analgesics" (p. 811) but not without the potential for complications particularly with long-term use. Across several studies, the authors found between 7% and 50% of athletes reported weekly use of analgesics and between 6% and 35% monthly use with a vast majority of athletes self-medicating, or obtaining through a parent, over-the-counter analgesics. Pedersen et al. (2022) found adverse events occurred in "3.3%–19.2% and included gastrointestinal symptoms, tiredness, lightheadedness, decreased perceived power, increased appetite, dry mouth, exacerbation of asthma symptoms, nausea, vomiting, headache, fatigue, allergy, non-immunomodulated adverse reactions, bronchospasms and anaphylaxis" (p. 814). The reasons given for using analgesics were to treat sport-related pain or injury, manage general muscle soreness or cramps, to improve performance, and treat illnesses such as headaches, fever, and colds. Additionally, athletes reported using NSAIDs and analgesics to prevent or block pain to enable participation in sport despite this being against guidelines for these medications' use. Pedersen et al. (2022) further describe, "As athletes from an early age may be introduced and socialized into the sport ethic culture of playing through pain, this finding may partly be explained by mediated cultural influences in sports communities including pain normalization, risk glorification, and external pressures, leading athletes to engage in risky behavior by ignoring and covering signs of fatigue, pain and injury" (p. 817).

Ford et al. (2018) describe past research investigating sport participation "among high school and college students shows that students involved in sports are less likely to be involved in delinquent/criminal behavior, have lower levels of marijuana and other illicit drug use, have better physical and mental health and better academic outcomes" (p. 15). However, Ford et al. (2018) found that "some research has found sports involvement to be a risk factor for certain types of risky or deviant behaviors. For example . . . high school and college students involved in athletics are at increased risk for alcohol use and binge drinking" (p. 15). In the mid-2000s, Ford et al. (2018) researchers found that "alcohol use is more prevalent among males that play hockey and females that play soccer, among athletes who play contact sports, and that team leaders have higher rates compared to other team members" (p. 15). Vandertuin (2021) noted that "Research has demonstrated that athletes frequently begin use of PRM (*Pain-Relieving Medications*) including opioids in adolescence, believing that their actions have few consequences other than allowing them to continue to play" (p. 5). Ford et al. (2018) found that at the college level "athletes, injured athletes, male athletes, and injured male athletes were at the greatest risk of NUPO (*Non-medical use of prescription opioids*) . . . 17.9% of injured male athletes indicated NUPO, this is more than two times higher than the average rate found within the college population used for the study" (pp. 19–20). Charest et al. (2021) shared their results that showed the difference "between collegiate and non-collegiate athletes may reflect differences in intentions to improve performance (e.g., steroids, stimulants), and pain management (e.g., opioids), stress management" (p. e450). Ekhtiari et al. (2020) performed a systematic review of opioid use in athletes in 2020 that concluded "Overall, opioid use is prevalent among athletes, and use during a playing career predicts post-retirement use. This issue exists even at the high school level, with similar rates to professional athletes" (p. 534).

The subset of athletes who may be prone to performance-enhancement drugs or opioids was conceptually, at least partially, described by the "Goldman dilemma" and encompasses the sport ethic. Goldman and colleagues authored *Death in the Locker Room* (Goldman et al., 1984) to argue that steroids and other performance-enhancing substances kill athletes. The use of the Goldman dilemma to drive rhetoric and narrative became an issue when peer reviews and scientific methods pertaining to the dilemma were applied to groups of athletes in the 2000s. Note: Goldman's dilemma was a nonscientific report that aligned with the narrative of athletes being willing to do anything for sport success. One anecdotal account such as in a 1997 *Sports Illustrated* article or chronicled in *Game of Shadows*, Tim Montgomery stated that "he won the gold medal in the 100 meters," "it would not matter if I died on the other side of the finish line," "demonstrate its appropriateness in explaining the extent of the sport ethic and mentality" (Fainaru-Wada & Williams, 2006, p. 95).

Moston et al. (2017) describe how the "Goldman dilemma has been used to argue that athletes differ from other members of the population, and that their single-minded obsession with winning necessitates the creation of anti-doping rules that contravene societal norms of privacy according to Waddington and also standards of justice" attributed to Whitworth and Van Geel (2013) (p. 3). Goldman's dilemma originates with Mirkin and Hoffman (1978) mentioning in their book, *The Sports Medicine Book*, their questioning of runners: "If I could give you a pill that would make you an Olympic champion and also kill you in a year, would you take it?" It was reported by more than half of the athletes that they would take the pill, but the authors provide no details, methods, design, or references to this "survey." Athletes may have changed their attitudes in the decades since the original questions were asked but Goldman's dilemma "fails the test of replicability" (Moston et al., 2017). The lack of scientific methodology is problematic in that when the "survey" was conducted for scientific purposes, the results are reversed: with athletes being no more likely to agree to a shortcut to success than non-athletes especially when life span shortening is considered (Moston et al., 2017). The pressure to succeed or sustain continued success can cause athletes to engage in behaviors they might not normally do, but feel are required to be competitive in their sport. Lance Armstrong described in his 2015 *Oprah* interview that he did not see doping as cheating but rather as leveling the playing field, as everyone was doing it (University of Texas in Austin, 2024). In decades past, Goldman's dilemma may have been at least somewhat true, but cultural attitudes toward alcohol and nutrition have changed and now how one treats one's body is very deliberate for many athletes. The attitude toward nutrition is an interesting one, as the *Games of Shadows* points to using the loose nutrition supplement regulations as a cover for athletes' anabolic steroid use in both track and field and baseball (Fainaru-Wada & Williams, 2006). Teenage risk-taking or views of themselves as indestructible has been in existence for a very long time. However, sports injuries show teenage athletes that pain can be real, and that their behaviors can have consequences. Some teenage athletes may view drugs as a way to mitigate those consequences which can create a slippery slope for a percentage of them.

In the secondary school setting, opioid use, even amongst athletes, was reported to be 28.4% to 46.4% based on data from 2009 to 2013 (Ekhtiari et al., 2020). This data includes both prescribed and nonprescribed cases, with cases being higher among football players and wrestlers. According to Ekhtiari et al. (2020), the key for healthcare providers is to find ways to be "sufficiently treating an athlete's pain while limiting the risk of adverse events" (p. 538), especially when the sport ethic culture exalts sacrifice of the mind, body, and soul for the sport. Vandertuin (2021) summarized research conducted by Outlaw et al. (2018) that concluded "20% of student athletes will sustain an injury during play with just short of 50% requiring surgery and concurrent prescription of opioids as a form of pain reliever" (p. 6). Vandertuin (2021) further reported that "Research has revealed that athletes have very little knowledge when it comes to PRM and will often consult unreliable sources such as peers, internet, and coaches for information if a healthcare practitioner is not available" (p. 4). These findings align with the great trust in coaches for everything by athletes, a mistrust of the medical community that emphasizes risks, and the influence of one's peers. Your peers often tell you what you want to hear rather than perhaps what you need to hear.

Rugg et al. (2022) investigated a single Division I athletic department for its opioid use patterns. The study found that 45.4% of athletes had pre-collegiate orthopedic surgeries or injuries, and 40.4% received an opioid prescription. The same athlete data describes 28.6% having collegiate orthopedic surgery or injuries, with 46.4% receiving an opioid prescription. The authors cited the most common reasons for taking opioids were for pain (84.6%) and sleep (46.2%), with 7.1% of individuals taking opioids outside of the prescribed indication. The investigation also found the length of opioid use was most commonly for two weeks or less. Aneizi et al. (2020) found "there is little consensus on proper postoperative narcotic prescribing practice, with wide variability in the quantity of opioids prescribed for even the most common surgical procedures" (p. 145). Dr. Wojtys (2020), in a *Sports Health* editorial, noted that "As the level of competition rises, so does the risk of significant injury and subsequent surgery" (p. 517). Additionally, the editorial noted that "4.7% of patients undergoing ACL reconstruction were still filling opioid prescriptions 12 months after surgery. . . . Despite having only 5% of the world's population, the United States consumes almost 80% of the world opioid production" (Wojtys, 2020, p. 517). Additionally, while opioid prescribing peaked in 2012, the number of orthopedic surgeries for those under 18 nearly doubled from 2004 to 2014 (McLean, 2022). While the actual number of individuals under 18 seeking opioids due to addiction is unknown, the opportunity for first-time exposure due to injury has risen as sport specialization and intensities of injuries have risen in the US youth sport landscape.

Miettinen et al. (2022) found that "Chronic pain and sleep problems frequently co-occur. Pain itself disturbs sleep, but other factors may also contribute to sleep problems in pain patients . . . those with sleep problems more often reported multiple health conditions than those sleeping normally (depression 31.6% vs 5.0%; angina pectoris 6.5% vs 0.0%; asthma 19.6% vs 1.7%; low back problems 55.1% vs 23.3%; joint disease other than rheumatoid arthritis 32.3% vs 18.3%)" (p. e815). Sleep is critical to recovery for athletes from workouts, for growth, as well as to recover from trauma and injuries. Miettinen et al. (2022) describe how "Pain medications more often regularly used by those with sleep problems than by the normally sleeping group included codeine combinations/tramadol, gabapentin/ pregabalin, NSAIDs, amitriptyline/nortriptyline, and venlafaxine/duloxetine" (p. e815). Additionally, "along with pain intensity and cognitive processes, physiological anxiety reactions to pain should be investigated in relation to pain and sleep. . . . The physiological anxiety component reflects a patient's experience when it is difficult to calm down, the body is trembling, and the heart racing, while in pain. It is easy to imagine that, if one has pain at bedtime, these reactions will make it difficult to fall asleep. But heightened physiological arousal may affect sleep problems in other ways" (Miettinen et al., 2022, p. e817). It is easy to see how an athlete could desire to use opioids or other pain modulators following trauma, surgery, and treatment to make one feel better or to lessen pain to lessen sleep disruption. To reduce opioid drug issues, Bridgewater State College (2019) faculty created a policy paper covering opioids and acute pain management in athletes where one recommendation was the implementation of a "Rule of Three." The rule of three was for patients to take no more than three opioid pills per day for no longer than three days. If patients needed more pain relief, then the patient's pain needed to be reassessed by medical personnel (Bridgewater State College, 2019). As of 2019, several states have enacted prescribing regulations for opioids, with the most common being seven days, the most restrictive being three days, and some allowing up to 14 days. Multiple states do not have hard limits on the amount per day (Chua & Kimmel, 2020).

Additionally, a factor in limiting opioid use in youth has occurred by conscientious parents ensuring limited use of opioids by their kids (McLean, 2022). Careful monitoring by parents can assist in decreasing the risk of addiction by youth post orthopedic or dental surgery, which are the two most common introductory events for athletes to opioids. It was noted by McLean (2022) that in some instances, "their parents' hypervigilance led to unmanaged pain" for some athletes, creating issues later on (p. 12). Additionally, doctors and dentists do not want to be burdened by individuals seeking more pain medications, so they have traditionally tended to overprescribe. This concept contrasts with the intercollegiate athlete, where the individual is usually an adult, but faces the same challenges as any student: academic demands, social demands, adjusting to college life, financial demands, altered support system, and living away from home. They also live life as athletes: with travel, team meetings, competition, and a higher likelihood of injury due to a higher level of competition and skill from teammates and opponents (Knettel et al., 2021). According to Knettel et al. (2021), overall "emotional distress is less common among student-athletes than their non-athlete peers; however, . . . student-athletes found high prevalence of self-reported depression (21% male, 28% female) and anxiety

(31% male, 48% female). . . . Additionally, student-athletes experiencing emotional distress are less likely than their peers to seek professional support" (p. 117).

Pain management is a divergent issue when investigated. Assa et al. (2019) noted that there may be differences in pain perception based on the activity. Assa et al. (2019) found that "endurance athletes exhibited improved pain inhibition and tolerability, whereas strength athletes exhibited reduced pain sensitivity" (p. 693). This is an area that is important in opioid usage, as the first encounter with an opioid is likely to be for pain management whether from injury or surgery; even something as common as wisdom tooth extraction. Additionally, pain management can encompass numerous medications, and few have been studied for their effects on exercise performance. Zandonai et al. (2021) cited several studies to conclude that "To the best of our knowledge, no studies have investigated codeine's effect on exercise performance. Tramadol used by athletes may be linked to its analgesic and mood enhancing effects" (p. 1). McLean (2022) found that "every interviewee who reported past non-medical opioid use also described the preset consumption of cannabis, specifically for sport-related pain. . . . While a range of motives for cannabis consumption were reported-general relaxation, sociality and team bonding-pain management emerged as the top reason" (p. 14). This is on top of "a large over-the-counter drug culture" found in many sports, but especially in baseball; in part as over-the-counter medications are seen as preventive self-medication and safe (McLean, 2022, p. 15). This use of over-the-counter (OTC) NSAID medication use begins early in sport culture, often provided by or through parents. Parents may say something like "Your arm/knee/ankle, . . . is sore just take ibuprofen to decrease inflammation and pain" (McLean, 2022, p. 586), ignoring that inflammation is necessary for tissue healing to take place and pain is there for a reason. Several of the studies mention that this attitude is pervasive in sport culture, especially since OTCs are seen as safe (McLean, 2022; Zandonai et al., 2021). Due to this mentality, many athletes have sought advantages over opponents using OTC medications since the beginning of athletic competitions. It is not necessarily always found solely in athletics, as numerous stories have described the "Tiger Mom," or parents who emphasize academic achievement or drive a musician to be the best. These strong parents are no different and their behaviors can lead to similar tracks toward drug use to relieve pressure (Knettel et al., 2021). Whether externally (from sponsors, coaches, parents, friends, fans) or internally (from oneself), the pressure to succeed or maintain success can lead individuals to seek methods to alter feelings, perceptions, and reality. Drug use and opioids can produce euphoria and reduce physical and mental pain. Reduction of pain, physical or mental, can be seen as a coping mechanism that allows for athletic performance. The idea that "If it does not hurt, then I can continue to work out/practice and push my limits physically and mentally" (Vandertuin, 2021).

Performance enhancement has been sought since the beginning of regulated athletic competition, with competitors willing to subject themselves to almost anything to gain an edge. This can be traced back to the original Olympic Games in Greece and its modern counterpart at the turn of the 20th century (Baron et al., 2007). The willingness of athletes, along with coaching, nutrition, and training technique improvements has produced progressively bigger, stronger, faster athletes; compared to the past. Some of these improvements have been chemical additions on an individual basis, or "state" sponsored as seen in the 1970s–1990s in East Germany. The East German's extensive use of chemical enhancement and how to beat detection was laid out in exhaustive detail in Steven Ungerleider's (2013) book *Faust's Gold.* The text lays out, in detail, how the German Sports Federation officials gave their athletes "vitamins" to improve performance leading to enormous successes and also personal individual consequences, including gender changes. The trust of the athletes in their coaches and medical staff was foundationally important to the success of the program; especially in women's sports and specifically track and field and swimming. The pursuit of the highest level of performance is a huge part of the sport ethic and a foundation for elite athletes (Hughes & Coakley, 1991). This quality has been studied for a very long time and the degree of willingness to push human limits, including death, has been explored as discussed in the Goldman dilemma. Hughes and Coakley (1991) state that the mental willingness to challenge their bodies was embraced by the "no pain, no gain" mentality that rose to prominence during various times, along with the social connection found within sport as described by the sport ethic. Charest et al. (2021) summarized from another study conducted by Massegale et al. (2017) that first-year collegiate athletes' social norms, such as alcohol consumption, were influenced by their choice of friends. The selection of mentors and advisors can greatly influence what acceptable behaviors an individual accepts or will be willing to accept. Previous experience with injuries and orthopedic surgery, in particular, has led individuals with more experience with strong medication, such as opioids, to use less than the amount prescribed to them (Aneizi et al., 2020).

The regulation of performance-enhancing substances came about in the 1980s when technologies were being developed to determine the presence of such substances. The initial drugs used for performance enhancement were anabolic steroids (1950s) and later the use of human growth hormone and other synthetic substances. Anabolic steroids were known to have some ill effects on the body which include male and female reproductive issues, liver, cardiovascular and hematological, endocrine, integumentary, urinary, immune, psychological complications, and issues (Haupt & Rovere, 1984; Maravelias et al., 2005). Medical science has not always reflected the realities of the athletic world. Medical science was not believed by athletes, as the athletes (especially those tied to bodybuilding and or weightlifting communities) knew from their experience that the information was wrong. The medical community in the 1980s was claiming that science proved that anabolic steroids were not effective in enhancing strength or size but actual users, especially in the bodybuilding world, demonstrated otherwise (Haupt & Rovere, 1984). Even though this discussion was started in the 1950s, Haupt and Rovere (1984) found the gap in perception still exists on this subject in 1984: "a large information and credibility gap concerning anabolic steroids exists between the athletes and the medical and scientific communities" (p. 469). So, from those early days, the bodybuilding community followed the results it found, not what was reported in the scientific literature. One of the major differences was dosage: the medical community was following pharmaceutical dosage guidelines and bodybuilders were regularly exceeding those dosages along with "stacking" or using multiple steroids at the same time during training. The steroids helped not only with the building process but with a faster recovery, to allow more lifting to also occur. Additionally, the medical community tended to emphasize the risks and not the rewards, as demonstrated in the real world versus laboratory-controlled experiments or as Haupt and Rovere (1984) described "the medical and scientific communities believe that inadequate scientific data exist to support the claim that anabolic steroids can improve athletic performance while overwhelming scientific data demonstrate their deleterious effects" (p. 470).

Within sport, the use of drugs and performance-enhancing drugs is traced to the 1920s in track and field and cycling when several competitors nearly died during the Olympic Games. The steroid culture evolved in the 1950s, with a Russian weight-lifting coach in a drunken state telling a US official about their program and the race was on. Furthermore, the drug use ethics and the ideals found in professional sports clashed with the "amateur" status of the Olympics. Bodybuilding pushed the limits of human knowledge and willingness to gain the "look" through chemical enhancement. Ungerleider (2013) discusses that many did not care about potential consequences so long as the results were achieved. Since trying to gain an advantage through biochemistry was international in scope with the Cold War being a proxy fought within sport, the demand for fairness, and a level playing field brought on attempts at drug testing. Early Olympians had a different culture and set of rules set up by society which looked down upon professional sports or the taking of money for participating in sport until 1992 when the US basketball's "Dream Team" went to Barcelona. Hiding from positive testing results, testing soon became a competition of its own as the attempt to regulate, monitor, and test athletes became an enduring enterprise especially for Olympic sports. Olympic drug testing moved forward significantly in 1983 with the introduction of mass spectrometry to identify even the smallest amounts of the drug or its metabolites within the urine (Kremenik et al., 2006). One key to the success or downfall of drug detection programs was the need to be able to exactly identify substances so they can be detected during testing. The testing could identify that something was there but not the substance unless it was already in the database for known drugs (Voy, 1991). Thus, a race between known and unknown substances, or the use of one substance to mask the existence of an "illegal" substance began and the possibility of "my chemist developing something to make me bigger, faster and stronger than your chemist" (Fainaru-Wada & Williams, 2006, pp. 101–3).

An incident with a famous baseball player, Barry Bonds, uncovered a whole industry dedicated to helping athletes in many sports use drugs to perform better. The book, *Game of Shadows: Barry Bonds, BALCO, and the Steroids Scandal That Rocked Professional Sports* (Fainaru-Wada & Williams, 2006) explored the use of steroids during the 1980s through the early 2000s in baseball, track and field, and other sports through the Bay Area Laboratory Co-Operative (BALCO), a nutritional supplement company, and its leader Victor Conte. Conte provided "I" insulin, "E"

EPO, the Clear, a custom synthetic anabolic steroid created by Patrick Arnold, and a cocktail of growth hormones and stimulants to boost talented sprinters from the regular ranks into superstars such as Tim Montgomery and Dwain Chambers (Fainaru-Wada & Williams, 2006, pp. 101–3). This so-called treatment was given to numerous track and field athletes, and for US and international competitors, as long as the money was paid, the goods would be delivered so the athlete could deliver their desired outcomes (Fainaru-Wada & Williams, 2006). The cat-and-mouse game between the drug creators and the antidoping agencies came into full force following the 1988 Olympic Games and continues today because athletes are willing to take and do whatever to achieve fame and glory, especially in the modern high-stakes world of athletics (Moore, 2013). To avoid detection in the late 1990s and early 2000s, Victor Conte's "drug cocktails were designed not only to be undetectable, but to enhance an athlete's specific needs. Conte's real blood and urine testing program . . . was designed to make sure that the drugs were working as intended, and to ensure that they would not be detected on a steroid test" (Fainaru-Wada & Williams, 2006, p. 115).

In its December 2021 news release, the World Anti-Doping Agency (WADA) updated its World Anti-Doping Code, stating, "samples can be stored for up to 10 years after their initial analysis and still retain the same legal impact if analyzed further and prosecuted" (Brennan et al., 2024). The rationale for these efforts was that "As detection methods are constantly being improved and updated, retaining samples for 10 years means that those who have cheated cannot rest easy for a full decade after they have been tested." As a result "further analysis of samples collected during Beijing 2008 and London 2012 has so far produced more than 130 Anti-Doping Rule Violations, which clearly highlights the effectiveness of such a program to provide more effective detection while also acting as a deterrence" (Brennan et al., 2024). The downside is someone caught cheating 10 years after the event has reaped the rewards of their status while their opponent is often anonymous and misses the presentation of awards and commercial endorsements that can follow athletic success (Mazanov, 2021). A recent example: "As a result of Valieva's four-year ban and subsequent disqualification of results, backdated to Christmas Day 2021, the US Figure Skating team will receive a gold medal for its 2022 Beijing Winter Olympic performance, after the then 15-year-old's Russian Olympic Committee was knocked down to third with the re-ranking of results" (Brennan et al., 2024). So, after two years of court fights, following a positive drug test that was not relayed to WADA, the US Team was awarded its medal in 2024. They were not able to gain the recognition most Olympians do, since the medals and medal ceremony were held up while this episode was sorted out in the Court of Arbitration for Sport (Brennan et al., 2024). The deterrence factor of testing may or may not truly be effective in minimizing drug use when the consequences are so far removed from the occurrence. Furthermore, the WADA determines annually what drugs are legal and at what levels they are and are not acceptable. The drugs that one can be banned for include performance enhancers and any medication that might mask the results of another banned substance. Charest et al. (2021) describe that the data from WADA show that approximately 2% of the athletes tested each year test positive for performance-enhancing substances. Opioids are a major component on every WADA prohibited list, including the newest list released in September 2023 (Brennan et al., 2024).

In non-Olympic sports, each sport has had its own rules: anabolic steroids were banned for the National Football League (NFL), but not Major League Baseball (MLB) until 1991 and drug testing did not begin at the MLB level until 2003 and ended in 2023. The NFL has asked for research into non-opioid pain management in funding a 2021 research study. This only occurred after legal action was taken by players against each NFL team regarding medication use and violation of federal and state laws regarding the administration and dispensing of medications. Non-US sports organizations such as the English Premier League (EPL) and other European football associations have their own rules and regulations regarding permitted and non-permitted drug use. Additionally in the United States, individuals have a hodge-podge of state regulations; with some permitting recreational use of items such as cannabis, others with medical use of pain relievers and anti-anxiety substances such as cannabis, while others do not permit its use under any circumstances. In 2022, Williston reported on doping violations within the EPL and lower division football leagues in England. The findings describe the difficulty of identifying individuals doing ethically questionable medicating and then leagues not enforcing bans as they are written. The substances included opioids, morphine, cocaine, and attention deficit hyperactivity disorder medications such as Ritalin. "Triamcinolone is an anti-inflammatory drug that can, for example, be injected locally to treat knee injuries. However, it can be used as a performance-enhancing drug by a non-injured athlete" (Williston, 2022). Which is a key to sport-related anti-doping lists and policies: when is a substance considered "getting to normal" versus for "enhancement"?

The NFL has a long history of trauma to players' bodies and brains. Players have long sought pain relief on an acute and chronic basis. According to Ekhtiari et al. (2020), opioid use among professional athletes at any given time is around 4.4% to 4.7%. In addition, as the amount of money and television exposure has grown, so has the pressure and stress to perform as well as stay on top and sustain careers that might have ended. Research by Dunne et al. (2020) describe that two out of three NFL players experience one serious injury per year, with such injuries leading to long-term chronic pain, disability, and increased risk for prescription opioid misuse. The average playing career in the NFL is 3.3 years depending on position; with running backs at the low average of 2.57 and punters and kickers at the high average of 4.87 years (Gough, 2023). With two out of three players sustaining at least one serious injury per year, the likelihood of sustaining at least one serious injury during a playing career is almost 100%.

Mannes et al. (2022) surveyed NFL retirees for risk factors for opioid use among retirees. One of many factors was whether a concussion was diagnosed or not: especially among older retirees with a history of concussion symptoms being associated with opioid use (Mannes et al., 2022). Among retired NFL athletes, as many as 80% report daily joint pain, with chronic pain being the most common difficulty during retirement (Dunne et al., 2020), and 25% of NFL retirees using opioids (Mannes et al., 2022). Dunne et al. (2020) conclude that "using prescription opioids may allow players to play through severe injuries and pain that otherwise would compromise their playing time and, subsequently, financial gain" (p. 547). Other risk factors found by Manne et al. (2022) included "the longer the retirement, the more concussions, and the more severe pain (was perceived) compared to non-users and retirees using only opioids or sedatives" (p. 324).

The initial use of opioids and other methods such as alcohol to cope with physical pain and mental stress issues makes those individuals more likely to continue to use the same coping mechanisms for their pain and other issues after their NFL career. Mannes et al. (2022) found that "After adjusting for all other variables in the model, greater pain intensity was associated with either opioid use only or co-use of opioids and sedatives" (p. 324). In addition to chronic pain, former players reported "drug and alcohol use, difficulty transitioning to retirement, trouble sleeping, and elevated risk of several psychosocial problems" (Dunne et al., 2020, p. 544). Charest et al. (2021) noted that while "collegiate athletes receive care for physical injuries, this may not be the case for depression or anxiety. Athletes struggling with mental health issues may be perceived as weak . . . with untreated features of mental health have been linked to substance abuse and a propensity for self-treatment" (p. e450). For those who finish their sporting career, a complication of the use of opioids is the fact that "While prescription opioids may be effective at managing acute pain, there is weak scientific evidence for long term opioid regimens to treat chronic pain" (Dunnes et al., 2020, p. 547). Furthermore, Dunne et al. (2020) noted that these retirees had high use rates of pain and opioid use during their playing days. Dunne et al. (2020) specifically stated that "56.8% of those currently using opioids reported prior opioid use in the NFL 'to function' compared to only 28.2% of those currently using opioids. . . . Former players using opioids in the past 30 days were significantly more likely than those not currently using opioids to report concurrent use of prescription sedatives (30.7% vs. 4.8%; OR=1.67, 95% CI: 1.38, 2.03, p<.001)"(p. 546). Former NFL players continue learned behaviors that have worked in the past (college) such that the "athletes may turn to substances such as cannabis, alcohol, and smokeless tobacco to cope with stress associated with injury, abnormally busy schedules, and pain" (Charest et al., 2021, p. e450). Many of these behaviors seem to link to the sport ethic mindset as described by Hughes and Coakley (1991): they are sacrificing long-term health for short-term sporting success.

Acute and chronic pain is not the sole factor in NFL retirees' opioid use. NFL retirees as reported by Dunne et al. (2020) "specifically, 35.2% of former NFL players currently misusing prescription opioids reported prior use in the NFL to relax or relieve stress compared to only 14.6% of players currently using opioids as prescribed" (p. 546). Dunne et al. (2020) also noted that there were "specific mental health disorders found to be associated with prescription opioid misuse in the general population including panic, depression, anxiety and personality disorder" (p. 547). Of concern is the mixing of opioids with either alcohol or sedatives, as these are known to depress the central nervous system and exacerbate mental health and sleep issues (Dunne et al., 2020). Mannes et al. (2022) noted that "the NFL has yet to enact formal policies aimed at mitigating the risks of prescription benzodiazepines or non-benzodiazepines sedatives" (p. 326). Again, Dunne et al. (2020) note that "While prescription opioids may be effective at managing acute pain, there is weak scientific evidence for long term opioid regimens to treat chronic pain" (p. 547) and Mannes et al. (2020) indicating that "opioid use is contraindicated for chronic pain" (p. 215). "NFL retirees using opioids and sedatives had higher rates of concussions, pain, disability, and moderate/severe physical and mental health impairment compared to those using opioids and sedatives individually" (Mannes et al., 2022, p. 324). "Opioid use while in the NFL as a means of relaxation and stress reduction appeared to heighten risk for current misuse compared to current use as prescribed" (Dunne et al., 2020, p. 548). The misuse or overuse of alcohol is alarming as "those misusing prescription opioids were over three times more likely to be drinking alcohol at risky levels when compared to those only using as prescribed" (Dunne et al., 2020, p. 547). The alarm is due to the "level of alcohol not only increases risk of overdose potential, but by reducing inhibition may also increase violence and suicidality" (Dunne et al., 2020, p. 547).

Mannes et al. (2020) summarized the works of Elliot et al. (2003) stating that "the literature on pain and depression reveals a complex bidirectional relationship, such that chronic pain negatively impacts mood and quality of life, while depression can intensify the experience of pain symptoms and interfere with pain management strategies" (p. 215). Mannes et al. (2020) then concluded from the work of Wasan et al. (2015) when stating that "chronic pain patients experiencing depressive symptoms were less likely to benefit from opioid analgesia and more likely to engage in opioid misuse behavior compared to pain patients without psychiatric comorbidities" (p. 215). According to Miettinen et al. (2022), there is still little knowledge of the mechanisms of the development of comorbid pain and sleep problems over time. Several factors may initiate the process, which is then advanced by reciprocal effects. It seems likely that with reciprocal relationships between many factors, there is a risk of self-reinforcing cycles, which may be involved in the development or maintenance of problems. The authors further describe a potential "vicious" cycle, involving pain, anxiety, and sleep problems with only modest improvements in sleep occurring when treatment is targeted solely on pain. The targeting of subprocesses such as biopsychosocial models to anxiety reactions to injury, biological pain, or treatments for these issues or possible interacting factors mental, emotional, or medical comorbidities may provide ways to break these cycles and achieve better outcomes. Pain management outside of opioids needs to be further explored and accurate information disseminated to the public needs to be done outside of marketing ploys by pharmaceutical companies.

Looking at the literature, there are no longitudinal studies that follow the athletes through their sporting lives to see what effect there is, long term, in using opioids, or their healthcare needs as a whole. There is minimal data comparing the healthcare needs of high school student-athletes to their youth sports peers especially as sport specialization becomes more and more prevalent in the United States. There is minimal data for individual sports such as tennis, golf, gymnastics, or many other sports. The data available is not necessarily reflective of the current practices found in place at high-level intercollegiate or professional sports teams. Based on the available data, there are subsets of athletes suffering different effects: with parents able to mitigate some misuse in youth sports, but a growth in risk-taking behaviors in collegiate sport, where name image and likeness deals can influence decision-making related to injury which can provide a gateway for opioid misuse and finally, elite and professional athletes whose learned behaviors during their careers may lead to use of opioids for perceived pain that was healed or is now chronic. Professional sport and post-career healthcare are unexplored areas outside a small pool of NFL data managed by players' association to some extent but there is a lack of understanding of the consequences of sport ethic and participation. There are many questions about whether opioids are an answer for post-injury pain management and if not opioids, what are alternatives such as cannabis or alternate techniques. This can also be seen outside of athletics, as pain management is a field that has new insights and has been changing rapidly in the last decade. Goldman dilemma appears to reflect the sport ethic on this point: athletes do use medications like opioids to be able to make sacrifices, gain recognition, play through the pain, and win at all costs. Understanding the potential physical or mental health cost is not always asked about nor given at the highest level. The costs for those extending their career by use of medicine, especially opioids, to mask the factors that may have slowed them down or ended their careers early are ever-evolving on a story-by-story basis.

CONCLUSION

In conclusion, analgesic use by athletes is common and is up to four times more often than their age-matched general populations. Most athletes report their first use of opioids in their late teens with the two most common events leading to an athlete's use of opioids being an orthopedic injury (leading to surgery and post-operatively) or through a dentist following wisdom teeth extraction. Overall, drug use is lower in high school–age athletes than the age-matched general population. A small subgroup of high school football players is seen as a higher-risk category as they engage in higher-risk behavior in general such as consuming alcohol, use of marijuana, and sexual encounters. Additionally, this subset sustains its risk profile through adulthood or at least while competing. Little data exists for post-collegiate or professional drug use outside the NFL and those applying to the overall population. The primary reason for opioid use or misuse is pain management. "Sufficiently treating an athlete's pain while limiting the risk of adverse is a challenging task" (Ekhtiari et al., 2020). Secondary factors for use include sleep issues and "to feel normal to function." Complications of opioid use and misuse include overdose death, but this is not commonly reported among athletes. Use of alcohol, cannabis, and sedatives are the most common co-use drugs for athletes using opioids. NFL retirees with a history of concussion symptoms in their past or diagnosed with a concussion and those with moderate to severe pain, impairment, or mental health issues are more likely to use opioids during and following the completion of their playing careers. There are differences between genders in pharmacological and non-pharmacological interventions but there is a lack of scientific data and sport-related data to determine best practices. A sample best practice for athletic departments and medical associates might include the Bridgewater State 3-3-3 policy of no more than three pills total, three times per day for three days before reassessing the root cause of the pain but also ensuring compliance with State and Federal laws are essential (Bridgewater State College, 2019).

REFERENCES

Aneizi, A., Wellington, I. J., Sajak, P., Ventimiglia, D. J., Burt, C. I., Santelli, J., Cothran, V. E., Packer, J. D., & Henn, R. F. (2020). Predictors of postoperative opioid use in NCAA Division 1 collegiate athletes. *Journal of Arthroscopy and Joint Surgery, 7*, 145–50. https//doi.org/10.1016/j.jajs.2020.06.009

Armstrong's doping downfall. (2024). Ethics unwrapped. McCombs School of Business, University of Texas at Austin. https://ethicsunwrapped.utexas.edu/video/armstrongsdoping-downfall

Assa, T., Geva, N., Zarkh, Y., & Defrin, R. (2019). The type of sport matters: Pain perceptions of endurance athletes versus strength athletes. *European Journal of Pain, 23*, 686–96.

Baron, D. A., Martin, D. M., & Magd, S. A. (2007). Doping in sports and its spread to at risk populations: An international review. *World Psychiatry, 6*(2), 118–23.

Brennan, C., Lev, J., & Deaton, J. (2024, February 8). *CNN Top sports court doesn't believe Russian skater's strawberry dessert defense.* https://www.cnn.com/2024/02/08/sport/kamila-valieva-doping-cas-ruling-spt-intl/index.html

Bridgewater State College. (2019, January 30). *Faculty members examine athletes and opioids.* US Fed News Service, HT Digital Streams Limited. Retrieved February 2, 2024, http://www.proquest.com/wirefeeds/faculty-members-examine-athletes-opioids/docview/2172580924/se2?accountid=12408

Charest, J., Grandner, M. A., Athey, A. B., McDuff, D., & Turner, R. W. (2021). Substance use among collegiate athletes versus non-athletes. *Athletic Training & Sports Health Care, 13*(6), 443–52.

Chua, K. P., & Kimmel, L. (2020, May 13). *Opioid prescribing limits for acute pain.* University of Michigan Institute for Healthcare Policy and Innovation. https://ihpi.umich.edu/news/ihpi-briefs/prescribinglimits

Dunne, E., Striley, C., Mannes, Z., Asken, B., Whitehead, N., & Cotter, L. (2020, November). Reasons for prescription opioid use while playing in the National Football League as risk factors for current use and misuse among former players. *Clinical Journal of Sport Medicine, 30*(6), 544–49. doi: 10.1097/JSM.00000000000000628

Ekhtiari, S., Yusuf, I., Al-Makadma, Y., MacDonald, A., Leroux, T., & Khan, M. (2020). Opioid use in athletes: A systematic review. *Sports Health, 12*(6), 534–39.

Elliot, T., Renier, C., & Palcher, J. (2003, December). Chronic pain, depression, and quality of life: Correlations and predictive value of the SF-36. *Pain Medicine, 4*(4), 331–39. doi:10.1111/j.1526-4637.2003.03040.x

Fainaru-Wada, M., & Williams, L. (2006). *Game of shadows: Barry Bonds, BALCO, and the steroids scandal that rocked professional sports*. Gotham.

Ford, J. A., Pomykacz, C., Veliz, P., McCabe, S. E., & Boyd, C. J. (2018). Sports involvement, injury history, and non medical use of prescription opioids among college students: An analysis with a national sample. *American Journal on Addiction, 27*, 15–22.

Goldman, B., Bush, P. J., & Klatz, R. (1984). *Death in the locker room: Steroids and sports*. Icarus Press.

Gough, C. (2023, September 5). *Average playing career length in the National Football League*. https://www.statista.com/statistics/240102/average-player-career-length-in-the-national -football-league/

Hainline, B., Turner, J. A., Caneiro, J. P., Stewart, M., & Moseley, G. L. (2017). Pain in elite athletes—neurophysiological, biomechanical, and psychosocial considerations: A narrative review. *British Journal of Sports Medicine, 51*, 1259–64.

Haupt, H. A., & Rovere, G. D. (1984, November–December). Anabolic steroids: A review of the literature. *American Journal of Sports Medicine, 12*(6), 469–84. doi: 10.1177/036354658401200613

Hughes, R., & Coakley, J. (1991). Positive deviance among athletes: The implications of overconformity to the sport ethic. *Sociology of Sport Journal, 8*, 307–25.

Knettel, B. A., Cherenack, E. M., & Bianchi-Rossi, C. (2021). Stress, anxiety, binge drinking and substance use among college student-athletes: A cross sectional analysis. *Journal of Intercollegiate Sport, 14*(2), 116–35. https://doi.org/10.17161/jis.v14i2.14829

Kremenik, M., Onder, S., Nagao, M., & Yuzuki, O. (2006). A historical timeline of doping in the Olympics. *Kawasaki Journal of Medical Welfare, 12*(1), 19–28.

Mannes, Z., Dunne, E., Ferguson, E., Cotter, L., & Ennis, N. (2020, October 1). History of opioid use as a risk factor for current use and mental health consequences among retired National Football League athletes: A 9-year follow-up investigation. *Drug Alcohol Depend, 215*, 108251.

Mannes, Z., Hasin, D., Abdallah, A., & Cotter, L. (2022, May 1). Co-use of opioids and sedatives among retired National Football League athletes. *Clinical Journal of Sport Medicine, 32*(3), 322–28. doi:10.1097/JSM.0000000000001007

Maravelias, C., Dona, M., Stefanidou, A., & Spiliopoulou, C. (2005). Adverse effects of anabolic steroids in athletes: A constant threat. *Toxicology Letters, 158*, 167–75. doi:10.1016/j.toxlet.2005.06.005

Mazanov, J. (2021, July 21). *Doping has become inevitable at the Olympics. And who wins gold in Tokyo might not be certain until 2031*. https://theconversation.com/doping-has-become -inevitable-at-the-olympics-and-who-wins-gold-in-tokyo-might-not-be-certain-until-2031 -163881

McLean, K. (2022). Policies in need of a problem? A qualitative study of medical and non-medical opioid use among college student-athletes in the United States. *Social Sciences, 11*, 586. https//doi.org/10.3390/socsci1120

Miettinen, T., Sverloff, J., Lappalainen, O. P., Linton, S. J., Sipila, K., & Kalso, E. (2022). Sleep problems in pain patients entering tertiary pain care: The role of pain-related anxiety, medication use, self-reported diseases, and sleep disorders. *Pain, 163*(7), e812–820.

Mirkin, G., & Hoffman, M. (1978). *The sports medicine book*. Little, Brown.

Moore, R. (2013). *The dirtiest race in history: Ben Johnson, Carl Lewis and the 1988 Olympic 100m final*. Bloomsbury.

Moston, S., Hutchinson, B., & Engleberg, T. (2017). Dying to win? The Goldman dilemma in legend and fact. *International Journal of Sport Communications, 10*(4), 429–43.

Outlaw, K., Carpenter-Aeby, T., & Aeby, V. (2018). Opioids and athletes: A growing problem and a deadly combination. *BMJ Open Sport & Exercise Medicine, 4*(3), 63–65. doi:https://dx.doi.org/10.17140/SEMOJ-4-163

Pedersen, J. R., Andreucci, A., Thorlund, J. B., Koes, B., Moller, M., Storm, L. K., & Bricca, A., (2022). Prevalence, frequency, adverse events, and reasons for analgesic use in youth athletes: A systematic review and meta-analysis of 44,381 athletes. *Journal of Science and Medicine in Sport, 25*, 810–19.

Rugg, C. M., Cheah, J. W., Vomer II, R. P., & Lau, B. (2022, November 6). Opiate use patterns among collegiate athletes. *Cureus, 14*(11), e31152. doi: 10.7759/cureus.311

Ungerleider, S. (2013). *Faust's gold: Inside the East German doping machine.* CreateSpace.

University of Texas in Austin. (2024). *Armstrong's doping downfall.* [Video]. Ethics Unwrapped. https://ethicsunwrapped.utexas.edu/video/armstrongs-doping-downfall

Vandertuin, J. (2021). Athletes, opioids and the athletic therapist. *Publications and Scholarship, 17.* https://source.sheridancollege.ca/fahcs_publications/17

Voy, R. O. (1991). *Drugs, sport, and politics: The inside story about drug abuse in sport and its political cover-up, with a prescription for reform.* Leisure.

Wasan, A., Michna, E., Edwards, R., Katz, J., Nedeljkovic, S., Dolman, A., Janfaza, D., Issac, Z., & Janison, R. (2015, October). Psychiatric comorbidity is associated prospectively with diminished opioid analgesia and increased opioid misuse in patients with chronic low back pain. *Anesthesiology, 123*(4), 861–72. doi: 10.1097/ALN.0000000000000768

Whitworth, R., & Van Geel, F. (2013, July 23). Toying with athletes. *Analytical Scientist, 0613*, 23–27.

Williston, E. (2022, April 16). Special Report: Fifteen top-flight stars fail drug tests but not ONE is banned, as 88 footballers in Britain return positive samples—but details of cases are withheld. *Daily Mail.* https://www.dailymail.co.uk/sport/sportsnews/article-10724919/FIFTEEN-Premier-League-stars-fail-drug-tests-NONE-banned-authorities-details-withheld.html

Wojtys, E. M. (2020). Drugs in sports. *Sports Health, 12*(6), 526–17. doi:10.177/1941738120963385

Zandonai, T., Escorial, M., & Peiro, A. M. (2021). Codeine and tramadol use in athletes: A potential for abuse. *Frontiers in Pharmacology, 12*, 661781. doi: 10.3389/fphar.2021.661781

13

Students Talking to Students

College Students and Prescription Medication Beyond Opioids

Kaylee Williams, Rebecca McGaughnea,
Sydney Wixtrom, Ally Mason, and Abigail Warf

Although this book is focused on opioids in general, this chapter looks at prescription medications beyond opioids, medication shortages, mental health disorders, and treatment options on college campuses. Students may be taking these medications in addition to opioids, or by themselves. The authors also address topics such as misdiagnosis, malingering, treatment options, and resources on college campuses.

This chapter features the perspectives and research of five undergraduate students from Methodist University. College students bring an important perspective to the table because they experience firsthand how mental health, medications, and services (or a lack thereof) regularly affect their community. These students offer insights and research on posttraumatic stress disorder (PTSD), anxiety, depression, attention-deficit/hyperactivity disorder (ADHD), and the nonmedical use of prescription drugs (NMUPD).

The purpose of this chapter is twofold. First, students struggling with mental illness need to know that they are not alone; students talking to students allows a direct conversation among peers. Second, the authors make recommendations directly to college and university administrators who have the ability and resources to impact meaningful change on their individual campuses.

POSTTRAUMATIC STRESS DISORDER

College students are at a high risk of experiencing potentially traumatic events (PTEs) that can ultimately lead to PTSD. PTEs are events that expose an individual to severe injury, sexual violence, potential death, or actual death. Once exposed to such an event, approximately 9% of college students will then develop PTSD (Read et al., 2014). The exact process by which a PTE transforms into PTSD is unknown, and certain categories of events, like sexual assault and military service, are more likely to develop into PTSD for students. Students who are suffering from PTSD are often misdiagnosed as having anxiety, depression, and acute stress disorder (Alison, 2022). This results in college students being improperly or inadequately treated and not receiving the help they need. Additionally, there is a lack of advancements in medical treatments for PTSD. Despite PTSD's increasing prevalence, there have not been any visible advancements in the last 20 years for medications that treat symptoms or aid in the remission of PTSD (Krystal et al., 2017). Research and development for the treatment of PTSD has come to a halt and this crisis is dramatically affecting college students. However, there are ways for colleges to respond to PTSD on their campuses by implementing education and treatment for students who may be suffering from PTSD.

Approximately 75% of college students have been exposed to PTEs (Read et al., 2011). Two PTEs affect college students the most. The first PTE is sexual assault. According to the Rape, Abuse & Incest National Network (RAINN; n.d.), 25% of female college students and 7% of male college students experience rape or sexual assault while in school. In a meta-analysis published in *Trauma, Violence and Abuse*, researchers found that 75% of sexual assault victims had significant symptoms of PTSD one month after the event and 41% had significant symptoms of PTSD one year after the event. The majority of PTSD recovery occurs within the first three months following the traumatic event (Dworkin et al., 2021). With such high numbers of the student population experiencing sexual assault while in school, it can be inferred that many of them are living with symptoms of PTSD months to years after the event.

The second PTE that affects college students the most is military-related service. The number of veterans with mental health challenges, such as PTSD, is growing on college campuses. Approximately 10% of individuals serving in the military go to combat, and in a 2014 study involving 3,157 US veterans, 87% reported exposure to at least one PTE during their military service (Midwest Disability, 2019; Zauderer, 2023). Additionally, 6% of college students have served or currently serve in the military, and a study surveying a national sample of student veterans pursuing higher education found that 45.9% experience significant symptoms of PTSD (American Association of Community Colleges, 2019; Morrissette et al., 2019). Therefore, it can be inferred that a significant percentage of these student veterans have experienced a PTE and are exhibiting symptoms of PTSD.

These statistics reflect that almost one-third of the student population have experienced a sexual assault PTE and 75% of those individuals will exhibit PTSD symptoms one month later. Additionally, almost half of the student veteran population will exhibit PTSD symptoms after experiencing a military-related PTE. Even though a considerable number of students have experienced a PTE, it is important to note that the seriousness of the PTE is not dependent upon the facts of the event but rather the individual's subjective interpretation and understanding of the event. Since no two individuals process an event in an identical manner, some PTEs will cause simple discomfort in some individuals and PTSD in others. Furthermore, students who have experienced a PTE and are exhibiting these symptoms may have PTSD without knowing it.

According to the American Psychiatric Association (2022), PTSD is "a psychiatric disorder that may occur in people who have experienced or witnessed a traumatic event, series of events, or set of circumstances." Diagnosis of PTSD requires exposure to an event that involves violence, serious injury, possible death, or actual death. The criteria for symptoms of PTSD include reexperiencing the event, avoidance of stimuli, and increased arousal. Reexperience of a traumatic event involves recurrent recollections, distressing dreams, acting or feeling as if reliving the event, and intense psychological distress. Avoidance involves efforts to evade thoughts, feelings, or conversations about trauma as well as efforts to evade places or people that arouse memories of the event. Avoidance may also include the inability to recall aspects of the trauma, diminished interest in significant activities, and feelings of detachment from others. Increased arousal includes difficulty falling asleep, irritability and outbursts of anger, difficulty concentrating, hypervigilance, and exaggerated startle response (Grasso et al., 2009). College students often exhibit many of these symptoms, and these symptoms can be overlooked because behaviors like avoidance of others or activities may seem normal for a college student. Additionally, difficulty concentrating, irritability, and detachment may also be considered a normal effect of the usual stresses of college.

Unfortunately, PTSD is not always recognized, so consequently, the disorder can be misdiagnosed or untreated. In ordinary doctor's visits, patients with PTSD often go undiagnosed. Only 2% to 11% have the diagnosis in their medical records and less than half of these patients receive treatment for PTSD (Meltzer et al., 2012). One reason for this misdiagnosis is that PTSD goes unnoticed not only by those suffering from it but also by those who observe it. In some circumstances, individuals may experience a PTE and not experience PTSD until years later. If individuals do not connect the traumatic event to the symptoms they are experiencing, it may go unreported and undiagnosed, or it may be diagnosed as a different mental health disorder. The implication for college students is that those who are suffering from PTSD are commonly misdiagnosed as suffering from other mental health conditions—such as anxiety, depression, and acute stress disorder—due to them having many similarities to PTSD (Alison, 2022). Instead of overlooking the symptoms or attributing them to another mental health disorder, students suffering from PTSD need to be educated on the criteria for diagnosis as well as proper treatment options.

In addition to being misdiagnosed, limited knowledge about pharmacological treatments for PTSD is another critical obstacle when it comes to effectively treating this disorder. There has not been a new medication approved to treat PTSD since 2001, and the only two medications approved by the FDA are sertraline (Zoloft) and paroxetine (Paxil) (Krystal et al., 2017). Sertraline and paroxetine are selective serotonin reuptake inhibitors (SSRIs), which are antidepressant medications that can reduce PTSD symptoms (American Psychiatric Association, n.d.). Unfortunately, no other sufficient medications are being prescribed to aid college students with PTSD. Students are then left to find relief through other means including polypharmacy, which means off-label medications not adequately studied for the treatment of PTSD. Therefore, most of these students are self-medicating by using medications or combinations that have little to no empirical evidence regarding benefits or risks. Other students may not be receiving any effective treatment at all. Students must be informed of other ways to treat PTSD since the lack of medical advancements is out of their control.

Despite the lack of advancements in medical treatments, there are other ways in which colleges can aid those suffering from PTSD. Colleges need to understand and recognize what PTSD is and how prevalent it is among the student population. The best way to do this is to provide education that will result in trauma-informed leaders and students. This education should include what PTSD is, what it looks and feels like, and how to treat it. Through this education, colleges can reduce the percentage of misdiagnosis on their campuses by giving students the knowledge that is necessary to recognize PTSD.

Additionally, colleges can provide services to students suffering from PTSD. One of the main treatments for PTSD is talk therapy, which can include group therapy, peer counseling, or professional counseling. Although professional counseling is important, some students are not comfortable sharing information about their traumatic experiences in this setting. At the University of Virginia, researchers found that about 75% of students reach out to a peer when they are in distress while only 11% contact faculty, staff, or administrators. Often the people who are least equipped to provide professional help are the ones most likely to provide it (Abrams, 2022). This is where group therapy and peer counseling become important. Students can be trained on things such as empathy, mentoring, and active listening. Although, unfortunately, not many students reach out to professionals, colleges can respond to this by providing education and other kinds of therapy for those suffering from PTSD. Overall, it must be a joint effort among college faculty, staff, and students to implement and utilize nonpharmacological treatments for PTSD.

ANXIETY

In 2017, the National Alliance on Mental Illness (NAMI) reported that about one-fifth of American adults have an anxiety disorder. Anxiety can be described as a feeling of worry, but an anxiety disorder is when anxiety can prohibit normal functioning in an adult and may include panic attacks, debilitating feelings of intense anxiety, and difficulty doing daily tasks. Anxiety disorders can be categorized into several different types including generalized anxiety disorder (GAD), social anxiety disorder (SAD), and panic disorder (PD) (NIH, 2024).

GAD is described as persistent and excessive worry, sometimes followed by physical symptoms such as restlessness, feeling on edge or easily fatigued, difficulty concentrating, muscle tension, and problems sleeping. SAD and PD both have similarities to GAD, but the cause of anxiety for SAD is social situations such as speaking in public, meeting new people, or answering a question in class. The main symptom of PD is panic attacks, which are characterized by symptoms of difficulty breathing, chest pain, a racing heart, sweating, and trembling (NIH, 2024).

Although there are different types, some anxiety disorders are more common than others. A study conducted by Harvard University revealed that among college-aged students, 4.3% were diagnosed with GAD, 13.3% with SAD, and 4.2% with PD (National Comorbidity Survey Replication [NCSR], 2007). Regardless of the number of students who have anxiety disorders, four common factors are shown to increase a student's risk for developing an anxiety disorder: loneliness, academic challenges, sleep disruption, and stress. As students are struggling with these risk factors, many students will look to self-diagnosis to attempt to explain their hardships in college. Additionally, when students cannot explain their challenges, they may look to gain accommodations through exaggerating or feigning symptoms of anxiety; this is called malingering.

College students are more stressed and anxiety-ridden than ever before. The loneliness students may experience when starting college can lead to a deterioration of their mental health which can increase their risk of anxiety disorders. When students are feeling lonely, they have a heightened risk level of anxiety (Richardson et al., 2017). Richardson et al. (2017) state, "loneliness may . . . [exacerbate] existing mental health difficulties or [lead] to a direct deterioration of mental health over time." Therefore, loneliness is a risk factor for college students to develop anxiety while they are attending college.

When students develop a high level of stress at college and experience that deterioration, their grades are often negatively affected. According to research conducted by the American College Health Association (ACHA) in 2019,

> Within the last 12 months, [27.8% of] students reported the following factors affecting their individual academic performance, defined as: received a lower grade on an exam, or an important project; received a lower grade in the course; received an incomplete or dropped the course; or experienced a significant disruption in thesis, dissertation, research, or practicum work. (p. 6)

Anxiety can directly impact a college student's academic performance, especially considering that just under a third of the population of students reported that they are struggling academically because of their anxiety (ACHA, 2019). School stress and disengagement from classes are closely associated with psychological distress, including anxiety, among college students. However, college students may also face challenges other than academics which can increase their risk for developing an anxiety disorder. These challenges may also cause difficulty with sleep schedules.

Sleep disruption is a common problem among college students but may be more of a challenge for students who struggle with an anxiety disorder. One study by the NIH found that 36.8% of college students with anxiety also reported that they had insomnia (Mbous et al., 2022). A large body of research supports the idea that students who are particularly stressed or anxious might find themselves processing the day's negative events at bedtime, making it much more difficult to fall asleep (Peltz et al., 2017). Working through stress and anxious conditions "can lead to mental health conditions like . . . anxiety" (MacPherson, 2024). Additionally, research finds that anxious college students often drink excessive caffeine and pull all-nighters to meet deadlines, which indicates that anxiety could cause sleep disruption among college students (MacPherson, 2024).

Another factor that can affect a college student's risk for an anxiety disorder is stress. It is normal for college students to be stressed and have intense feelings of anxiety, especially during midterms and finals; however, it is abnormal when students become so stressed that they start worrying about topics that are unrelated to what initiated their stress. The stress of college can be a catalyst for anxiety disorders, particularly in vulnerable individuals such as those who may have a predisposition for anxiety, sometimes leading to initial symptoms during this time (Kadison & DiGeronimo, 2004). Over time, stress can increase anxiety symptoms and cause students to develop an anxiety disorder, making it important to examine stress levels.

Anxiety is an alarming issue that is affecting the majority of college students. Nearly two-thirds of students report that they have anxiety (ACHA, 2019). Thirty percent of college students are self-diagnosing a variety of mental health issues (Redshaw, 2023). Anxiety is the most commonly self-diagnosed mental health disorder, accounting for 48% of the 30% of college students who self-diagnose (Redshaw, 2023). However, students may tend to exaggerate their symptoms and even brag to their friends about how they stayed up all night, were stressed out about a test, or missed class. These students might simply be facing typical college stress and may not need a diagnosis, particularly if their symptoms do not align with those of an anxiety disorder.

In conjunction with self-diagnosis in students comes the question of if they are malingering. Malingering is the dishonest and intentional production or exaggeration of physical or psychological symptoms for external gain. One study indicated that "94% of students reported that they would, to different extents, be motivated to fabricate symptoms for the incentive, regardless of its quality" (Boskovic, 2020). In the same study, "students estimated that 97.6% of their peers, although with varying frequency, engage in malingering" (Boskovic, 2020). College students may feign symptoms to seek accommodations, like getting an extension on a test or assignment, because they did not get their work done. Others may try to get out of group projects claiming they have bad social anxiety. Anxiety is one of the most common mental illnesses associated with malingering (Saberi et al., 2013). However, malingering is a topic deserving of more intensive research as it is difficult to get reliable data on rates of malingering, and further research should be conducted to determine how many college students are feigning anxiety disorders.

Anxiety can be treated with therapy or medication, and sometimes a combination of the two. The most common form of therapy for anxiety disorders is cognitive behavioral therapy (CBT): "CBT is by far the most consistently empirically supported psychotherapeutic option in the treatment of anxiety disorders" (Otte, 2011). CBT is a method that helps clients effectively manage emotions to break negative habitual thoughts and patterns. CBT works by helping clients work through their anxiety through the use of self-monitoring their symptoms, mind exercises, and cognitive reconstructing. However, the effectiveness of the treatment varies depending on the type of disorder. CBT proved to be 92% effective for GAD, 62% effective for SAD, and 35% effective for PD (Otte, 2011). These differing results provide information for college students to gravitate toward different treatment pathways such as medications.

Anxiety can be treated with about 54 different medications. About 17% of college students with diagnosed anxiety take medications (Marconi et al., 2023). These medications for anxiety could be SSRIs, serotonin-norepinephrine reuptake inhibitors (SNRIs), or benzodiazepines. SSRIs include citalopram (Celexa), escitalopram (Lexapro), fluoxetine (Prozac), fluvoxamine (Luvox), paroxetine (Paxil), and sertraline (Zoloft). SNRIs are medications like duloxetine (Cymbalta) and venlafaxine (Effexor XR). Finally, benzodiazepines include alprazolam (Xanax), chlordiazepoxide (Librium), clonazepam (Klonopin), diazepam (Valium), and lorazepam (Ativan). If used as prescribed, these medications can reduce students' levels of anxiety, heighten energy levels, and improve stress levels thus improving the student's ability to focus, concentrate, and complete assignments. Although many of the most common anxiety medications are relatively safe to take and have minimal side effects, recent shortages of these medications have made them difficult to obtain.

Shortages for anxiety medications have become more prevalent in recent years. In the past five years clonazepam and lorazepam have been in short supply several times. Additionally, benzodiazepines including diazepam, lorazepam, and chlordiazepoxide have been in short supply more frequently in recent years (Whitledge et al., 2023). A "proactive emergency management plan to address critical medication shortages has become an increasingly necessary [action to take] and would have been appropriate for use during this national shortage" of medications (Marks et al., 2023). Shortages can cause a client to change their medication and changing medications can have medical consequences.

Transitioning to different anxiety medications because of shortages can cause issues in terms of tolerance, dependency, and addiction—especially with medications like clonazepam. Some anxiety benzodiazepines such as diazepam, alprazolam, and lorazepam can only be used short term because of the body's ability to build up a resistance to them. However, some SSRIs and SNRIs can take up to six weeks to be effective (Guina & Merrill, 2018). Prescription medications can work well for treating anxiety; however, students and educators must be aware of these potential issues that may arise.

College has proven to be a difficult time in students' lives when it comes to mental health, this could cause students to "withdraw and become anxious" (Kadison

& DiGeronimo, 2004, p. 12). A university can have profound, positive effects on college students battling mental health disorders. According to Kadison and DiGeronimo (2004), aiding students in coping with stress, anxiety, and the uncertainties of relationships with peers and professors is a vital aspect of education. Additionally, "[n]inety percent of [students] reported that counseling helped them meet their goals at the university and helped reduce stress that was interfering with their schoolwork," and "77 percent of students . . . reported that they were more likely to stay in school because of counseling" (Kadison & DiGeronimo, 2004, p. 158). Therefore, colleges need to accept reasonable responsibility for the psychological well-being of their students by putting more resources into their staff and facilities.

Universities need to be aware of and prepared to handle this pressing issue. The reality is that many colleges do not have the budget or resources to handle the excess of college students who need mental health services. A 2019 survey from the ACHA showed that in the last academic year, 66% of students self-reported that they had felt overwhelming anxiety. Approximately 24% of those students reported being diagnosed or treated by a mental health professional (ACHA, 2019). This 42% gap should be concerning to colleges because college counseling centers are not prepared to handle more clients. Conversely, as self-diagnosed data continues to show higher numbers than medically diagnosed anxiety, it is up to universities to decipher which students have true anxiety and which students have malingered symptomatology. Universities need to clarify and improve their efforts to address the issue of anxiety of their students. Universities also need to call attention to the serious nature of anxiety among college students and address the negative aspects of self-diagnosing and malingering.

Students commonly face barriers that prevent them from seeking help from mental health professionals. These "[p]reference[s] for informal consultations, concerns about confidentiality, and preference for self-diagnosis were the most commonly reported barriers to mental healthcare seeking" (Arun et al., 2022), along with negative stigma, time constraints, and lack of convenience or quick access to counseling. Colleges and universities need to seek to eliminate these barriers for their students to enable their students access to mental health support when necessary. It would be best for colleges to help students by encouraging all students with anxiety to get an official diagnosis, or simply seek counseling so that they can obtain appropriate accommodations and get more specialized treatment from doctors and mental health professionals.

DEPRESSION

College students are depressed, and universities need to do better at treating and providing assistance to these students. Depression is one of the most common mental health disorders on college campuses. According to the National Institute of Mental Health (NIH), "[d]epression (also known as major depression, major depressive disorder, or clinical depression) is a common but serious mood disorder [that] causes severe symptoms that affect how a person feels, thinks, and handles daily activities, such as sleeping, eating, or working" (NIH, n.d.). College students with depression can experience a wide variety of symptoms that may affect them daily, such as losing interest in activities they once enjoyed; feeling irritable, fatigued, and guilty; having impacted sleeping habits; and being persistently sad (MHA, n.d., *Depression*). These symptoms can cause college students to have difficulties at home and school. There are several possible reasons why college students are depressed, such as "societal pressures, peer pressures, academic pressures, stress, and challenges in [their] social [lives]" (Renzoni, 2023). Academic pressures, stress, and other challenges can make it difficult for college students to manage their academic performance, which could lead to the development of a substance use disorder, dropping out of school, or even committing suicide.

There are multiple methods mental health professionals use to treat depression, such as a combination of therapy and antidepressants. The first method of treatment for depression is typically therapy, and there are different types of therapy that mental health professionals can utilize. These different types can include psychotherapy—also known as talk therapy—behavioral, cognitive, interpersonal, psychodynamic, and supportive therapies (Clinical Practice Guideline for the Treatment of Depression, 2019). The most common form of therapy is psychotherapy, which can include a combination of all the aforementioned types of therapy. In addition to therapy, antidepressants are commonly prescribed to further treat depressive symptoms. Of all the medications that could be prescribed to those with depression, the five most commonly prescribed are Prozac, Celexa, Zoloft, Paxil, and Lexapro.

As with all medications, there are potential negative side effects. The medications discussed may also be known under other generic forms. Prozac, also known as fluoxetine, has been used to treat depression, panic disorder, and bipolar depression. Some potential negative side effects of this medication include the patient experiencing nausea, drowsiness, and a lower sex drive. A positive of taking Prozac includes its ability to be prescribed to children and teens, unlike most other antidepressants. Celexa, also known as citalopram, has been prescribed to treat people with depression and panic disorder. There are several potential negative side effects of taking this medication such as nausea, sweating, drowsiness, lower sex drive, and painful erections. A positive for this medication is that most people do not experience any side effects, but if they do, the side effects do not last longer than a few weeks. Zoloft, also known as sertraline, is used to treat a wide variety of mental illnesses, such as depression, obsessive-compulsive disorder (OCD), and PTSD. This medication has several potential negative side effects, such as nausea, diarrhea, lower sex drive, and effects on blood sugar levels in patients with diabetes. Zoloft is less likely to cause drowsiness than other antidepressants. Paxil, also known as paroxetine, is used to treat depression and anxiety. The potential negative side effects of this medication include diarrhea, drowsiness, nausea, a lower sex drive, and an increased risk for diabetes. A positive of taking Paxil is that it may be easier for some patients to sleep while taking the medication. Lastly, Lexapro, also known as escitalopram, is used to treat a wide range of mental health issues such as depression, anxiety, and OCD. Lexapro has several potential negative side effects, such as excessive sweating, difficulty sleeping, nausea, a lower sex drive, and painful erections. However, Lexapro can improve the patient's sex life, and the medication can be prescribed to teenagers.

All these medications have side effects that college students need to be aware of while finding a medication to take for their depression. According to the *Medical Research Journal* (2013), most "students felt that being on [antidepressant] medication did not help them cope with depression any better than not being on medication." Nevertheless, antidepressants have been shown to improve the quality of life for those with depression. Therefore, with a combination of both therapy and prescription medication as a course of treatment, college students can learn to cope with their depression.

Counselors are overwhelmed by the sheer number of college students who require assistance with their mental health diagnoses. College students are seeking the help they require for their mental health, but they are being let down by the lack of funding and the low number of mental health counselors that universities are willing to have on staff. What makes this situation all the more problematic is that "some colleges have sought to cut spending by cutting counselors' jobs" (Flannery, 2023). Cutting spending and reducing professional counseling positions are not the solutions universities should be seeking when they are informed about the mental health crisis on campuses across the United States. Universities need to hire an adequate number of counselors—available 24 hours a day, 7 days a week—to help with the growing mental health crisis on college campuses.

If universities provide college students with more counselors, students will have a much better chance of receiving the help they need to cope with their depression through therapy, antidepressants, or a combination of the two. For college students, "[h]aving a provider that understands a patient's experience more first-hand can make a true difference during treatment" (Flannery, 2023). Students can view counselors as more than just paid employees because they help them develop lifelong strategies to cope with their mental health. University administration must allocate more funding to the counseling services already guaranteed to students once they are enrolled in their universities.

ATTENTION-DEFICIT/HYPERACTIVITY DISORDER

ADHD is a neurological disorder that affects an individual's behavior, which is often described as a pattern of symptoms that revolve around hyperactivity, impulsivity, as well as inattention (American Psychiatric Association, 2024). The three sublevels of ADHD are "predominately inattentive," "predominately hyperactive/impulsive," and "combined" (American Psychiatric Association, 2013). These sublevels have symptoms of concentration issues, such as trouble focusing or getting bored easily, and symptoms of hyperactivity and impulsiveness, such as fidgeting or yelling out at inappropriate times.

Regardless of age or gender, ADHD is commonly discovered in children. Based on a study conducted in 2019, "approximately 5.3 million children (8.7%) in the United States, ranging between the ages of 3–17, have a current diagnosis of ADHD" (Children and Adults with Attention-Deficit/Hyperactivity Disorder [CHADD], 2023). Often, children diagnosed when they are young can grow out of the diagnosis; however, ADHD can last into adulthood. A 2022 study indicated that 5.6% of college students in the United States are diagnosed with ADHD (Hotez et al., 2022).

Historically, the diagnosis of attention-deficit disorder (ADD) encompassed the symptoms of inattention and impulsiveness, which was what females were frequently diagnosed with, and a subcategory of ADD with hyperactivity which is what males were commonly diagnosed with. By 1987, ADD was no longer recognized as a diagnosis (Holland, 2021). The rationale given was that the symptoms of hyperactivity are more prominent than originally thought, leading psychologists and therapists to invent a new term that incorporates it; therefore, ADHD was entered into the *Diagnostic Statistical Manual* (DSM), a set of guidelines that psychologists and therapists use to diagnose someone with a mental disorder.

Current numbers show that males are twice as likely to be diagnosed with ADHD than females (Ramtekkar et al., 2010). Traditionally, research on ADHD has been focused more on males. However, research is starting to focus more on females and has allowed researchers to understand how females differ in ADHD symptoms as compared to males. For instance, females will exhibit more internal symptoms such as inattention and concentration issues compared to males' external symptoms of hyperactivity.

College students with ADHD often face challenges in the classroom due to their struggles with "time management, organization, and procrastination" (Frida Care Team, 2023). These challenges can cause a lower GPA and fewer credits earned compared to college students without ADHD and may stem from the impacts of ADHD on their "academic and psychological functioning" (Fleming & McMahon, 2012). Lower grades can affect the self-confidence and self-perception of college students. Some reports show that students with ADHD "are more concerned about their academic performance, report higher levels of emotional distress and social concerns, and rate themselves as less emotionally stable" (Blase et al., 2009, p. 306). About half of college students with ADHD develop comorbidities, which are two or more diagnoses occurring in the individual simultaneously, because of the effects that ADHD symptoms have on a student's academic and social life (Anastopoulos et al., 2016). Comorbidities can include disorders such as anxiety, depression, oppositional defiant disorder, mood disorders, and opioid usage disorder (OUD). College students with ADHD are three times more likely to drop out by their second year compared to those who do not have this neurological disorder (DuPau et al., 2018, pp. 161–78). For college students, the combination of ADHD symptoms with co-occurring disorders, diminished self-confidence, and poor academic performance can culminate in the decision to drop out of school (DuPau et al., 2018).

There are many treatment options for ADHD; often, CBT is suggested by therapists and psychologists before prescribing medication such as Adderall. The use of CBT aims to help reduce symptoms of mental disorders using self-help strategies which has proven to be the most effective way to change an individual's mindset. CBT is beneficial to college students with ADHD because it improves ADHD symptoms and acquaints students with accommodation services and other resources (Anastopoulos et al., 2018). In addition, CBT helps students improve their organizational skills which directly impacts grade point averages and graduation rates of these students. When CBT does not work due to the symptoms being too severe, doctors will prescribe medication in addition to therapy to help aid in the reduction of ADHD symptoms.

The most well-known medication treatment for ADHD is Adderall; however, there are other stimulants available such as Ritalin and Concerta. Most ADHD medications contain dextroamphetamine, amphetamine, or dextro-methylphenidate. These are chemicals that affect the central nervous system, which is where the brain controls hyperactivity and impulse control (Drugs.com, 2023). The benefits of using medication can include an increase in concentration abilities as well as a decrease in behavioral issues such as interrupting people and fidgeting (Hobbs, 2022). However, there are also side effects of the medication such as headaches, dizziness, and insomnia. Additionally, there are ongoing shortages of ADHD medications which can make filling prescriptions difficult. While stimulant medications like Adderall can help manage ADHD symptoms, college students with ADHD who take these stimulants face an increased susceptibility to developing an OUD compared to the general population. Research has found that more than 16% of people with ADHD who used stimulants, such as Adderall, also used opioids (Hlavinka, 2018).

Colleges and universities should provide aid for those with ADHD to accommodate them in ways that were not possible before. Resources that can be beneficial for students with ADHD can involve tutoring and CBT sessions which can help with skills such as time management and organization. CBT would also be beneficial in learning self-help tools to aid students with their ADHD symptoms such as hyperactivity and impulsive tendencies.

Another way for colleges to address the problem of ADHD among students would be for colleges to individualize resources and aid for each student. Schools that provide the same resources to every student instead of individualizing what each one needs can cause more of a disservice to the students than it does assisting them. Research revealed that students who sought assistance from college teachers, tutors, or other support services reported that the assistance did not help as previously expected (Wallace et al., 1999). A potential reason these services failed could be due to schools and programs providing the same resources for each student with ADHD and/or other mental disabilities. Each student needs an individualized set of resources that can better accommodate them, rather than receiving a baseline of resources given to everyone. To improve the outcomes of these resources, schools need to be able to communicate with the students and provide tailored resources to each student's needs (Álvarez-Godos et al., 2023). The improvement of mental health outcomes for students can be accomplished through the use of CBT sessions and therapy sessions on campus and educating students who have ADHD about resources that can be provided for them while attending college. Providing an area on campus where students can go for these services could also be beneficial. Providing a more accommodating environment for those who face daily challenges due to ADHD not only benefits these students but also assists the colleges themselves by improving retention rates, ultimately satisfying both parties.

Finally, colleges can assist students in obtaining their medications. Depending on the school, on-campus doctors can prescribe medications and, depending on state law, dispense medications to students (Phillips & Turner, 2020). This medical service may allow students to receive ADHD medications such as Adderall and Ritalin. Even with the ongoing shortage, universities may be able to obtain medications more easily than an individual. If schools are unable to prescribe and dispense medications, on-campus therapists and counselors can refer students to off-campus psychologists (Mana, n.d.). This service can also assist undiagnosed students to receive a diagnosis and be prescribed medication using outside resources. Creating individualized plans can improve outcomes and retention for students struggling with the distinct challenges ADHD presents in higher education.

NONMEDICAL USE OF PRESCRIPTION DRUGS

Prescription misuse and drug abuse without a prescription are illegal and can have serious social and physical consequences. The NMUPD can be defined as drug use "without a prescription or use for reasons other than what the medication is intended for" (Martins & Ghandour, 2017, pp. 102–4). The World Health Organization (WHO) defines misuse and abuse similarly as substance use that is unrelated to or not consistent with medical guidelines (WHO, 1994). It is important to understand that the use of prescription medication is serious, and the consequences of misuse are likely to have severe negative impacts.

Although anyone who has access to prescription medication could potentially misuse or abuse drugs, about 10% of college students have misused prescription medication (Kenne et al., 2016). While college students across all demographics are at risk for NMUPD, studies show that certain members of the student population are more likely than others to exhibit a propensity toward NMUPD. One predictive factor is age. Researchers found that "being in the third or higher year of [college] was associated with significantly increased odds of misusing" (Benson et al., 2018, p. 484). Another predictive factor is involvement in Greek organizations. Research found that "fraternity/sorority members were significantly more likely to misuse" (Benson et al., 2018, p. 485). The same study shows that there was "no significant relation between race and misuse" (Benson et al., 2018, p. 484). The 10% of college students who misuse prescription drugs are affected by different factors that influence their NMUPD.

Mental health disorders may be the underlying reason for NMUPD in some students. When considering the role of ADHD and stimulant misuse, research indicated that "participants who met criteria for ADHD . . . diagnosis were 2.80 times more likely to report academic motives for misuse compared with those who did not" (Benson et al., 2018, pp. 481–82). Results of the same study showed that the increased severity of ADHD increased the likelihood of NMUPD for academic motives (success). Students with ADHD are attempting to treat their symptoms through NMUPD.

A study conducted by Peck et al. (2019) found that the reason for some NMUPD in college students is the self-treatment of anxiety and depression. These studies collectively illustrate the correlation between NMUPD and college students suffering from mental illnesses. In a 2022–2023 study of 76,406 college students in the United States, 46% reported a previous or current diagnosis of mental illness (Eisenberg et al., 2023). In the same study, undergraduate students made up 83% of the respondents. Not including the undiagnosed students who suffer from mental health disorders, almost half of all undergraduate students are at an increased risk for NMUPD. The correlation between mental health and NMUPD among college students is significant because of the large percentage of students who suffer from mental illnesses and mental disorders.

According to the CDC (2023), two of the most commonly misused prescription drugs among college students are opioids and stimulants. Opioids are prescribed to treat moderate to severe pain and can cause feelings of euphoria. Some of the most frequently prescribed opioids are hydrocodone (Vicodin) and oxycodone (OxyContin or Percocet). Stimulants speed up the body's systems promoting wakefulness, a sense of exhilaration, and mental focus. Two regularly prescribed types of stimulants are amphetamines (Adderall and Dexedrine) and methylphenidate (Concerta and Ritalin), which are used to treat ADHD (Drug Enforcement Administration [DEA], 2022).

The top four reasons given by college students for misusing prescription opioids are to relieve pain (47.6%), to feel good (19.8%), to relax (13.2%), and to experiment (6.8%) (Peck et al., 2019). Research shows that certain groups are more likely to engage in NMUPD for a specific reason. Biological sex is predictive for certain reasons for opioid misuse. Males are more likely than females to misuse prescription opioids to get high or feel good (Peck et al., 2019). Age can also be a predictive factor when considering reasons why students misuse opioids. Research indicates that younger college students are more likely than older college students to abuse opioids for recreational use, while older students are more likely than younger students to list pain relief as their main reason for NMUPD (Peck et al., 2019).

College students often misuse prescription stimulants, such as Adderall and Ritalin, in an attempt to enhance academic performance. While the prescribed use of stimulants supports academic success in students who have ADHD, misusers of stimulant medications do not achieve the goal of higher academic performance, although some do experience a few of the positive effects of the drugs (Weyandt et al., 2018). In a 2018 study conducted by Weyandt et al., researchers administered Adderall and placebos to groups of students who did not have ADHD and found that Adderall positively affected attention performance but negatively impacted students' working memory, confidence in problem-solving, and their ability to complete tasks and interact with others. Instead of fulfilling students' expectations, the side effects of misusing prescription stimulants outweigh any of the positive effects and decrease overall academic and social performance in students who do not meet the requirements for ADHD.

College students' perception is the driving factor of prescription stimulant misuse, more than the actual experienced neurocognitive and physical effects. Students believe that taking stimulants will help them study better and perform at a higher academic level, leading to the labeling of stimulant medications as "study drugs." Stimulant misuse among college students "may be perceived in the same way as is underage alcohol [consumption]; that is, as part of the 'normal' college experience and as a rite of passage for college students" (Kennedy et al., 2019, p. 838). This casual perception and normalization of the use of "study drugs" encourages NMUPD among college students.

Finally, there is an internal pressure to fit into the perceived social norms, which affects substance use for prescription drugs as well as alcohol, tobacco, and cannabis (Isaacs et al., 2021). The problem of NMUPD among college students begins with the spread of false beliefs. Research shows that "[c]ollege students' perceptions of peer substance use are higher than actual levels of peer use and this misperception is thought to drive increased use to fit in with perceived norms" (Isaacs et al., 2021, pp. 2587–94). Unfortunately, students' internal desire to fit in adds to the appeal for NMUPD.

There are many medical side effects associated with NMUPD of both opioids and stimulants. "Nonmedical use of prescription stimulants can lead to irregular heart rate, hypertension, cardiovascular system failure, stroke, and seizures, while non-medical use of prescription opioids can cause respiratory suppression and overdose" (Martins & Ghandour, 2017, pp. 102–4). While students think that pain relief and academic success are the only effects of NMUPD, there are serious health risks associated with the misuse of these medications. Stimulants have also been known to cause insomnia, hallucinations, and anorexia (Gibbs et al., 2016; Martins & Ghandour, 2017). These side effects of NMUPD actively work against the academic success of students, making college life more difficult.

College students with undiagnosed ADHD are at risk for prescription stimulant misuse, which could also put them at risk for illicit drug use. Prescription stimulant misusers are at a greater risk for amphetamine and cocaine addictions because these illicit forms of stimulant medication have more intense effects on the central nervous system (Upadhyaya et al., 2010). As the effectiveness of prescription drugs decreases over continued use, the likelihood that students will turn to illicit drugs to satisfy their addiction increases. These addictions support the hypothesis that many students who misuse prescription stimulants and become addicted to illicit stimulants are self-medicating to treat undiagnosed ADHD (Upadhyaya et al., 2010). While illicit substances may satisfy the dependence and work to relieve symptoms of ADHD, illicit drug use is not sustainable and may lead to serious health problems.

The nonmedical use of opioids and stimulants can cause suicidal ideations among college students. Kuramoto et al. (2012) found that "[23%] of nonmedical users with past-year prescription opioid disorder, reported ideation in the past year; in contrast only 9% of nonmedical prescription opioid users who did not meet criteria for dependence and/or abuse report ideation" (pp. 178–84). Approximately one out of four college students who consistently misuse opioids will experience suicidal ideations, affecting both their academic and their social lives. College students who self-medicate with prescription drugs to treat pain or symptoms of ADHD are increasing their risk of suicide.

The treatment of NMUPD should be a major health concern for colleges and universities. "There is a large portion of the student population that is indicating untreated or inadequately treated symptoms of ADHD and executive functioning deficits" (Benson et al., 2018, p. 485). In addition, to decrease the misuse of prescription opioids, students' physical pain needs to be effectively treated and long-term solutions need to be sought. "Young adults with a recent history of NMUPD [opioids] are less likely to receive adequate pain treatment and subsequently are more likely to report continued self-medication with prescription opioids and intravenous drug use" (Peck et al., 2019). These studies show that the overwhelming purpose of NMUPD in college students is to treat legitimate illnesses and address physical ailments.

To assist colleges in "systematically measuring the scope of drug misuse issues, building relationships with key stakeholders, and planning and implementing a drug misuse prevention effort," the DEA funded the publication *Prevention with Purpose: A Strategic Planning Guide for Preventing Drug Misuse Among College Students* (Educational Development Center, 2024). Every college campus should have NMUPD prevention plans and treatments available or assist students in finding off-campus treatments. An example of a college providing prevention material is Harvard University, as it released the free online course *HarvardX: The Opioid Crisis in America*, to allow students to "learn about the opioid epidemic in the United States, including information about treatment and recovery from opioid addiction" (Harvard University, 2024). This course encourages the self-education of students on NMUPD while increasing students' awareness of the realities of opioid misuse. Additionally, universities across the country are encouraging the use of helplines, establishing student wellness centers, hosting workshops and public speakers, implementing policies and regulations, and providing resources to educate students regarding NMUPD. In fact, "51.4% of students were aware of resources, either on or off campus, that help with prescription drug safety . . . [and] 73.1% of [these] students knew where to go to get help if they were worried or concerned about misuse" (Ohio State University, 2022). It is apparent that some colleges and universities have made resources accessible for students who are misusing prescription drugs.

NMUPD among college students is treatable and can be prevented. When providing treatment for students, NMUPD should be handled as a mental health crisis. Severe punishments for the illicit use of drugs are not beneficial to the student or the institution. Punishments such as suspension, academic probation, or expulsion do nothing to address the underlying issues of NMUPD. These harsh responses are likely to deter students from seeking help if they fear punitive measures. While NMUPD is a choice, the physical pain, mental distress, and mental disorders that students live with are not a choice. By treating NMUPD as a mental health crisis, schools can find healthy and sustainable solutions that address the primary reasons for NMUPD. This approach provides students with the care they need and allows them to seek help without fear of punishment. In preventing and treating NMUPD among college students, it is first the students' responsibility to avoid misuse and seek acceptable means of help. Second, it is the colleges' responsibility to appropriately respond to NMUPD in a way that benefits students' long-term physical and academic success.

CONCLUSION

This chapter examined mental health disorders, prescription medications beyond opioids, medication shortages, and treatment options on college campuses. The ways these issues affect college students were also explored. The student authors provided their perspectives and their research on these issues to reassure college students across the country that they are not alone in their struggles. Furthermore, the authors used their experiences and research to make recommendations to college and university administrators so that they can help students who may be struggling with mental health issues.

Students and administrators must understand in detail the effects that mental health disorders such as PTSD, anxiety, depression, and ADHD have on students as well as the effects of NMUPD. A coordinated response to these issues is necessary. Universities need to provide adequate resources and services on their campuses so that students can get the help they need. Colleges and universities have obligations to their students that extend beyond providing an education. Those obligations extend to recognizing and providing treatment for mental health and medication concerns. By following the recommendations offered here, colleges and universities will be taking concrete steps to ensure that the mental health needs of their students are respected and met in ways that will only aid the schools in completing their educational mission.

REFERENCES

Abrams, Z. (2022). Student mental health is in crisis. Campuses are rethinking their approach. *American Psychological Association, 53*(7).

Alison. (2022, June 30). *Is PTSD commonly misdiagnosed?* Preferred Research Partners. https://preferredresearchpartners.com/is-ptsd-commonly-misdiagnosed/

Álvarez-Godos, M., Ferreira, C., & Vieira, M. (2023). A systematic review of actions aimed at university students with ADHD. *Frontiers in Psychology, 14.* https://doi.org/10.3389/fpsyg.2023.1216692

American Association of Community Colleges. (2019). *Students serving our country, 7* (19).

American College Health Association. (2019). American College, Health Association-National College Health Assessment II: Reference Group, Executive Summary Spring 2019.

American Psychiatric Association. (n.d.). *What is posttraumatic stress disorder (PTSD)?* https://www.psychiatry.org/patients-families/ptsd/what-is-ptsd

American Psychiatric Association. (2013). *Diagnostic and statistical manual of mental disorders* (5th ed.). https://doi.org/10.1176/appi.books.9780890425596

American Psychiatric Association. (2022). *What is post traumatic stress disorder (PTSD)?* https://www.psychiatry.org/patients-families/ptsd/what-is-ptsd

American Psychiatric Association. (2024). *What is ADHD?* https://www.psychiatry.org/patients-families/adhd/what-is-adhd

American Psychological Association. (n.d.). *Medications for PTSD.* Clinical Practice Guideline for the Treatment of Posttraumatic Stress Disorder. https://www.apa.org/ptsd-guideline/treatments/medications

Anastopoulos, A. D., DuPaul, G. J., Weyandt, L. L., Morrissey-Kane, E., Sommer, J. L., Rhoads, L. H., Murphy, K. R., Gormley, M. J., & Gudmundsdottir, B. G. (2016). Rates and patterns of comorbidity among first-year college students with ADHD. *Journal of Clinical Child & Adolescent Psychology, 47*(2), 236–47. https://doi.org/10.1080/15374416.2015.1105137

Anastopoulos, A. D., King, K. A., Besecker, L. H., O'Rourke, S. R., Bray, A. C., & Supple, A. J. (2018). Cognitive-behavioral therapy for college students with ADHD: Temporal stability of improvements in functioning following active treatment. *Journal of Attention Disorders, 24*(6), 863–74. https://doi.org/10.1177/1087054717749932

Arun, P., Ramamurthy, P., & Thilakan, P. (2022). Indian medical students with depression, anxiety, and suicidal behavior: Why do they not seek treatment? *Indian Journal of Psychological Medicine, 44*(1), 10–16. https://doi.org/10.1177/0253717620982326

Benson, K., Woodlief, D. T., Flory, K., Siceloff, E. R., Coleman, K., Lamont, A., & Stoops, W. W. (2018). *Is ADHD, independent of ODD, associated with whether and why college students misuse stimulant medication?* https://pubmed.ncbi.nlm.nih.gov/29952616/

Blase, S. L., Gilbert, A. N., Anastopoulos, A. D., Costello, E. J., Hoyle, R. H., Swartzwelder, H. S., & Rabiner, D. L. (2009). Self-reported ADHD and adjustment in college. *Journal of Attention Disorders, 13*(3), 297–309. https://doi.org/10.1177/1087054709334446

Boskovic, I. (2020). Do motives matter? A comparison between positive and negative incentives in students' willingness to malinger. *Educational Psychology, 40*(8), 1022–32. https://doi.org/10.1080/01443410.2019.1704400

CDC. (2023, August 22). *Basics about prescription opioids.* Retrieved March 6, 2024, from Center for Disease Control. https://www.cdc.gov/rxawareness/information/?CDC_AAref_Val=https://www.cdc.gov/rxawareness/information/index.html

CHADD. (2023, September 26). *General prevalence of ADHD.* Retrieved January 31, 2024, from https://chadd.org/about-adhd/general-prevalence/

Clinical Practice Guideline for the Treatment of Depression. (2019, August). *Depression treatments for adults.* APA. https://www.apa.org/depression-guideline/adults

DEA. (2022, October). *Stimulants.* Retrieved March 6, 2024, from Drug Enforcement Administration: https://www.dea.gov/sites/default/files/2023-04/Stimulants%202022%20Drug%20Fact%20Sheet.pdf

Drugs.com. (2023, August 23). *Adderall.* Retrieved February 1, 2024, from https://www.drugs.com/adderall.html

DuPau, G. J., Franklin, M. K., Pollack, B. L., Stack, K. S., Jaffe, A. R., Gormley, M. J., Anastopoulos, A. D., & Weyandt, L. L. (2018). Predictors and trajectories of educational functioning in college students with and without attention deficit/hyperactivity disorder. *Journal of Postsecondary Education and Disability, 31*(2), 161–78.

Dworkin, E. R., Jaffe, A. E., Bedard-Gilligan, M., & Fitzpatrick, S. (2021). PTSD in the year following sexual assault: A meta-analysis of prospective studies. *Trauma, Violence, & Abuse, 24*(2), 497–514. https://doi.org/10.1177/15248380211032213

Educational Development Center, Inc. (2024, January). *Prevention with purpose: A strategic planning guide for preventing drug.* Retrieved March 8, 2024, from https://www.campusdrugprevention.gov/sites/default/files/2024-01/DEA-CollegeDrugPrev-010324_web_v5.pdf

Eisenberg, D., Lipson, S. K., Heinze, J., & Zhou, S. (2023). *The healthy minds study: 2022–2023 data report.* Retrieved March 8, 2024, from https://healthymindsnetwork.org/wp-content/uploads/2023/08/HMS_National-Report-2022-2023_full.pdf

Flannery, M. E. (2023, March 29). *The mental health crisis on college campuses.* NEA Today. https://www.nea.org/nea-today/all-news-articles/mental-health-crisis-college-campuses

Fleming, A. P., & McMahon, R. J. (2012). Developmental context and treatment principles for ADHD among college students. *Clinical Child and Family Psychology Review, 15*, 1–27 https://pubmed.ncbi.nlm.nih.gov/23053445/

Frida Care Team. (2023, April 3). *How ADHD impacts college and university students.* Retrieved February 20, 2024, from https://www.talkwithfrida.com/learn/adhd-college-university-students/.

Gibbs, E. L., Kass, A. E., Eichen, D. M., Fitzsimmons-Craft, E. E., Trockel, M., & Wilfley, D. E. (2016). ADHD-specific stimulant misuse, mood, anxiety, and stress in college-age women at high risk for or with eating disorders. *Journal of American College Health, 64*(4), 300–308.

Grasso, D., Boonsiri, J., Lipschitz, D., Guyer, A., Houshyar, S., Douglas-Palumberi, H., Massey, J., & Kaufman, J. (2009). Posttraumatic stress disorder: The missed diagnosis. *National Institute of Health, 88*(4), 157–76.

Guina, J., & Merrill, B. (2018). Benzodiazepines I: Upping the care on downers: The evidence of risks, benefits and alternatives. *Journal of Clinical Medicine, 7*(2), 17. https://doi.org/10.3390/jcm7020017

Harvard University. (2024). *HarvardX: The opioid crisis in America.* Retrieved April 3, 2024, from https://www.edx.org/learn/drugs/harvard-university-the-opioid-crisis-in-america#!

Hlavinka, E. (2018, August 10). *Opioid use rising in ADHD patients on stimulants.* Medical News MedPage Today. Retrieved February 2, 2024, from https://www.medpagetoday.com/psychiatry/adhd-add/74520

Hobbs, H. (2022, May 4). *The effects of Adderall on your body.* Healthline. Retrieved February 20, 2024, from https://www.healthline.com/health/adhd/adderall-effects-on-body#how-it-works

Holland, K. (2021, October 28). *The history of ADHD.* Healthline. Retrieved February 5, 2024, from https://www.healthline.com/health/adhd/history#1987

Hotez, E., Rosenau, K. A., Fernandes, P., Eagan, K., Shea, L., & Kuo, A. A. (2022, January). A national cross-sectional study of the characteristics, strengths, and challenges of college students with attention deficit hyperactivity disorder. *Cureus, 23*, 14(1), e21520. doi: 10.7759/cureus.21520

Isaacs, J. Y., Thompson, K., Yakovenko, P., Dobson, K., Chen, S.-P., Hudson, A., . . . Stewart, S. H. (2021). Social norms of college students engaging in non-medical prescription drug use to get high: What's sex got to do with it? *Journal of American College Health*, 1–8.

Kadison, R., & DiGeronimo, T. F. (2004). *College of the overwhelmed: The campus mental health crisis and what to do about it*. Jossey-Bass.

Kenne, D. R., Hamilton, K., Birmingham, L., Oglesby, W. H., Fischbein, R. L., & Delahanty, D. L. (2016). Perceptions of harm and reasons for misuse of prescription opioid drugs and reasons for not seeking treatment for physical or emotional pain among a sample of college students. *Substance Use & Misuse*, *52*(1), 92–99.

Kennedy, S., Allen, M., & Kennedy, G. J. (2019). Using latent profile analysis to assess college students' attitudes about underage drinking and prescription stimulant misuse. *North American Journal of Psychology*, *21*(4), 831–41.

Krystal, J. H., Davis, L. L., Neylan, T. C., Raskind, M., Schnurr, P. P., Stein, M. B., Vessicchio, J., Shiner, B., Gleason, T. D., & Huang, G. D. (2017). It is time to address the crisis in the pharmacotherapy of posttraumatic stress disorder: A consensus statement of the PTSD psychopharmacology working group. *Biological Psychiatry*, *82*(7), 51–59.

Kuramoto, S. J., Chilcoat, H. D., Ko, J., & Martins, S. S. (2012). Suicidal ideation and suicide attempt across stages of nonmedical prescription opioid use and presence of prescription opioid disorders among U.S. adults. *Journal of Studies on Alcohol and Drugs*, *73*(2), 178–84.

MacPherson, R. (2024, February 6). *This one type of drink might be to blame for college students' sleep loss*. Sleepopolis. https://sleepopolis.com/news/energy-drinks-cause-sleep-loss-college/

Mana. (n.d.). *Therapist vs. psychologist vs. psychiatrist: What's the difference?* Retrieved March 13, 2024, from https://mana.md/psychologist-psychiatrist-or-therapist/

Marconi, A. M., Myers, U. S., Hanson, B., Nolan, S., & Sarrouf, E. B. (2023). Psychiatric medication prescriptions increasing for college students above and beyond the COVID-19 pandemic. *Scientific Reports*, *13*(1), 19063. https://doi.org/10.1038/s41598-023-46303-9

Marks, Y., Demler, T. L., & Matecki, C. (2023). Impact of the medication shortages on psychiatric patients: Exploring the consequences of lorazepam injection scarcity. *Innovations in Clinical Neuroscience*, *20*(10–12), 23–28.

Martins, S. S., & Ghandour, L. A. (2017). Nonmedical use of prescription drugs in adolescents and young adults: Not just a Western phenomenon. *World Psychiatry*, *16*(1), 102–4.

Mbous, Y. P. V., Nili, M., Mohamed, R., & Dwibedi, N. (2022). Psychosocial correlates of insomnia among college students. *Preventing Chronic Disease*, *19*, E60. https://doi.org/10.5888/pcd19.220060

Medical Research Journal. (2013, January 15). College students on antidepressants. *Medical Research Journal*. https://medicalresearchjournal.org/index.php/GJMR/article/view/416/5-College-Students-on_html

Meltzer, E. C., Averbuch, T., Samet, J. H., Saitz, R., Jabbar, K., Lloyd-Travaglini, C., & Liebschutz, J. M. (2012). Discrepancy in diagnosis and treatment of post-traumatic stress disorder (PTSD): Treatment for the wrong reason. *Journal of Behavioral Health Services & Research*, *39*(2), 190–201.

MHA. (n.d.). *Depression*. Mental Health America. https://mhanational.org/conditions/depression#:~:text=Basic%20Facts%20About%20Depression,are%20affected%20by%20major%20depression

Midwest Disability. (2019, December 13). *What percentage of soldiers see combat?* Midwest Disability. https://www.midwestdisability.com/blog/2019/12/what-percentage-of-soldiers-see-combat/

Morrissette, S. B., Gonzalez, C. R., Yufik, T., DeBeer, B. B., Kimbrel, N. A., Sorrells, A. M., Steiker, L. H., Penk, W. E., Gulliver, S. B., & Meyer, E. C. (2019). The effects of PTSD symptoms on educational functioning in student veterans. *Psychological Services, 18*(1), 124–33. https://doi.org/10.1037/ser0000356

NAMI. (2017). *Anxiety disorders.* https://www.nami.org/About-Mental-Illness/Mental -Health-Conditions/Anxiety-Disorders

NCSR (by sex and age). (2007). https://www.hcp.med.harvard.edu/ncs/ftpdir/table_ncsr _LTprevgenderxage.pdf

NIH. (n.d.). *Depression.* National Institute of Mental Health. https://www.nimh.nih.gov/ health/topics/depression

NIH. (2024). *Anxiety disorders.* National Institute of Mental Health. https://www.nimh.nih .gov/health/topics/anxiety-disorders#:~:text=There%20are%20several%20types%20of,and %20various%20phobia%2Drelated%20disorders

Ohio State University. (2022). *2022 college prescription drug study.* Campus Drug Prevention. Retrieved March 6, 2024, fromhttps://www.campusdrugprevention.gov/sites/default/files /2022-06/CPDS_Multi_Institutional_Key_Findings_2022.pdf

Otte, C. (2011). Cognitive behavioral therapy in anxiety disorders: Current state of the evidence. *Dialogues in Clinical Neuroscience, 13*(4), 413–21. https://doi.org/10.31887/DCNS .2011.13.4/cotte

Peck, K. R., Parker, M. A., & Sigmon, S. C. (2019). *Reasons for non-medical use of prescription opioids among young adults: Role of educational status.* Retrieved from https://www. sciencedirect.com/science/article/abs/pii/S0091743519301239?via%3Dihub

Peltz, J. S., Rogge, R. D., Pugach, C. P., & Strang, K. (2017). Bidirectional associations between sleep and anxiety symptoms in emerging adults in a residential college setting. *Emerging Adulthood, 5*(3), 204–15. https://doi.org/10.1177/2167696816674551

Phillips, M., & Turner, C. (2020, August 31). *Dispensing medications at student health clinics. Healthcare law insights.* Retrieved March 13, 2024, from https://www.healthcarelawinsights .com/2020/08/dispensing-medications-at-student-health-clinics/

RAINN. (n.d.). *Campus sexual violence: Statistics.* https://www.rainn.org/statistics/campus -sexual-violence

Ramtekkar, U. P., Reiersen, A. M., Todorov, A. A., & Todd, R. D. (2010, March). Sex and age differences in attention-deficit/hyperactivity disorder symptoms and diagnoses: Implications for DSM V and ICD-11. *Journal of the American Academy of Child and Adolescent Psychiatry, 49*(3), 217–28.e1-3.

Read, J. P., Griffin, M. J., Wardell, J. D., & Ouimette, P. (2014). Coping, PTSD symptoms, and alcohol involvement in trauma-exposed college students in the first three years of college. *Psychology of Addictive Behaviors, 28*(4), 1052–64. https://doi.org/10.1037/ a0038348

Read, J. P., Ouimette, P., White, J., Colder, C., & Farrow, S. (2011). Rates of DSM–IV–TR trauma exposure and posttraumatic stress disorder among newly matriculated college students. *Psychological Trauma: Theory, Research, Practice, and Policy, 3*(2), 148–56. https:// doi.org/10.1037/a0021260

Redshaw, L. (2023, August 2). *Is self-diagnosis on social media helping or hurting people's health?* The Intake. https://www.tebra.com/theintake/medical-deep-dives/tips-and-trends/is-self -diagnosis-on-social-media-helping-or-hurting-peoples-health

Renzoni, C. (2023, May 8). *Depression facts and statistics.* The Recovery Village. https://www .therecoveryvillage.com/mental-health/depression/depression-statistics/

Richardson, T., Elliott, P., & Roberts, R. (2017). Relationship between loneliness and mental health in students. *Journal of Public Mental Health*, 16(2), 48–54. doi:https://doi.org/10.1108/JPMH-03-2016-0013

Saberi, S. M., Sheikhazadi, A., Ghorbani, M., Nasrabadi, Z. N., Meysamie, A. P., & Marashi, S. M. (2013). Feigned symptoms among defendants claiming psychiatric problems: Survey of 45 malingerers. *Iranian Journal of Psychiatry*, 8(1), 14–19.

Upadhyaya, H. P., Kroutil, L. A., Deas, D., Durell, T. M., Van Brunt, D. L., & & Novak, S. P. (2010). Stimulant formulation and motivation for nonmedical use of prescription attention-deficit/hyperactivity disorder medications in a college-aged population. *The American Journal on Addictions*, 19(6), 569–77.

Wallace, B. A., Winsler, A., & NeSmith, P. (1999). Factors associated with success for college students with ADHD: Are standard accommodations helping? Paper presented at the Annual Meeting of the American Educational Research Association (Montreal, Quebec, Canada, April 19–23, 1999). https://eric.ed.gov/?id=ED431350

Weyandt, L. L., White, T. L., Gudmundsdottir, B. G., Nitenson, A. Z., Rathkey, E. S., De Leon, K. A., & Bjorn, S. A. (2018). Neurocognitive, autonomic, and mood effects of Adderall: A pilot study of healthy college students. *Pharmacy*, 6(3), 58.

Whitledge, D. J., Fox, E. R., & Mazer-Amirshahi, M. (2023). Benzodiazepine shortages: A recurrent challenge in need of a solution. *Journal of Medical Toxicology: Official Journal of the American College of Medical Toxicology*, 19(1), 4–6. https://doi.org/10.1007/s13181-022-00917-z

WHO. (1994). *Lexicon of alcohol and drug terms*. World Health Organization.

Zauderer, S. (2023, January 11). *51 PTSD statistics and facts: How common is PTSD?* Cross River Therapy. https://www.crossrivertherapy.com/ptsd-statistics

Index

About the Contributors

Dr. Josiah R. Baker is Nimocks professor of international business and professor of financial economics at Methodist University in Fayetteville, North Carolina. For nearly 25 years, Dr. Baker has taught college courses in Kentucky, Florida, the Washington, DC, area, and North Carolina. In Washington, DC, he completed his dissertation on the economic history of the construction of Sweden's welfare state. He has also lived in six countries (including Norway, Japan, Bolivia, Russia, and Sweden) and studied six languages (French, Norwegian, Spanish, Japanese, Swedish, and Russian). Dr. Baker has authored more than 60 academic publications, as well as dozens of newspaper and magazine articles.

Madison Brunson is from Saint Petersburg, Florida. She received her BS degree from Methodist University in May 2024. While at Methodist University, she studied performance psychology, clinical/counseling psychology, and management. She plans to continue her education at the Florida Institute of Technology to pursue an MS in industrial/organizational psychology.

Dr. Matthew L. Dobra holds a PhD and MA in economics from George Mason University, a graduate certificate in higher education from Monash University, and a BA in history from Loyola University, New Orleans. He is currently professor of economics and Nimocks endowed professor of business in the Reeves School of Business at Methodist University in Fayetteville, North Carolina. His primary research interests lie in the fields of resource economics, public economics, and political economy.

Dr. Robert Gmeiner is assistant professor of financial economics at Methodist University. His work focuses on monetary economics and international trade. He holds a PhD and MS in economics from Florida State University as well as a BA in economics and Russian.

Dr. Hugh Harling holds a bachelor's and master's in exercise and sport sciences from the University of Florida as well as a doctorate of education in healthcare education from Nova Southeastern University. Dr. Harling began his career as an athletic trainer for Santa Fe Community College and then moved to Florida Southern College. Dr. Harling began teaching at Methodist in August 1999 as its athletic training program director and is currently a professor in the Department of Kinesiology. His primary focus is emergency care, anatomy, and injury prevention and care. Additionally, Dr. Harling continues to be active clinically as an athletic trainer for a variety of events and sports in North Carolina.

Dr. Mark Kline is a full professor of psychology and assistant dean of MU Online for Methodist University. Dr. Kline received his PhD in psychology from Indiana University and has been at Methodist University since 2011. He has specialized in research on trauma, PTSD, and alcohol abuse.

Dr. Paul Knudson is associate professor of sociology at Methodist University. Knudson earned his PhD in sociology in 2011 from the State University of New York at Albany. His research focuses on urban and metropolitan affairs, urban schools and families, and race and ethnic relations. His latest project explores the work lives of recent refugees who have arrived from Venezuela. An earlier project examined upper-middle-class families who have chosen to remain in a struggling central-city public school district despite having the resources to relocate to suburban schools or enroll their children in private schools. Another recent project examined African American parents' views of charter schools in New York State.

Dr. J. Scott Lewis earned his PhD in sociology from Bowling Green State University. He is associate teaching professor of sociology and sociology program coordinator at Penn State Harrisburg. He is the author of more than a dozen academic publications. His current research involves exploring how narratives about social problems intersect with race and gender to become weaponized against marginalized groups.

Dr. David A. Mackey is professor of criminal justice at Plymouth State University. He earned his PhD in criminology from Indiana University of Pennsylvania. With Kristine Levan, he co-edited *Crime Prevention*. With Kathryn M. Elvey, he co-edited *Society, Ethics, and the Law*. He is a lifetime member of the Academy of Criminal Justice Sciences and the Northeastern Association of Criminal Justice Sciences. In 2023, he was awarded the Northeastern Association of Criminal Justice Sciences Founders Award.

Dr. Laura Mars is assistant professor of psychology at Methodist University. While in the US Army, Dr. Mars attended and graduated from Methodist College. She received her PhD and MS in health psychology from Walden University. Her love of education began almost 20 years ago when she left the military to teach. As a veteran, she is primarily interested in the challenges and topics related to the military family. Her areas of expertise include veterans and spouses, child development, and health psychology.

Ally Mason received her BS degrees in forensic science and criminal justice from Methodist University in May 2024. She was the president of the Criminal Justice and Forensic Science Association at Methodist University; she also worked as a lab assistant with the forensic science department. Ally has always enjoyed researching and taking on the next major project or task that comes her way. She plans to make the most of all opportunities that come her way in all her future career endeavors.

Rebecca McGaughnea is an undergraduate student at Methodist University majoring in biology, criminal justice, and forensic science with a minor in chemistry. She works as a criminal justice research assistant in the criminal justice department. McGaughnea presented a poster at the 2024 Academy of Criminal Justice Science Conference in Chicago, Illinois. She is also a member of the basketball and track and field teams at Methodist University.

Dr. Deborah L. Morris, MD, is professor of clinical medicine and has taught in the Methodist University Physician Assistant Program since 2007. Her career in medicine spans more than 40 years as a physician assistant and primary care doctor. She has published scholarly works and creative nonfiction and, recently retired, continues adjunct teaching, writing, and supervising advanced practice providers.

Michael Potts is professor of philosophy at Methodist University. His areas of specialization include professional ethics and philosophy of religion. He is the author of numerous peer-reviewed articles and book chapters. He is the editor-in-chief of *Beyond Brain Death: The Case Against Brain-Based Criteria for Human Death* (2000).

Eric S. See holds a PhD in criminology and is professor and the division head for the Department of Criminal Justice and Military Science at Methodist University. He has published on a variety of topics including gadget guns, the right to own and carry firearms, police use of force, terrorism, methamphetamine abuse, and the mentally ill in the criminal justice system. He won the Distinguished Professor of the Year award at Methodist University in 2012. He previously served as an editor and author of *Guns 360: Differing Perspectives and Common-Sense Approaches to Firearms in America.*

Sarah A. See is an assistant professor at Methodist University in the Department of Criminal Justice and Military Science. She received her bachelor's in psychology and a master's in criminology from Indiana University of Pennsylvania. Her previous research and publications have been focused on the mentally ill in our jail and prison systems, concealed carry, and police use of force. She previously served as an editor and author of *Guns 360: Differing Perspectives and Common-Sense Approaches to Firearms in America.*

Dr. Kevin Swift is associate professor of broadcast at the University of North Carolina at Pembroke. He is a veteran of broadcasting in many capacities. He worked as a writer, producer, and reporter for several broadcast, cable TV, and radio stations in the Youngstown, Ohio, and Pittsburgh, Pennsylvania, areas. He served as an anchor and reporter at WVLK radio in Lexington, Kentucky. As a professional announcer, he has recorded voiceovers for organizations including the Red Cross, NPR/Health Beat, Ford, and hundreds of TV and radio spots in the Midwest and on the East Coast.

Abigail Warf received her BS degrees in criminal justice and forensic science with a minor in psychology from Methodist University in May 2024. She was the past president and treasurer of the photography club and event coordinator in the Criminal Justice and Forensic Science Association. She is also a member of the American Academy of Forensic Science, the North Carolina International Association for Identification, and Delta Delta Epsilon. Warf aspires to become part of the criminal investigation division in the US military or work as a crime scene investigator.

Kaylee Williams is an undergraduate student at Methodist University. She is double majoring in criminal justice and forensic science with a minor in psychology. Williams previously co-authored a blog for the child advocacy center titled, "Stranger Danger: It's Time to End the Rhyme and Talk to Strangers."

Sydney Wixtrom received her BS degrees in criminal justice and forensic science from Methodist University in May 2024. She received the Outstanding Criminal Justice Research Achievement award from Methodist University for her work in this publication. Wixtrom served as the secretary for Methodist University's Criminal Justice and Forensic Science Association and is a member of Delta Delta Epsilon.

www.ingramcontent.com/pod-product-compliance
Lightning Source LLC
Chambersburg PA
CBHW060036030426
42334CB00019B/2348